FOOD/ENERGY AND THE MAJOR FAITHS

FOOD/ENERGY
AND THE
MAJOR FAITHS

Presented by JOSEPH GREMILLION

ORBIS BOOKS
Maryknoll, New York 10545

Library of Congress Cataloging in Publication Data

Gremillion, Joseph B
  Food/energy and the major faiths.

  Includes bibliographical references.
  1. Food supply—Congresses. 2. Energy policy
—Congresses. 3. Religion and international
affairs—Congresses. I. Interreligious Peace
Colloquium, 1st, Bellagio, Italy, 1975. II. Ti-
tle.
HD9000.1.G73   338.1'9   77-17975
ISBN 0-88344-138-1 pbk.

The Catholic Foreign Mission Society of America (Maryknoll) recruits and trains
people for overseas missionary service. Through Orbis Books Maryknoll aims to
foster the international dialogue that is essential to mission. The books published,
however, reflect the opinions of their authors and are not meant to represent the
official position of the Society.

CONTENTS

Foreword, *by Cyrus R. Vance and Henry Siegman*   vii
Letter from the Secretary-General of the United Nations,
     Kurt Waldheim   1
The Food/Energy Crisis: A Challenge to Peace, A Call to Faith, *A State-
     ment from the First Interreligious Peace Colloquium*   3
The Setting—and Since, *by Joseph Gremillion*   5

SESSION ONE
THE FACTS OF THE FOOD/ENERGY CRISIS

1. The World Food Council, *presented by John A. Hannah*   11
2. Production and Technology, *presented by Norman Borlaug*   17
3. Discussion: Facts and Their Meaning   25

SESSION TWO
IMPACT OF THE CRISIS ON WORLD PEACE AND SOCIAL JUSTICE

4. Economic Consequences and Political Context,
     presented by Edwin M. Martin   37
5. The Crisis of Western Society, *presented by Shlomo Avineri*   46
6. Political Change and Religious Institutions,
     presented by Paul Moore   50
7. Discussion: Intertwining Political and Economic Power   54

SESSION THREE
THE ROLE OF RELIGION IN POLITICS AND SOCIETY

8. Divisiveness and Unity, *by Wilfred Cantwell Smith*   71
9. Distinction, Identity, and Community,
     a Hindu response presented by K. Sivaraman   86
10. Buddhist Social and Political Thought, *by W. Ananda Thera*   91
11. Faith and Ideology,
     a Buddhist response presented by M. Palihawadana   109
12. A Strategy of Ideological Self-Restraint,
     a Jewish response presented by Norman Lamm   113

13. Food, Faith, and the Political Process,
    from comments by Irwin Blank   120
14. The Religious Reply to World Crisis: Islamic Potentiality,
    presented by Hasan Askari   122
15. Comments from a Modern Muslim,
    presented by Mohammed Al-Nowaihi   133
16. Faith, Church, and World,
    a Christian response by Charles Moeller   140
17. Discussion: Toward a World "Community of Communities"   152

SESSION FOUR
STRATEGIES FOR MEETING THE FOOD/ENERGY CRISIS

18. Political and Economic Structures Demanded by Our Interdependent
    World, *by S. L. Parmar*   175
19. Programs Undertaken by Some Religious Bodies, *extracts from a
    survey by Peter Henriot and Frank Harris*   202
20. New Styles of Life in Faith Communities,
    presented by Krister Stendahl   216
21. Discussion: The Powerless vs. the Powerful: Faceup for Faith   226

SESSION FIVE
THE WORK GROUPS AND A HAPPENING OF THE HEART

22. The Work Groups and Their Reports   239
23. Discussion and Finale: Shalom and Salam   249

THE TWO YEARS SINCE BELLAGIO

24. A Call for Follow-Up   261
25. The Interreligious Peace Colloquium   264
26. The Food/Energy Situation in 1977   274
27. Personal Notes, *by Joseph Gremillion*   277

Appendix
    Participants in the Bellagio Colloquium   280
    Sponsors, Officers, and Board Members   281
    Outline and Questions for Work Groups   282
Index   285

Foreword

Thirty-five participants were present for the first Interreligious Peace Colloquim held in Bellagio, Italy, May 1975. The majority were religious leaders from the five world faiths—Hindus, Buddhists, Jews, Muslims, Christians. The rest were from political, business, and academic circles; most had special competence in our wide-ranging subject: The Food/Energy Crisis: A Challenge to Peace, A Call to Faith.

Our purpose was to help believers of these five faiths, so often in conflict, to work together on issues affecting the fate of the whole human family—above all to work for peace. The food/energy crisis challenges peace and justice and human rights—for what right takes precedence over the right to eat? It raises questions about the value of life, social ethics, and the meaning of the human person that are so basic that they call upon faith for adequate response. So the food/energy crisis became our first focus.

This volume tells about our week-long exchange at Bellagio. It is not a mere reproduction of papers and transcribed discussions. This is an account of what was said and done and lived together, written by one of our number, Joseph Gremillion. We who are responsible for the follow-up to the Colloquium have asked him to give a personal interpretation, utilizing the papers and tapes as he judged fitting. This was done for two reasons:

First, full reproduction of the ten formal papers and the three hundred pages of transcribed discussion would require a very lengthy book indeed.

Second, our days at Bellagio represent more than a printed report can convey; we lived a human experience that can be communicated only by personal interpretation, and then but partially.

We hope that our first meeting marks the beginning of a wider, deeper movement among believing men and women who must deal daily with critical world issues. The Interreligious Peace

vii

Colloquium was originally sponsored by a temporary Steering Committee composed of such persons. They named the undersigned, together with Father Gremillion, as a "continuation committee" charged with follow-up and future planning. We are pleased to present his account to the public in partial fulfillment of this responsibility.

The Colloquium and its Committee came into being in 1974 at the invitation of the president of the Synagogue Council of America, Rabbi Irwin M. Blank. In opening the Bellagio meeting, Rabbi Blank credited a layman, Matthew Rosenhaus, for having "prodded us and provided us with funds to come together for this period of sharing. He was dismayed and angry," Blank continued, "that given the presumed strength of the religious community throughout the world, we should go from crisis to crisis, from conflagration to conflagration—that the religious community should have such apparently ineffective input into the management of our global village. We share that dismay with him and feel much of his anger. Beyond that, we are most grateful to him." Mr. Rosenhaus now serves as president of the Colloquium. We thank also a vice-president of the Synagogue Council, Moses Hornstein, for his moral and financial support.

Gratitude is expressed as well to the Rockefeller Foundation for its helpful grant and for inviting us to be their guests at Villa Serbelloni, its Conference Center in Bellagio. Unfortunately, we were too numerous to accept the Foundation's hospitality.

Finally, those who presented papers and all participants are warmly thanked. The future of our initiative is discussed near the close of this book. Those of us who became friends—we can even say a COMMUNITY—during our days together know that such experiences shared among believers are precious gifts from God—from the Great Reality underlying our respective faiths. These gifts must be shared with others; this is the purpose of this publication.

We the few who are "alumni" of Bellagio know that countless others yearn and strive for human rights and betterment, for world peace built upon social justice. Many share in one or the other of our five faith traditions; many do not. With the latter, we wish to communicate respectfully and frankly some of our concerns in the light of our belief in God, in a Reality that transcends secular experience.

We want to share the call we heard at Bellagio for fresh joint approaches to our faith commitments in terms of the new fact of global interdependence. It is a call which we Hindus, Buddhists, Jews, Muslims, Christians do need to hear, because too often our differences of faith have kept us apart, sometimes in violence and hate.

At Bellagio we became especially conscious of the conflicts, past and present, among those of us who share most: we who are believers in the one personal God of Abraham and Moses, of Jesus and Muhammad. Reflecting upon this paradox, we asked whether the new fact of economic and political interdependence among all our peoples provides (perhaps by Providence) a sign calling for greater interdependence among our faiths.

Such were the gifts of Bellagio, which we now share with friends of all faiths. As we did there, each in our own tradition, we meditate upon these gifts. We pray and wish well for and with each other—for all our brother and sister humans, especially those most in need of food and justice, peace and hope.

CYRUS R. VANCE*
HENRY SIEGMAN

New York City
August 1976

*Mr. Vance resigned as an officer of the Interreligious Peace Colloquium in January 1977, when he became Secretary of State of the United States.

Letter from
the Secretary-General
of the United Nations

The United Nations
May 20, 1975

Interreligious Peace Colloquium
Villa Serbelloni Hotel
Bellagio, Italy

I am very glad that the first meeting of the Interreligious Peace Colloquium will be devoted to the global challenges of food and energy, and that such a large number of distinguished individuals from many countries and backgrounds are attending this important conference.

The two closely interrelated problems of food and energy were the topics of major international conferences held under United Nations auspices last year, and these complex and vital issues will continue to be of crucial importance to the international community. At the United Nations World Food Conference and the Sixth Special Session of the General Assembly devoted to the subject of raw materials and development, important initial steps were taken to meet the urgent problem of malnutrition and hunger and to create the outlines of a new international economic order. But these were only the first steps of global approaches to meet these massive challenges, and it is essential that we achieve the political will to make practical reality out of these beginnings.

In this task, the positive contributions of governments and individuals everywhere will be crucial, and I welcome the initiative that has been taken in bringing together leaders of major religious faiths with public figures to consider the issues upon which human survival and the preservation of our world for future generations will depend. I look forward to reading the results of this meeting, and I wish you all success in your deliberations.

KURT WALDHEIM

1

The Food/Energy Crisis:
A Challenge to Peace,
A Call to Faith

A Statement from the First
Interreligious Peace Colloquium

We met, conscious of the four hundred million—one-tenth of the world population—who lack sufficient food, one-half of that number being children; a world of starvation and malnutrition causing permanent damage to brain and life; a world where many of the attempts at rectifying this situation have not worked but rather have tended to make the rich richer and the poor poorer; a world which may double its population from the present four billion to eight billion prior to the year 2020.

Under different symbols—powerful in our various traditions —there emerged a common vision in which "bread" and "rice" are far more than a commodity manipulated by the laws of market and commerce. The right to breathe the air and to drink the water becomes coupled with the right to eat. Some would even speak of the holiness of bread. To others, the basic human need for food leads to similar reverence for the fruits of the earth. In short, food is not just a commercial commodity among commodities and cannot be so treated by society. And an enhanced dignity of the farmers must consequently be translated into improved economic status for them and for their almost sacred service to us all.

We were made aware of how the scarcity of food and the scarcity of energy are closely related, and we became convinced that the first claim on resources of energy should be made for agricultural development, in terms of fertilizers and irrigation, and that at a price acceptable to the less developed countries.

3

We rejoiced in the efforts now getting under way through the World Food Council of the United Nations, grateful that this amount of cooperation between sovereign nations has been possible. We appreciate its emphasis on local development where it is most needed and promises more lasting effects. We hope reserves of grain will be so located that they can reach people in need speedily and efficiently.

We were strengthened in our convictions that neither short-term nor long-term alleviation of hunger and malnutrition can be achieved without structural changes in the societies of which we are a part. In a world of scarcity, the increased affluence of the affluent is intolerable. And it is unacceptable that the economic burden of a slowdown in the increasing standard of living in the affluent nations be borne by the unemployed and the poor in those countries. Scarcity calls for a just distribution of resources, both within and among nations. In developing countries no less than in the developed ones, the first and last aim must be that of just distribution.

As members of religious communities and as individuals we consider it our immediate duty to hold up this simple truth before ourselves and our political leaders and our leaders of industry and finance, so that the poor may be assured their rights to eat. We shall do so through organizations available to us and through local and national "food councils," working in cooperation with whatever agencies are formed to administer the programs of the World Food Council of the United Nations.

The deepest and strongest expression of any religion is "the style of life" that characterizes its believers. It is urgent that religious communities and individuals scrutinize their lifestyles and turn from habits of waste, overconsumption, and thoughtless acceptance of the standards propagated by advertisements and social pressures.

The cry from millions for food brought us together from many faiths. God—Reality itself—calls us to respond to the cry for food. And we hear it as a cry not only for aid but also for justice. The spirit of one of the prayers heard in our meeting sums up not only our hope but our resolve: "Give bread to those who have hunger, and to those who have bread, give a hunger for justice."

The Setting—and Since

The setting of this Statement is already clear from the Foreword of this book. It sums up views expressed by participants in the first Interreligious Peace Colloquium during our five unusual days of study and prayer, exchange and fellowship, May 26 to 30, 1975, in Bellagio, Italy.

We Buddhists, Hindus, Jews, Muslims, and Christians speak here and throughout this book in a personal manner only. We do not *represent* our faiths, our temples, churches, mosques, monasteries, or religious bodies, in any official way, although some occupy high rank therein. In like manner, leaders from secular fields do not voice their views on behalf of the governmental, business, professional, or academic position they might hold.

Nor does this Statement present formally adopted resolutions or policies; much less is it "a message to the world." Its nature is much more modest, a sort of agreement among friends. These terse paragraphs, first drafted by Dean Krister Stendahl, are a simple reminder of the intention of the Colloquium participants to work for the alleviation of hunger, each by the means available to him or her, each in our own national, cultural, and faith communities. It is shared with others as a gift we received at Bellagio.

Indeed, all that follows is offered in the same spirit. I have been requested by my fellow officers to present my account of our Colloquium with a personal interpretation of its meaning, present and future. I gladly accept this charge. This book is then my own report; as can be judged from the context, it contains the views of others as I understand them, as well as my own views. For both I alone am responsible. For any misinterpretation, I request correction and indulgence from my confreres.

But, as indicated by the Foreword, our followup to Bellagio has taken other forms besides this book. The "continuation committee," composed of Cyrus Vance, Henry Siegman, and myself, was expanded to include Matthew Rosenhaus. In the two years since Bellagio, we have met twelve times.

In August 1976, the Interreligious Peace Colloquium was legally incorporated, with the four of us as founding directors and officers: Mr. Rosenhaus, president; Mr. Vance, vice-president; Rabbi Siegman, treasurer; myself, secretary and directing officer with the title of coordinator. In December we opened an office in Washington, with William Ryan as executive secretary. Cyrus Vance resigned as an officer in January 1977, when he became Secretary of State of the United States. A dozen additional members have been invited to serve on the board of directors; its composition is given in the Appendix of this book, together with the Colloquium's original sponsors.

The final section of this account is entitled, "The Two Years Since Bellagio." It tells what has happened, and of our hopes and plans for the future.

JOSEPH GREMILLION

Notre Dame, Indiana
May 1977

SESSION ONE

THE FACTS OF THE
FOOD/ENERGY CRISIS

The bleak facts of the food/energy crisis opened our Colloquium. They were presented by two distinguished experts: John A. Hannah, executive director of the World Food Council, a post to which he was appointed by the secretary-general of the United Nations in January 1975; and Nobel Peace Prize winner Norman Borlaug, director of the Maize and Wheat Improvement Center, Mexico City.

In sum they told us:

More than 400 million people, 10 percent of the human family, are not getting enough food to maintain good health. More than half of these individuals are children. Many are starving to death. Many more will die of diseases that invariably accompany gross malnutrition.

The world's population will double to about eight billion within the coming forty years. It is now growing at the rate of about eighty million persons each year; most of this increase is—and will continue to be—in countries already beset by poverty and hunger. Just feeding these extra mouths will require an increase in grain production of thirty-three million tons each year.*

*The American ton is used throughout this book; it is ten percent less than the metric ton.

7

Production of so much additional food will call annually for about five million extra tons of nitrogen, phosphorus, and potash for use in making the required fertilizer. Producing this much more fertilizer each year will demand an additional capital investment of $5 billion to $8 billion each year—a total of about $30 billion new investment by 1980.

The principal cost in producing fertilizer is the purchase of petroleum and gas; their price has quadrupled since 1973. The thirty poorest countries, who most need food and, therefore, fertilizer, have little or no petroleum. Among them are India, Bangladesh, and the countries of the African Sahel; now called the Fourth World, these nations today have a population of about one billion humans. Tens of millions live there on the thin edge of famine, starvation, death. Even in a "normal" year for crops, tens and hundreds of thousands do not survive. Malnutrition is the norm. Further oil hikes will result in less fertilizer for them, and less food.

Despite the Green Revolution, the long-range growth rate of food production has actually been slowing down. But population growth remains high and steady, especially in the Third and Fourth Worlds. The trend is toward more mouths to feed and relatively less to feed them, even when harvests are normal.

The present food crisis emerged in 1972, when for the first time in twenty years world food production fell. A fair harvest in 1973 was followed by disastrously poor crops in 1974. That year, the per-capita food production of developing countries, excluding China, fell below that of the early 1960s.

These recent crop failures, caused in large part by drought and colder winters, drained grain reserves and created shortages. Prices shot up. Meanwhile, the more affluent populations consumed more grain by eating more meat. (It takes about seven pounds of feed to produce one pound of beef.)

And the Soviet Union and China made huge surprise purchases from the food-rich countries—Canada, Australia, and the United States—which drastically cut reserves and further increased prices.

As the energy and fertilizer squeeze got tighter, grain reserves lower, and food prices higher, citizens of the rich countries began to see television pictures of starvation in the Sahel in living color. Nations and peoples bestirred themselves. Representatives of 133 governments met in Rome for a World Food Conference in

November 1974. From this came the World Food Council of the United Nations.

(As I listened to Dr. Hannah and Dr. Borlaug, I saw that it is healthy for religious leaders to learn about the things of the world from lay experts of high competence. The striking lesson comes through that while feeding the hungry is a simple religious imperative it is not a simple undertaking. Technology and economics, ideology and political will, inner motives, religious and cultural values, all enter in. It's a complex business, feeding the one human family. Can it be done in freedom? Is force required? Can it be done at all?)

1

The World Food Council

presented by John A. Hannah

Dr. Hannah's paper, which formed half of the backbone of the Colloquium's first session, focused on the World Food Council—its goals and organization. He explained that its purpose is to stimulate and coordinate implementation of the resolutions of the World Food Conference, the meeting held in Rome, November 1974, at the headquarters of the Food and Agriculture Organization of the United Nations (FAO).

The World Food Council has been established at the ministerial or plenipotentiary level to function as an organ of the United Nations reporting to the General Assembly and the secretary-general. It serves as a coordinating agent to provide overall, integrated, and continuing attention for the successful coordination and follow-up of policies concerning food production, nutrition, food security, food trade, food aid, and other related matters, by all the agencies of the United Nations system.

"The role and purpose of the World Food Council is to stimulate the implementation of the resolutions of the World Food Conference, to assure coordination of U.N. and other international and bilateral programs in food and agriculture, and to serve as an overall monitoring mechanism concerned with both short-range and long-range programs in all areas of food and agriculture."

The Council, explained Dr. Hannah, consists of thirty-six U.N. member nations elected to it by the General Assembly. He noted its composition by region: Africa, nine countries; Asia, seven; Latin America, seven; the developed countries of the West and

11

Japan, nine; the socialist countries of East Europe, four. Dr. Hannah's note suggested that although individual nations still form the de jure membership units of the United Nations, the significant reality de facto is their coalescing into regions, groups, and blocs. He spoke of the deep concern for the food crisis which "was true of every group—the Group of 77 (the non-aligned countries and the largest bloc in the U.N.), the developing countries, the developed countries; the Soviet Union, the People's Republic of China, and the other socialist countries; the Latin Americans, the Africans, the Asians, the OPEC* countries—all of them."

(As a church official, I immediately began to correlate these regions and blocs with the religion which is present—and probably of some influence—within each. I asked myself whether the values and ethical system of this faith relate in any way to government, regional, and bloc policies of the United Nations? To decisions in the World Food Council? To this corporate humanity-wide undertaking to feed the hungry? As confreres in faith at Bellagio we continued to ask these questions of each other as individual believers, as disciples of our five religious traditions, and as members of the community in faith that we began forming together. And we who are full-time officers of religion must ask our associates from the secular world similar questions: In their view, should we relate the world food crisis to the world faiths, particularly within their nations and regions? If so, how?)

From Dr. Hannah's paper, the Colloquium participants learned that the Food Council is now becoming "a coordinating mechanism" for various organizations dealing with the food crisis. Because the crisis is expected to last a long time, the World Food Conference called for the establishment of five new intergovernmental bodies, most of them under U.N. sponsorship, to work specifically on production and investment, funds for agricultural development, food reserves and security, food aid for emergencies, and information and warnings about the future. The work of these five new creations must be correlated with that of several older U.N. agencies and the World Bank (and the various regional banks), and with bilateral aid from some thirty individual rich nations to about eighty poorer countries.

(The bureaucratic complications seemed to pile up for us "of simple faith"; this heavy machinery might well crush us "of little

*Organization of Petroleum Exporting Countries.

faith." So we followed Dr. Hannah's briefing carefully, step by step, with admiration for the human drive, mixed perhaps with religious hope, by which our secular leaders are trying, block by ponderous block, to build up peace and justice by and for feeding the hungry.)

The Consultative Group on Food Production and Investment is getting started on its "responsibility for increasing, coordinating, and improving the efficiency of financial and technical assistance to agricultural production in developing countries." In a few minutes, Dr. Borlaug would tell us a lot about production practices and technology. He, Dr. Hannah, and all the experts seemed to agree that increasing production where the food is needed must get top priority. Most admitted that many countries will require outside funds and technical assistance to do this. Some doubted whether several key areas can increase production enough to catch and keep up with population growth. All were convinced that it is an enormous undertaking, fraught with possible failure.

The International Fund for Agricultural Development is in formation. Dr. Hannah reported enthusiastically on the meeting he attended for setting up this fund only three weeks before. Representatives of forty-eight countries, from the developed and the developing world, had participated in this session in Geneva, May 1975. The OPEC countries had taken the lead: "The Minister of Agriculture of Saudi Arabia proposed an initial budget of 1 billion Special Drawing Rights* (equivalent to about U.S. $1.25 billion) for the capital of the Fund, which could be increased in light of the success achieved by the Fund in realizing its objectives and additional needs as they arise. This proposal was supported by Algeria, Iran, Kuwait, Libya, Nigeria, Qatar, the United Arab Emirates, and Venezuela."

The nine countries supporting the proposal are all members of OPEC. In fact, the very idea of this Fund for Agricultural Development had been initiated by the OPEC bloc as its major contribution to the 1974 World Food Conference. During that meeting, it had been "generally agreed that the magnitude of the Fund

---

*Special Drawing Rights are units of credit which a country has with the International Monetary Fund. The value of an SDR (about $1.25 in 1975) derives from the average value of the participating national currencies; consequently its worth fluctuates, but the system still provides a unit of international exchange more stable than the U.S. dollar, the deutsche mark, or pound sterling. The SDR system has been in use only since 1970; a major purpose is to provide loans and help liquidity problems, short-term or long-term.

should be approximately $1 billion per year at the outset, which would be contributed one-half from the OPEC countries and one-half from the traditional donors—the DAC* of Western Europe, Japan, Australia, New Zealand, Canada, and the United States —and that the Governing Board would be divided one-third from the OPEC countries, one-third from the DAC countries, and one-third from the recipient developing countries."

Since October 1973, the oil-producing bloc has increased its economic power and political leverage in quantum leaps, by embargo, nationalization, and quadrupling the price of its product. The liquid resources of these countries are now actually much greater than are those of the West, and they are able to offer aid to others even though they are still quite rightly classed as developing countries themselves.

(In the context of this Interreligious Colloquium, I find it noteworthy that of the nine OPEC countries backing this $1.25 billion, seven are dominantly Muslim, and an eighth, Nigeria, is heavily so. They are now offering to match the industrialized West, dominantly Christian and Jewish in heritage, in providing these and similar aid funds. In the history of nations, religious self-confidence and influence can often be correlated with the economic political power of the believing people. The two or three centuries of western world dominance saw Christian missionary zeal reach new dimensions. The more recent rise of the State of Israel is not unrelated to the economic and political power achieved by many Jews, especially in the United States.

(Perhaps we will now see a rise of self-confidence among Muslim peoples, especially in North Africa and the Middle East. Perhaps the world's "religious power equation" will shift, as does the economic power balance. Perhaps economic and political interdependence are in some way related to religious interdependence, and vice versa. I confess that I have become more interested in Islam now that Muslim peoples wield such economic power and, in the case of this Fund for Agricultural Development, are beginning to use it with wisdom and compassion worthy of true followers of Allah, the All-Wise and All-Merciful. And Allah is the same one omnipotent and compassionate God worshipped by Jews and Christians.)

*Developing Assistance Committee of the Organization for Economic Cooperation and Development; i.e., the aid-giving arm of the organization of the developed countries of the West plus Australia, New Zealand, and Japan.

The Committee on World Food Security was the third new body Dr. Hannah introduced to us religious officials. It will "make periodic evaluations of the adequacy and distribution of world food stocks, including those for food aid . . . , and recommend policy actions necessary to assure cereal supplies for minimum food security."

In other words, the human family is learning to look ahead. Over three thousand years of history has taught us the same lesson that divine vision revealed to Joseph in Egypt: Fat years will be followed by lean, so we had better keep a goodly supply of grain in storage.

Since this lesson seems fairly obvious, perhaps a few of the less knowledgeable among us wondered a little if such a committee might not be an example of too much organization, of bureaucracy for its own sake. Any such doubts were dispelled a few hours later when Dr. Borlaug elaborated on how suddenly the last three years of poor crops came upon us, depleting reserves. So now the world's warehouses are truly almost empty. He also stressed the continuing danger: "I think that the leadership of the world even now fails to realize how close we were to a tremendous disaster. It is not only that thousands or even hundreds of thousands perished in the last two years. More frightening is the fact that we were a step away from a situation in which *millions* could have perished. That is how thin the line was. . . . We are not out of the situation yet because there has been virtually no build-up of stock, of cereal grains in the last three years."

A *Committee on Food Aid Policies and Programmes*, Dr. Hannah explained, is also being formed. When crop failure does occur (as happens every year somewhere in the world), the suffering country, which is usually among the world's poorest, needs aid. It rarely has sufficient cash to purchase food from the warehouses of the rich, whose prices shoot up precisely because of shortages in less fortunate regions. These people need the equivalent of U.S. food stamps. But these have no value if they are not backed up by a food supply set aside and pledged as aid available when emergency calls.

Dr. Hannah praised the Food Conference for introducing this "concept of forward planning of food aid." He believed "that the committee's target goal of ten million tons of cereal grain for food aid per year for three years could be met. The generous action of the United States, Canada, Australia, and others has placed the goal within reach."

A *Global Information and Early Warning System on Food and Agriculture* is the last group now being organized. Hannah gave few details, but the title seems descriptive enough.

(By mental association, the phrase "Early Warning" brings to mind the U.S.-Canadian radar network in the Arctic Circle, ready to alert Washington and Ottawa of impending nuclear catastrophe. What a relief to hear the term put to a peaceful purpose—to a purpose almost religious, because we at Bellagio became very conscious that in most of our faiths bread and rice take on holy meaning as the sign or sacrament of life, even of the divine, especially when given to the hungry. But we also became more and more aware that we faithful often regard wars, too, as holy, as calls of the divine.)

Dr. Hannah concluded that "if nations will not agree on a food policy which will benefit them all, they are not likely to agree on anything. But if they can make real progress toward solving the food problem, it could well lead the way to solving some of the other difficult problems the world now faces: the need for an international monetary system that works, the economic problems that grow out of the energy crisis, inflation, and the rest.

"All 133 nations at the World Food Conference last November resolved that within a decade no child will go to bed hungry, no family will fear for its next day's bread, and no human being's future and capacities will be stunted by malnutrition. This was a pledge that the whole world joined in—a solemn pledge taken freely by the entire international community.

"The real challenge is whether people like you will take a leadership role in making this pledge possible of fulfillment. Political leaders move in response to the attitude of their people. This audience represents a broad cross-section of the religious leadership of the world. You are in a position to play a key role if the necessary national and international actions are to be taken.

"There will be no abiding peace in this world unless we can solve the basic problem of food for hungry people everywhere. History will judge the adequacy of our actions. Let us hope and pray that we shall not fail."

2

Production and Technology

presented by Norman Borlaug

Norman Borlaug, father of the Green Revolution, opened the
next address with a somber warning of the magnitude of the
production problems that face the goals described by Dr. Hannah.
Layer by interconnecting layer, he unrolled the technical and
production factors that make any attempt to solve the food crisis
so complex.

LIMITED ARABLE LAND

The two primordial restrictions on increased food production
are the limitations of arable land and of available water, from
rainfall or irrigation. "As we fly across one continent after
another, we get the impression that the world is very large from
the standpoint of land area. But when we get down to analyzing
the situation, we see that only about 11 percent of the total land
surface area of the earth can be classified as arable, meaning that
it is either cultivated now, or has the potential or being cultivated
within the near future." This 11 percent of the earth's surface
adds up to about 3.3 billion acres of land which can be annually
plowed and planted in grain, potatoes, and other root crops, coffee,
tea, etc.

Additionally, about twice that area, 6.6 billion acres, is classified
as grazing land, fit for livestock production. But some of that is
subject to periodic drought, such as occurred in recent years in the
Sahel, the grass plains just south of the Sahara Desert. Peoples

living on grazing lands tend to build up economies—and eating habits—based on livestock. When rainfall fails, the cattle and goat herds which had built up in good years are decimated. So are the people.

THE NEED TO INCREASE GRAIN PRODUCTION

Dr. Borlaug focused on production of cereal grain because wheat, rice, oats, corn or maize, millets, and barley do constitute the staff of life. They provide most of the calories that humans consume. These grain fields now occupy half the world's arable surface. But because population growth is now adding eighty million persons to the world each year, grain production must increase by some thirty-three million tons annually just to keep food supply at the same level—a level often inadequate to begin with.

In the past, when a population outgrew the production capacity of its land, some of the people migrated or expanded their land borders—sometimes across oceans—through empires or trade. There was always more land for the taking somewhere.

"But today," Dr. Borlaug insisted, "there exists little new land that can be brought into cultivation. Brazil, Paraguay, and several African countries do have such areas, but these are exceptions. Now we suddenly find that many of the developing nations have huge and growing populations, but no additional land that can be brought under the plow rapidly without tremendous irrigation development—which is both expensive and slow to bring results."

Worse still, grain production from some normally good soil dropped in recent years, because of drought in some areas and colder, longer winters in others. It was this added chill which reduced the Soviet wheat crop in 1972. "Although the total world production dropped by only about 3.8 percent, some forty-four million tons, it took this much out of the warehouses. Prices began to soar, indicating that we hadn't calculated very well what reserves were needed in order to keep prices more or less reasonably stable."

THE TRUE SHORTFALL

Forty-four million tons of grain sound like a lot, but it is really only one-thirtieth of worldwide output. The fact that recent harvests were down only that much can be laid partly to modern agricultural methods, partly to the relatively small proportion of grain-producing land which was hit by unfavorable weather conditions. But it must be remembered that besides equalling the previous year's production each of those recent harvests should have increased by an amount sufficient to feed the new mouths added to the population in that year. That increase of about eighty million persons requires about thirty-three million additional tons of grain annually. So, to arrive at the true shortfall, one must add the increase that did not materialize to the actual drop in production.

In 1974, this simple equation gave a true shortfall of about seventy million tons. (In that year, world grain reserves dropped from 189 to 119 million tons.)* And thus, Dr. Borlaug pointed out, reserve stocks were drained by even a moderate drop in annual production, *plus* the steady rate of population growth. Worse still, he deplored, is the fact that "no one knows the magnitude of the stocks held in many countries. These are economic secrets."

We must ponder the morality of such secrecy in the context of social justice, whether in planned economies, where the food supply may be a political and military secret, or in free-market economies, where confidential data will enlarge the "killing" possible through speculation in grain futures. Such secrecy ties in with the collusion we glimpse occasionally between western agribusiness and government bureaucrats and politicians, and with the constant coordination between economic and political commissars—perhaps too, with economic and strategic espionage. The systems of reserves and of early warnings that Dr. Hannah is putting together will have to combat such secrecy and the profitable deals it makes possible.

FERTILIZER, THE KEY

Dr. Borlaug then concentrated on how to increase production during the five years 1976–80 on the land now under cultivation, in order to provide for the eighty million new humans expected to be added to the population annually (about 400 million in the five-year period). For his calculations, he assumed that the natural disasters of 1972–74 were temporary aberrations and used as his

---

*As I go over this text for final editing, reserves for 1976 are estimated at 110 million tons. Daily world consumption is about 3.6 million tons, so the human family has reserves for only 31 days. (Lester Brown, *Worldwatch*, Paper 2, p. 6.)

base the world's record harvest of 1971 (1.32 billion tons of cereal grains). "To maintain per capita food consumption at the 1971 level, without drawing down on stocks that are held in reserve (as was necessary in 1972 and '74), will take on the order of thirty-three million tons of additional grains."

Fertilizer, said Dr. Borlaug, is the key input for increasing production rapidly. "To produce those thirty-three million tons of grain will require about 3.3 million tons of nitrogen, half that much of phosphorous, and a third that much of potash." To obtain this six million tons of additional fertilizer, "there will have to be investments of about $6 billion per year for the next five years. This is no small item."

So by 1980, something like $30 billion of new investment will have been needed for fertilizer alone. We see here the tie-in with two of the newly formed bodies described by Dr. Hannah: the Group on Food Production and Investment, and the International Fund for Agricultural Development. Providing more fertilizer is a prime purpose for them also.

Dr. Hannah, the highly respected worldwide administrator who deals with governments and magnitudes, seems more optimistic than Dr. Borlaug, the Iowa-farmboy-become-global-production-technician. Dr. Borlaug deals with drought and frost, illiterate peasants, village practices, and local politics. Dr. Hannah, true to his intergovernmental role, rightly rejoiced at the prospect of aid transfers from have to have-not nations; he believes they will meet Dr. Borlaug's fertilizer needs at least in part.

"The World Food Conference in 1974 pointed out that external input into the developing countries of up to $5 billion per year would be required by 1980 to achieve the desired food production goals. In 1973, about $1.5 billion was being made available. The actions already taken by the World and Regional Banks and by the bilateral aid donors have increased the availability to almost double the previous $1.5 billion, for a total now of almost $3 billion. As soon as the International Fund for Agricultural Development gets underway at the hoped-for levels, we will be well on our way to achieving the goals that seemed unattainable one year ago." Such are Dr. Hannah's hopes.

THE MYTH OF ORGANIC FERTILIZERS

Dr. Borlaug paused in his briefing on production needs to address an issue often raised in today's environment-conscious world: the use of organic fertilizers. "Now there are a lot of people who think that we're going to produce this thirty-three million additional tons of grain each year by using things like organic fertilizers. Let me say here and now that the use of organic fertilizers for growing a few rose bushes or a few tomato plants in someone's backyard is wonderful. But it's completely unrealistic to think that we are going to produce the food that's needed by relying on organic matter. There isn't that much organic matter around.

"That does not mean that we should not try to use all waste to the maximum of our ability to do so. Indeed, I have great respect for the People's Republic of China where, as part of a long cultural tradition, they do use all types of waste to increase food production.

"But let me also point out that no country today is putting more capital investment into chemical fertilizer plants than the People's Republic of China. In 1960, they consumed no chemical fertilizer whatsoever. From 1960 until about 1973, they constructed something on the order of 800 small chemical nitrogen fertilizer plants, dispersed throughout their cultural areas. These produce ammonia from coal and convert it to a solid form of fertilizer. Now they're building newer and larger plants based on natural gas."

FERTILIZER AND ENERGY

Next Dr. Borlaug spoke to the environmentalists' concern over using nonreplaceable resources to manufacture fertilizers. This is one of many places where the food and energy crises knot themselves together. The major inputs for producing chemical fertilizers are petroleum and natural gas.

"People say we can't afford this kind of investment because it's wasteful of energy." But the needed energy is already wasting away. "When I fly over vast areas of gas fields and petroleum fields in the world today, I see gas being flared off* in quantities so large that one year's worth would produce all the fertilizer that is needed until the end of the century. Something is wrong in that environment equation."

*The outflow of liquid oil from wells is often accompanied by an outflow of gas, such as methane. Many fields do not have the apparatus for capturing this gas and directing it into pipelines for human use. It is allowed to escape into the atmosphere, and as it does so it is set afire and blazes like a huge flaring torch.

In the discussion that followed Dr. Borlaug's remarks, Dr. Hannah said he found this estimate of the fertilizer potential of "gas that is being flared in the Middle East a little higher than I thought it was, but there *is* a tremendous waste. We're trying to get the producing countries to use the gas as near the well heads as possible, to build fertilizer plants there, and to offer the produce for sale at cost where it's needed. And where the fertilizer is most needed is in Asia and Africa." Dr. Hannah went on to stress the substantial saving to be gained from "the difference in the freight rate—the difference in cost between producing fertilizer there, and exporting it from New Orleans to Africa and Asia."

Dr. Borlaug added more concretely: "I was in Saudi Arabia last week, talking to the Minister of Agriculture. A big project is now under way there to capture all of this gas, channel it into pipe lines, and establish a large chemical fertilizer industry. At least there is some progress all along this front, which has been neglected too long."

(A starry-eyed believer in the prophets and their promises, I had visions of a Middle East development plan for a region flowing with milk and honey, fertilized by liquid ammonia made by modern technology from the flood of gas our one God-Creator stored in the bosom of our one mother earth for our common use. Will we Jews-Muslims-Christians, children by blood and by the Spirit of Abraham, awaken to our one God and his call to justice and compassion, love and peace? And we officials of temple-mosque-church, minister-mufti-iman-rabbi-priest, what example do we give to leaders of government and business, research and media, the Hannahs and Borlaugs of this world? They strive and cooperate more than we do to feed the hungry.)

THE OTHER INPUTS OF FOOD PRODUCTION

Dr. Borlaug called us back to a reality even more down-to-earth than fertilizer. That is but one of the inputs for increased food production, and probably the most simple. Three others are also decisive: moisture, seed, and cultivation practices.

"It's all a very complex situation down on the farm at the production level. It looks very easy to organize all these things from modernized, isolated command centers. . . . When you get down on the firing line, where the food is produced, it's most frustrating, a most difficult situation."

Dr. Borlaug stressed that there is no magic in the special high-yield seeds (which caused the Green Revolution and for the development of which he was given the Nobel Peace Prize). "These have the built-in potential to produce abundantly if there is sufficient water and soil nutrients, and if cultural practices permit the seeds to reach their potential. But too often the peasant farmer is trying to cultivate at mere survival level. The soil has been mined for decades, centuries, sometimes for thousands of years. The nutrients have been removed." Suppose fertilizer is added, if available—which it seldom is, for the subsistence farmer. Unless cultivation practices are changed, "weeds will use up the fertilizer rather than the plant you are trying to cultivate."

Why is it so difficult to change the habits of farmers?

"You must reach largely illiterate people. In the developing nations, anywhere from 60 to 85 percent of the people are rural (compared with about 5 percent in North America). They have not had the benefit of education that more privileged people even in developing nations have had. This is a great bottleneck in applying the new technology."

REDISTRIBUTION AND NATIONAL POTENTIALS

Dr. Borlaug had a final word on land policies and on national potentials. Mere quantitative redistribution of land usually has little or no value for raising production. Optimum farm size, he said, varies enormously between "say, a semitropical country where you can produce two or three crops a year on the same plot, and a semidesert country where for three out of four years inadequate moisture will limit production." On this sort of question, Dr. Borlaug lashed out at planners working "from command posts isolated from the drudgeries and misery of the people who till the soil, more than half the people of the world."

He also criticized "the allocation of economic resources in the developing nations, which have always given agriculture a very small percentage of what it merits, based on the basic needs of the peoples."

Dr. Borlaug is convinced that opportunities for increasing food production are greater in hungry countries that now have low yields per acre (compared with high-yield countries, such as Holland or North America) if agriculture is given priority. "As Dr. Hannah has pointed out, we have the capacity if we can apply our technology, if we can get these different sectors pulling together, if we can get these new investments functioning in the developing world."

But, he hastened to add, even this theoretical technical capacity does not obtain in all places. "Unfortunately there are some new nations that have a soil-rainfall base which will never permit them to be self-sufficient in food production. The base is too limited. Too many nations have come into being with political lines drawn without any regard for the possibilities of producing a decent standard of living for the citizens of those countries. This is another problem that will make it impossible for some developing nations ever to produce the food that will be needed; they will always have to obtain part of that food, in some cases great percentages of it, from beyond their borders."

3

Discussion: Facts and
Their Meaning

Colloquium participants then asked questions and brought up new facts. Six issues wove in and out, already grouping the threads which would merge into major themes throughout the Colloquium. Because the discussion, like all live encounters, circled and overlapped itself, I have made no effort to reproduce it consecutively or in its entirety. Rather I have selected statements and paraphrases representing the general drift and clustered them by topics.

FACTS: PERSONAL AND IMPERSONAL

Two opposed meanings of "fact" were spotted right off by Wilfred Cantwell Smith. "In modern western thought 'facts' seem to be those things with which natural science deals. Realities such as will, resolve, commitment, concern, sympathy are not 'facts.' But to Dr. Hannah and Dr. Borlaug the most important thing has apparently become the will—the will to act in this realm, political decisions, discernment of problems, and the like. I get a feeling that they are skirting the distinction between impersonal facts and personal facts. . . . But I would guess that in part the real heart of our Colloquium, of the larger problem we are concerned with, is precisely this feeling that the facts are impersonal."

Professor Hasan Askari partially echoed Dr. Smith. He urged "from my experience of the Indian situation" that food-crisis facts be balanced by a proper emphasis "on the structural questions within a given society. . . . I have witnessed many programs fail in India, seen planning collapse. . . . The food crisis is certainly interrelated with the question of certain political and ideological options, . . . with a will to solve problems on the political level."

Dr. Borlaug agreed that nontangible facts, such as dedication and commitment, are very important. He stressed the need for agricultural scientists "who are willing to give to the best of their ability and can stimulate others. We find very few of them. . . . Agriculture has no prestige. After you get an education, you don't want to work with your hands." His approach to developing new agriculturists is "to bring young graduates outside their environment, to a place such as Mexico, and teach them to sweat the honest sweat of producing the bread each of us consumes every day, and takes for granted."

Dr. Hannah disdained semantics. "Nothing happens unless the real leaders—political, economic, social, religious—make the decision that the production of food is important, which is what the People's Republic of China has done."

In addition to the necessity of leadership, Dr. Hannah admitted that "when you get down to cold hard facts—even further down the line than Dr. Borlaug did—you have to make agricultural production attractive to the people who are doing the farming. Especially the subsistence farmer needs incentives to produce more than the family can eat; then he exchanges this surplus for goods not produced on the farm—things like clothes or spices to make food palatable, or an education for the kids, or even a lamp, any of the basic things they need to make living interesting and satisfying."

FOOD PRODUCTION IN CHINA

Maoist China's apparent success in increasing food production—and the meaning of this success—drew more attention than any other subject during this session.

Shlomo Avineri, Dean of Social Sciences at the Hebrew University of Jerusalem,* asked the first question. He wanted data on China's food imports and on the very large percentage of food "locally grown under highly non-industrialized conditions. I would especially appreciate any suggestion about the reason which enables China to do things that other countries in a similar situation aren't able to do, or at least haven't been able to do until now."

---

*Dean Avineri was named Director General of the Foreign Ministry of the State of Israel a few months after our Bellagio meeting.

Dr. Borlaug replied that China has not "published official figures for more than fifteen years. But experts estimate production at probably 250 million tons of what the Chinese call 'equivalents of cereal grains.' They use that term in production statistics because they have a way of including root crops, such as yams, potatoes, and all sorts of other things, using a correction factor to equate that figure with cereal grains." As for imports, Dr. Borlaug reported that in 1974 China brought in six to nine million tons of grain, mostly wheat, "to rebuild stocks that were depleted following the 1972 harvest, which was bad."

From observations made during a visit to China last year and from other data, Dr. Borlaug stated that Chinese agriculture "has improved very greatly."

"It is very labor intensive. Between 80 and 85 percent of the total population is engaged in producing food. During the Cultural Revolution, university people—even professors—were sent to the countryside to till the soil and to work with the peasants. There is no question that part of the change has had to do with that. It is now general policy that a professor will spend one out of three years on a collective farm working with production brigades. I have seen also the work that is being done by what I call the Youth Corps, which each year has recruited about 800,000 young people from the urban areas and sent them out to work on rural projects. Some are building roads, others digging new canals or cleaning out old ones—all sorts of work, most of it related to agriculture.

"This is a very drastic change. Obviously it is related to preventing the bureaucracy from separating itself as an elite, from isolating itself from the problems of the masses, in relation to the production of food.

"They are also applying much newer technology. For example, as I mentioned earlier, vast investment is now going into fertilizer plant capacity. When you add all this up, you see that the People's Republic of China has given the expansion of food production a very high order of importance—both in capital investment and labor input."

Professor Mohammed Al-Nowaihi, of Cairo, and Father Joseph Spae, of Geneva and Tokyo, pressed for opinions on the applicability of China's experiment to other nations. The Egyptian returned to the "difficulty of getting illiterate rural people to apply modern techniques. We in the Middle East have been hearing a lot about China's use of simple, even primitive methods. This has been very attractive to us. I'd like to ask to what extent what we've heard is true, and if true, how much can be applied to other undeveloped countries?"

Fr. Spae cited returning U.S. experts who have said "only China can, in the final instance, give the world a lesson in agriculture." But, he continued, the head of FAO, Dr. Addeke Boerma, had reportedly retorted: "This is true. But it is unthinkable from a political point of view. So, here again we see that hunger is a political problem."

Professor Askari also linked the Chinese experiment to the deeper politics "of ideological option. Should we say that a food crisis is better resolved if a government operates on cultural, ideological, and economic regimentation?"

Dr. Borlaug did not admit that "only China can show the way. I think there are several roads that lead to the same place. Which one to take depends entirely on the stage of cultural evolution that a given country finds itself in at a given point in time. There is no single way to solve these problems.

"Also, if everyone were to choose the road of China—putting 85 percent of the people back on the land—in an industrialized country, what would happen to the industry? What would happen to the whole way of life? Would it even be possible? In the industrialized nations most of the people have lost contact with the soil. They would be the most inept people in the world to put back on the soil without a very intensive program of indoctrination. But the real question is, would they accept?"

Dr. Borlaug asked Dr. Hannah to comment. It was at this point that the latter stressed the importance of leaders making tough decisions, "whether it's in China or Bangladesh or the Central African Republic." In China, when things didn't look very good, "they decided that they had to be certain they could feed their own people. And so they made the tough decision that no matter how disagreeable it might be for human beings, they were going to harness this one and get it done."

Dr. Avineri concluded "that the same problem in two different economic systems is a completely different problem." The Chinese can do everything necessary to make their fertilizer industry function by a single political decision. Whereas the market economies of the West and the OPEC countries operate "within the pricing system—things have to be profitable to everyone concerned. Now, isn't that a consideration of the first order—that the survival of so many people depends on a political system? Can this question really be ducked?"

ECONOMIC STRUCTURES AND FAITH COMMUNITIES

The linkage of social and economic structures with political and ideological options became quite clear. The corollary link with faith communities was quickly pointed out, first by Professor Askari. This was, of course, a key Colloquium issue and received detailed treatment in later sessions. Now I need only note that at this early moment in the meeting Professor Askari charged that "our faith communities, as they are located in their respective home constituencies, are not existing in a vacuum. They are related to economic structures, structures that perpetuate inequality, oppression, exploitation." (Another Indian, Professor S. L. Parmar, formally presented this central theme in a major paper during Session Four.)

INTERNATIONAL AID AND TRADE

The discussion looped back to the shaky structures of international aid. Rabbi Irwin Blank wanted clarification on the "tremendous gap between need and response. Dr. Borlaug says $5 billion is needed annually to produce fertilizer only, but Dr. Hannah's Aid Fund falls very far short of what the requirements are."

Fr. Spae followed up on the role of the rich countries, especially the United States. He cited Dr. Borlaug's statement to the U.S. Senate, some months before, that "famine and widespread death of millions would bring the world to an understanding of the enormity of the problem (*New York Times*, July 6, 1974). Surely Dr. Borlaug knows better than all of us that in many areas of the world this is already happening, that these millions of people are dying silently."

Dr. Hannah agreed that the reality could only worsen unless the United States, Western Europe, and the OPEC countries do their fair share. But, he pointed out, it is not simply a question of direct food aid, no matter how well intentioned. Fertilizer and other inputs must be provided for the production of food in or near the needy countries themselves. "Raising more food in North America offers no basic answers. It wouldn't do the trick because the hungry people are going to be in some place like Bangladesh. To get the food to them you have to get it distributed.

"Two years ago, when the Soviet Union bought twenty-six million tons of cereal grains in the United States and Canada, that completely demobilized North America's transportation system.

Some freight cars took fourteen months to get the darn stuff from where it was stored all the way to the port."

Getting food to the Sahel, continued Dr. Hannah, is still more difficult. They are inland countries, far from the African ports. Further, "you're dealing with nomadic people who are scattered all over the landscape. You've got to get them centralized and you've got to get the food to them—maybe even haul it by air—and distribute it. If the food-exporting countries could produce it, it wouldn't solve the problem. The real problem is how to produce more food in the poor countries where there are hungry people."

This distribution problem is why Dr. Hannah again stressed the Development Fund, which will raise food production in the hungry countries themselves, particularly through increasing local production of fertilizers and pesticides. Because those inputs require petroleum and natural gas, he insisted again on the key role of the oil exporting countries:

"We're not going to get anywhere in the Development Fund unless the OPEC countries stay with the commitment that they made in Rome last November. And there are lots of reasons why they might become less enthusiastic. But for the idea to work, four or five of the OPEC countries will have to stay with it and determine to move toward their goal of funding half the total cost of this Agricultural Development Fund."

And those countries will have to include Saudi Arabia and Iran, Dr. Hannah went on, because they're the big oil producers. Algeria is important for a different reason; it does not have much in the way of resources, but it occupies a leadership role among the OPEC countries. The other really important countries are the United Arab Emirates and Kuwait, because they are well-intentioned people, and Venezuela because it has substantial resources outside the Arab world. "Unless the United States does its fair share, we're going to have trouble. Not because it is an absolute key, but because if it doesn't do its share, the French and the West Germans aren't going to. Because the Common Market countries will say that so large a fraction of the responsibility belongs to the United States."

(We see here the intertwinings of the food and energy crises, the interdependence of the rich regions, the enormous shift of economic and political power toward the Arab, Muslim countries. We see the West, predominantly Christian and Jewish, assume only second place in Dr. Hannah's funding requirements. And I wonder about the consequences of this new alignment of interdependence—political, cultural, religious consequences.)

Dr. Marga Klompe, minister of state in Holland, once a colonial power, worried about charges of neocolonialism being leveled against aid-giving countries. "Perhaps they really want to help people at the grassroots, but the government of the receiving country wants to give priority to industry rather than agriculture, or wants very huge agricultural projects which do not help the poorest. This is, I think, an ethical problem which embarrasses many people who have the best intentions and want to help the poorest especially."

Dr. Hannah answered Dr. Klompe by saying that there won't be enough aid to go around, so resources and technical assistance should go where they will produce best results. This problem faces bilateral programs as well as the new World Food Council, and must always be answered by giving "first priority to the poor people in the poorest countries with a food deficit. But help should also go to a place like Sudan where a lot of food can be produced for export to nearby neighbors in the needy Sahel."

Professor Askari raised the related danger of cultural colonialism. He asked whether Dr. Hannah's approaches did not "presuppose superimposition of western concepts on the perceptions of the other parts of the world regarding the food crisis. This is important sociologically, because food is not only a biological commodity. It is something cultural and spiritual. It is part of ritual. And hence, I submit to Dr. Hannah that the question invites a much more complex discourse than a mere reference to statistics and the enormity of the problem."

Dr. Hannah assured Professor Askari that the World Food Council will not try to impose unacceptable views on countries, each of which has its own values, cultures, and problems. The thirty-six nation members will decide what priorities the Council should follow in dealing with the world food problem. Thereafter, "the right answer has to be written in the country you're talking about. The right answer in India is the Indian answer, and it doesn't make a darn bit of difference what the people in Rome or New York think about it. But nothing is going to happen without leadership by the people who make decisions in the individual countries. And remember, right now there are 138 separate countries. Maybe that's too many, but that's the way it is." (Ten more nations came into existence during the fifteen months I worked on this book.)

WASTE, LIFESTYLE, AND POPULATION

Another major theme of the Colloquium surfaced briefly: waste, lifestyle, and population. Dean Krister Stendahl, due to give a paper the next day on "New Styles of Life in Communities of Faith," introduced the subject here. "I would like to know whether waste and overuse in the developed countries is a substantial factor in projecting the future food and hunger situation, or whether this is a romantic self-occupation, especially in religious circles. I would also like data about the relation between cereal needs and that enormous amount of cereal that goes into meat production. None of this was mentioned, which gives me an eerie feeling."

The World Food Council, said Dr. Hannah, is definitely concerned about waste and overuse. Elimination of waste by rodents, poor storage, spoilage, and the like has high priority. Proper use of land for meat production, however, presents a different and more complex problem. In the United States, Dr. Hannah explained, most cattle start out on the grazing range, eating grass in dry areas which would not be used otherwise. Then they are fattened with grain which may or may not be fit for human food. "A substantial fraction of the Iowa-fattened steer came out of grass or poor forage." Dr. Hannah expects similar dry grasslands in Africa to produce large quantities of lean stringy beef that has high protein value. "It's not the kind of beef that we like to eat in the western world but it's got a lot of nutriment. If we can control the tse-tse fly and diseases carried by it, we're going to be feeding a lot of people with that stringy beef."

Dr. Hannah did urge that his compatriots eat less meat. "That's good for your health of body and your peace of mind. But the big question is: How do you translate what you don't eat in New York or Boston into feeding hungry people in Chad? This is the step that counts. Figure out how you take what you save and turn it over so that it's available to people who are hungry in the poor country."

Bishop James Rausch objected that he was not satisfied with focusing the problem on spoilage rather than misuse through western overconsumption. "It does seem to me that there are consumption choices that have to be made and that the religious community has to speak to that issue. It also seems to me that there are choices that have to be made regarding production. For example, Monsignor Gremillion has reminded those of us at this

end of the table that we are using arable land to burn up smoke."
(He was referring to my effort as Colloquium traffic officer to seat
non-smokers and smokers at opposite ends of the table.)

The population aspect was brought up by Dr. Mohammed Al-
Nowaihi. "We will not be really living up to our duty if our Colloquium sticks only to food production, avoiding, either deliberately
or accidentally, the other side of the problem—restricting the
terrible explosion of population." But Dr. Hannah chose "not to
get into the population business" for the moment.

At several points in the discussion, however, Dr. Hannah did
comment on lifestyle and meaning, "being philosophical for a
moment." He warned "you people who are religious leaders,
. . . you don't want to buy a formula and say this is it. As religious
leaders, let's look down the road. Somehow or other, we've got to
develop a philosophical realization that what we are really talking
about is the content, qualities, factors that make life meaningful
and satisfying to the people who are living. It won't be satisfying if
you don't feed them. But far beyond—what is it that makes life
interesting?"

BARGAINING AND INFORMATION

Fr. Bryan Hehir concluded the period by noting the gap between the bargaining power of consuming and producing nations
on the world commodity market. He cited his experience in working on a scheme for the international regulation of cocoa prices.

The producers, Fr. Hehir explained, needed to know what stocks
the manufacturing countries held over from last year, while the
buyers needed to know production prospects for the coming year.
"The producers are very weak countries who could not say no to
anything. So they gave all the information they had. But the
information on available stocks was not forthcoming from the rich
and strong buyers. So it was never possible to work out a proper
regulation scheme. I bring this up because I keep wondering how
you are going to work out a proper food bank when the people who
stock these products refuse to disclose what they have in their
stocks? I just want to know how the Food Council is tackling this
little problem."

Discussion time was up. So that little problem dangles still.

Cardinal Evaristo Arns, of São Paulo, Brazil, closed our first
session, which he chaired, by calling upon the great religions to

agree on joint action for serving the human family: to save the earth and give it to the humble; to work together to assure that the world's resources reach those of our brothers and sisters who are now excluded by social injustice; to cooperate with the world of development and science.

SESSION TWO

IMPACT OF THE CRISIS ON
WORLD PEACE
AND SOCIAL JUSTICE

Ambassador Edwin M. Martin, distinguished for his long career in international organizations and politics, aid, and development, gave the principal paper for Session Two. As requested, he placed the facts of the food/energy crisis within the context of economic and political structures, with a view to promoting world peace and social justice. Brief extemporaneous presentations followed by Dean Shlomo Avineri, of Jerusalem, and Bishop Paul Moore, of New York. They formally began the Colloquium's basic purpose of relating the realities of economics and politics, peace and justice, to the sphere of ethics and faith. Chief Simeon Adebo, longtime delegate of Nigeria to the United Nations, chaired this session; now and again he shared of his rich experience as a global, national, and tribal leader.

4

Economic Consequences
and Political Context

presented by Edwin M. Martin

Ambassador Martin drew heavily from his four decades with international organizations, most recently the World Bank,* where he is chairman of the Consultative Group on Food Production and Investment in Developing Countries. This position he translates as the Bank's "energy-food crisis focus." Before his "retirement" in 1974 to this post, Ambassador Martin chaired the Development Assistance Committee (DAC) of the Organization for Economic Cooperation and Development (OECD).†

Ambassador Martin evolved his subject around four themes, all related to upbuilding global peace and social justice, which are either promoted or impeded by the structures of economic and political power.

BASIC ETHICAL ASSUMPTIONS

"I suppose that my basic assumptions about the rights of all mankind," Ambassador Martin began, "owe something to the fact

*The World Bank is the colloquial name for the International Bank of Reconstruction and Development (IBRD).

†The OECD is a continuation of the Marshall Plan cooperative experience; it is formed by the nations of the industrialized West, plus Japan, Australia and New Zealand. The DAC is its aid-giving arm. Headquarters are in Paris.

that my father was a YMCA secretary with a puritanical but social view of the gospels. . . . I am profoundly convinced that all people born have an equal right to benefit from the earth's resources. To me, this is the basic human right. Facing it, national boundaries, ethnic differences, and the like, have no relevance.

"The most important goal is to enable each person to have the minimum of material good necessary to choose his lifestyle and to fulfill whatever potential he may have and chooses to pursue. This can perhaps best be put as 'equality of opportunity.' It has, of course, political and moral, as well as economic, aspects. It is clearly *not* equality of income. It is utopian in the traditional sense, but I find it helps me to make choices.

"Another of my working assumptions is to be quite selective in my concerns about the well-being of future generations. As long as so many members of this generation must lead such restricted lives, I believe we have to think primarily in the present tense. Even more important, I lack faith in our ability to foresee the future. So many variables keep me humble here: Our capacity for both constructive and destructive actions; the many alternative lifestyles among which our descendants will choose; the current rapidity of technological change and its tendency to throw off little-guessed-at, far-reaching byproducts; our ignorance of such elementary determinants of our lives—what the weather will be, how economics really functions, and so forth.

"In the same vein," the ambassador went on, "I am somewhat skeptical about 'the facts' on most issues. We usually don't know which are important ones; we face wide gaps in our knowledge about the past and the present; we can only guess about the future." For these reasons, he was loathe to project material needs too far into the future or even worry about them past the next five years.

He does, however, feel the need to guard the environment and to conserve nonrenewable resources, especially petroleum and natural gas, which "may have some special uses, which it will be very difficult to synthesize and replace from other resources. So it might be worth our while to avoid exhausting them completely before the end of this century, or even early in the next."

THE POWERFUL THREATEN JUSTICE AND PEACE

The ambassador's basic ethical assumptions made it clear that in his view all inequality in distributing basic human needs—whether on a national or international scale—contradicts minimal social justice. But his comments on food and energy shortages centered on the political aspects of the crisis, the focus we had asked of him as an experienced diplomat.

In the short run, Ambassador Martin did not see the well-publicized food shortages as an *immediate* threat to world peace. "In our modern age of highly-organized, capital-intensive forces of order, hungry people are no direct threat to the establishment. They may well arouse the consciences of various middle-class intelligentsia, especially those with military or political connections, who will use them (sincerely or not) as part of the rationale for overthrowing present regimes. . . .

"But even such revolutions would pose no military threat to the established world power system, unless we fail (as we may do) to stop nuclear proliferation. Where our world system is increasingly vulnerable is in the trend to confrontation, rather than collaboration, in seeking solutions to the increasingly complex issues that face all of us—environment, population, trade and finance systems, the law of the sea, and so forth. Unless most nations see a common interest in finding practical courses of common action to deal with each of those issues and their interrelations, we will all suffer. . . .

"Yet I cannot believe that nations with large percentages of their population struggling to survive on inadequate diets will have much interest in working out solutions which promote the interest of all. . . . A far more attractive alternative will be the destruction of present structures for cooperation in the hope that a new order cannot help but be better. Fundamental to such an attitude is that most basic of human needs—enough to eat.

"The richer countries are fortunate in this deadly game because they are surplus producers of food. They cannot be blackmailed by food embargoes. But neither can they effectively use their food surplus to force concessions from the food-deficit countries. In the first place, grains are hard to follow in international trade; for short periods they can be bought from a wide variety of sources if the price is right.

"But more important," Ambassador Martin explained, "the political fallout from a grain embargo could be highly counterproductive—the image would be of starving babies, and not merely curtailed Sunday driving in gas-guzzlers. Food not grown is lost for good, while oil not pumped remains in the ground and probably increases in value."

On the other hand, generosity with food can win friends. "In the diplomatic game, food serves better as a carrot than as a stick."

Ambassador Martin felt that there are no insurmountable problems "of a physical or technical sort which will prevent us from removing scarcity and malnutrition, which are now obstacles to equality of opportunity." He also thinks that "general energy scarcity seems unlikely at an early date if we manage our affairs, including our research efforts, with reasonable wisdom."

He did add some caveats concerning research into various energy sources—including rapid transfer to alternatives for fossil fuels. Great care must be taken with nuclear energy until we develop better safeguards against "the terrible threat inherent in widespread nuclear proliferation which nuclear power makes possible." But he saw no insoluble technical problems.

However, it is in the area of energy that Ambassador Martin did see serious problems for world peace. "Transitions from one type of energy to another are possible but may be difficult, and relative costs will fluctuate. In such circumstances, it will be the powerful, public and private, whose interests will be threatened first. And these people can take action, whereas people who don't get enough to eat are not in the position to wield political power. I see a much greater threat to peace from energy shortages and cost raises than from food shortages.

"Therefore, anything we can do to make lifestyles less energy-intensive, to use energy more efficiently, to limit the number of people whose opportunities on earth depend on an articifial energy supply, to spend wisely on research for the long-term future, will be a contribution to peace."

A PROPOSED FOOD PROGRAM

The food program Ambassador Martin envisaged corresponded closely to that outlined by Drs. Hannah and Borlaug. Only new elements or political emphases are noted here.

1. Like the previous speakers, the ambassador feared that a bad crop year will completely wipe out reserves; indeed he was "a little less optimistic for the immediate future" than were Dr. Hannah and Dr. Borlaug. Therefore, "adequate global reserves of something like sixty million tons of grain" must be built up. But there are innumerable political and economic problems in the way of accomplishing this goal. Farmers object to bigger reserves "because they fear it will depress prices." The U.S. government wants to keep reserves low because of high storage costs. The Soviet Union is "unwilling to participate in the reserves scheme; they did not attend the last meeting on the subject." The U.S.S.R. frankly

admits that secrecy about its own harvests, reserves, and needs permits it to "go in and buy on the cheap market. Perfect capitalistic doctrine!"

2. This surplus grain must be reserved for poor countries, "by government action if necessary, and not allowed to be swallowed by the richer importers." In other words, the free market system cannot take care of the hungry poor on a global scale. Both market control and aid are needed.

3. The developed countries must be prepared to help not only with direct food aid but with a transfer of sufficient resources "to enable the food-deficit countries to buy what they need, despite the fact that most of them are critically short of foreign exchange. . . . Any country with a financial surplus can help them. It is important to remember that, under our current system, food aid normally means not a gift of food but a purchase order to buy grain."

4. "Some years—and 1974 was such a year—it may be more helpful to share fertilizer and, if necessary, the money to buy it, than grain. . . . In 1974, buying and shipping grain that a ton of fertilizer would have grown cost about seven times more than the fertilizer would have cost." Pesticides must also be shared, and the use of fertilizer for non-critical purposes—such as lawns and golf courses—must be reduced, as the 1974 Food Conference requested.

5. "Supplementary feeding programs conducted by various charitable organizations, often religious in inspiration," can provide disaster relief and some nutrition improvements, but they cannot reach the 500 million malnourished rural poor. Neither will trickle-down from GNP growth* or massive income redistribution help much. The rural poor must increase production of their own food. "They must be helped to help themselves, without dependence year to year on a generous world or an efficient and just national government. Their own government must, in most cases, change price, tax, investment, educational, and bureaucratic policies and priorities to favor more the needs of farmers and the rural sector generally, as against the urban, industrialized claimants." If developing nations do this, financial and technical aid will be required from richer countries in much larger amounts than in the past. It will not be easy, or cheap in the long run, to give these farmers the incentives, skills, inputs, and marketing oppor-

---

*GNP refers to "gross national product," that is, an estimate of the financial value of all goods produced and services performed within a nation during a given year.

tunities to make better use of their labor, their solar energy, their land and water. But it can be done, and equality of opportunity for a large percentage of the world population demands it.

6. Reaching these 500 million rural poor "has been made the central point in Mr. McNamara's new development program."* After all, "only farmers raise wheat, so until farmers decide to act differently, we haven't solved the problem."

The World Bank program, according to Ambassador Martin, is commendable for two reasons. First, it should bring direct assistance to those who most truly need it, "the subsistence farmer, the landless laborer, the urban dwellers who have come to the city in the unfulfilled hope of getting food that doesn't exist in the countryside. . . . The evidence is convincing that much of our present assistance goes for dairy products to feed the children of the middle-class elites, not for grain to feed starving people." Most developing countries place far greater emphasis on industrialization and the urban sector, rather than on food production and the rural sector. Yet "we cannot act except through the governments of the countries in which people live. . . . Perhaps the only way we can make sure assistance reaches the poor people is through projects in which the money goes directly to them, not through intermediaries. On the other hand, if countries do adopt new priorities, they will need substantial additional help."

The second reason for praising these continuing programs "is that people have short memories. Disasters excite many well-meaning people in many parts of the developed world; but just because we don't have a headline-making disaster doesn't mean that hunger has gone away." In both developed and developing countries, "a lot of people take these large numbers of permanently malnourished people for granted, as part of life the way it is." Even a small gain—or lack of loss—in food availability is regarded as a bonanza.

"That's the kind of complacency we must get away from."

7. "Meeting essential food and energy needs for all will happen sooner, the fewer 'all' are. In addition, the poor farmer, on whom my concern centers, will have that much better chance of increasing his yields and the food consumption of his family if there are fewer mouths to feed, thus increasing family savings for investing in his land. The population dilemma will not go away."

*Robert McNamara has been president of the World Bank since 1968.

THE NEW INTERNATIONAL ECONOMIC ORDER

Ambassador Martin sees nationalism as a major obstacle to "equality of opportunity" and to solving the food and energy crisis. The real problems to finding answers are not physical or technical, but "in people's attitudes and the institutions that reflect them. These are buttressed in many cases by continued narrow loyalty to each person's in-group, most conspicuously the nation-state. . . . Concern for equality of opportunity weakens fast as the national border is crossed. We here are becoming more and more aware of global interdependency and the obsolescence of much that passes for nationalism, but we are far away in most countries from seizing the lever of political power."

He admits that we still live in the "age of nationalism" despite little steps here and there: "A prime objective for many proponents of the New International Economic Order* is to match economic and political power with us (the rich, industrialized nations), perhaps by the unity of OPEC with the Third World. It is a necessary first step, no doubt, but a better sharing in the management of the world must also seek better goals for all mankind than up to now, particularly the goal of equality of opportunity."

Ambassador Martin, a forty-year veteran of the U.S. Foreign Service and vastly experienced in international realities, takes the Third World initiative for a New International Economic Order very seriously. He explained that one of its key elements is "how to break or reduce developing-country dependence for their GNP growth on rich-country GNP growth. We industrialized countries rely on increasing per capita use of energy to sustain production increases. Without that, developing-country export

*The New International Economic Order (NIEO) is a plan for changing major structures which determine economic relations among nations, particularly those between the industrialized North and the developing nations of the Third World. Such an undertaking was formally called for by the Sixth Special Session of the General Assembly of the United Nations, April–May 1974.

In September 1975, the Seventh Session of the U.N. General Assembly was convened to debate this subject. It adopted a Resolution on Development and International Economic Cooperation which "set in motion" measures in seven key areas: international trade, transfer of resources for financing development and international monetary reforms, science and technology, industrialization, food and agriculture, cooperation among developing countries, and restructuring the economic and social sectors of the United Nations system. For a full account of the NIEO, including official documents, see *A New International Economic Order*, by J.S. Singh (New York: Praeger Publishers, 1977).

markets within our rich natons will shrivel up. Then they will become unable to import from us the capital goods essential to their development or for food and other necessities of their poor."

In other words, the GNPs of rich countries now grow principally through constantly improved technology which requires ever larger inputs of nonhuman energy, especially from petroleum. The cost of these added energy inputs increases the price at which we sell poor countries the manufactured goods which they need for development, such as railroad and mining equipment, chemical and fertilizer plants. Additionally our technology often makes new synthetics which substitute for poor countries' commodities, such as cotton and hemp. The result is that their exports and the prices we pay for them fall, while our exports and the prices we get climb higher.

But now the New International Economic Order—or some new and more just ordering of world trade and the monetary system —may be possible because OPEC has given the Third World a new economic weapon. Most of the rich countries need to import the petroleum which provides the energy to increase their production. (Western Europe and Japan import about 80 percent of their petroleum needs from the Middle East, which is predominantly Muslim.) But new profits from the sale of that same petroleum are providing the OPEC countries with the wherewithal to pay for the industrialized countries' products. Therefore this region has acquired new and significant leverage in the economic power equation between the rich North and the poor South—and new political voice as well.

Ambassador Martin closed by recounting that just before coming to Bellagio he had attended a conference on the New International Economic Order which gave attention to these new possibilities for development patterns. "I look with interest to the future work of the newly-established Third World Forum.* It aims

*The Third World Forum is a network of social scientists and scholars from Africa, Asia, Latin America, and the Middle East who seek new and creative conceptual frameworks for meeting the problems faced by Third World countries. It aims at reaching opinion and decision makers with its research findings. The Forum was constituted at a meeting in Karachi in 1975; it is an independent organization, with no governmental or institutional affiliation. The Chairman of its executive committee is Dr. Ismail Sabri Abdalla, of Cairo. Coordinator is Dr. Juan Somavia, with headquarters in Mexico City. Regional offices are located in Dakar, Colombo, and Cairo. The views of Dr. Mahbub ul Haq are thus far exercising significant influence within the Third World Forum. He gives an integrated presentation of these in his book, *The Poverty Curtain: Choices for the Third World* (New York: Columbia University Press, 1976).

to mobilize the best brains of the developing countries to tackle this and other key development issues, hitherto largely studied by rich-country economists in rich-country institutions. I am particularly interested in this effort as it has pledged itself to give top priority to poverty and to stress power relationships only as they effect the elimination of poverty."

5

The Crisis of Western Society

presented by Shlomo Avineri

The Colloquium next heard the production and technical facts of Drs. Hannah and Borlaug, together with the political realities presented by Ambassador Martin, placed into the wider context of history, social theory, ethical ambiguity, and religious practice. The speakers were Shlomo Avineri, dean of the Social Sciences Faculty, Hebrew University, Jerusalem, and Paul Moore, Episcopal Bishop of New York and an activist for twenty years in civil rights and peace movements at national and local levels. As scheduled, both men spoke extemporaneously, opening paths and patterns for the wider discussion.

During his eighteen minutes Professor Avineri, with admirable daring, plunged into the philosophy of history, Hegel's societal dialectics, Marx's insistence on "spiritual power," a critique of structures, and the politico-ethical dilemmas that result. Each sentence outlined the chapter of a thick book which Professor Avineri should write—and I must dare sketch his outline: "Since 1971–72, a certain period in history and self-understanding of the western world has come to an end." We are discovering now that the quarter-century from 1945 to 1970 was an interlude of complacency that had deluded the West.

THE PROBLEM IS STRUCTURAL

"Until 1945, the consensus in Europe and America had been that the world was basically sick. The system as we knew it then was facing a series of challenges." Around 1935, especially, there was "a very deep feeling of crisis, of dissatisfaction and unease about the western economic system." Signs of this were: "Communism in Russia, as well as the great following the communist movement had in the West; also the social democrat movements in the West. . . . Certainly fascism, too, whether in Germany, Italy, or the other countries where it was a quite powerful challenge, was also one of the responses of western industrialized society to the crisis of modern western society itself.

"Then the Allied victory in World War II, as well as the containment of communism that followed, created in the West a false illusion that we had really mastered the structural problems of the modern industrial world."

During the postwar years, Professor Avineri contended, the structural causes of the basic crisis—which had been perceived during the two decades between the world wars, which had brought about depression, communist revolution, totalitarian fascism, and World War II—were never removed. It was only illusion during the 1950s and 1960s that permitted us to believe that "the prophecies of doom, of Marx and the communists, and of the later fascists" were answerable by a gradual reform which would retain the old western system, "with a little bit of economic tinkering, with a little bit of decolonization—politically, not economically, speaking. In the field of social sciences, the slogan 'the end of ideology' was the ideological expression of that field."

It was because of these illusions that the combined "energy and food crisis of the early 1970s has brought such profound shock. It has proven most of the disciplines of social sciences wrong." We must now go back to basic questions about society that were asked from the mid-nineteenth century until 1940, back to structural problems which are not purely economic, but also socio-political.

In explaining this last point, Professor Avineri cited two fairly recent examples of political factors determining economic structures. First, for political reasons, cheap oil was long available to the West, making it unnecessary to seek alternatives, such as coal or solar energy, both of which are more sensible economically. Second, in many African countries, "the decision to go into export crops had to do not only with the market system, but with the fact that the rules of the market system could be determined by the old western colonial power, even after nominal independence."

Turning to the food crisis, Professor Avineri questioned the technical and purely quantitative answer of "more fertilizers, more cereal production, a palliative that can, for the moment perhaps, best save people from starvation. But have we really done much to create a new structure? The inequalities prevailing before the 1970s continue and are becoming even more exacerbated. Therefore, our critique should address structures, not passing policies."

MASTER AND SLAVE

Professor Avineri continued his explication of the West's crisis by evoking the paradox of master and slave from Hegel, one of his favorite philosophers. Two men struggle "in a primal fight for survival." The stronger wins. "The victor becomes the master, the vanquished becomes the slave; ... then what happens dialectically is that the master becomes dependent on the labor of the slave." The nominal master's freedom and lifestyle depend upon the subjected slave, who "through his labor acquires power over his master. And then, at the dialectical turning point, the slave becomes the real master. Something of that," he asserted, "is happening before our eyes. It is a fact that, twenty-five years after the end of World War II, Western Europe is dependent on the oil production of a number of Middle Eastern countries that had been its colonies only a few years ago—one of those dialectical changes of slaves and masters."

Does the dialectic now enter a new stage and continue indefinitely? "We can gladly accept that the old domination is over, but the alternative should not be new forms of new domination."

SPIRITUAL POWER

"What should be the role of religious leaders here?" Professor Avineri quoted Marx, of all people, as saying, "Power can be vanquished only by power, but spiritual power is also power once it has mastered the masses." This is not just a naive materialistic statement. Spiritual power *is* also power. Particularly in the context of political power, he repeated, "spiritual power is a power as well." That is why the exercise of influence on politics through intellectual and interreligious impact is one aspect where all the institutions with which we are connected play a role.

POLITICO-ETHICAL DILEMMAS

"But I'd like to end on a note of covenant rather than preaching. Given our moral premises, I can best do this by posing several dilemmas:

"How should we deal with a ruling elite who don't serve the needs of their own poor? Do we introduce welfare gunboat diplomacy to force that country to send that food out of the city to the countryside? Suppose we are convinced that in a given country a change in the political system, a radical change, would solve the problem of starvation. What do we do?"

The fact of China again intruded. Suppose a country opts for the Maoist solution to food production; Professor Avineri asked, leaving aside the question of American security, "Would the United States go along with that? Would we, as people who also cherish freedom, let them exchange whatever minimal freedom they have for whatever minimal nourishment they would get in return for a change to a Communist Chinese system?"

Finally, in Professor Avineri's judgment, the mechanisms described by Dr. Hannah, Dr. Borlaug, and others abstract from political issues and concentrate on the purely technical agricultural distribution level. "Given the political reality, what mechanisms does the world community have to insure that questions of food scarcity or energy scarcity are not going to become one more trump card in a political game? They have done this in the past few years—the United States bargaining for political concessions from the Soviet Union in return for the wheat deal, some of the Arab countries clamping an oil embargo on the world within the context of political demands."

Professor Avineri concluded that we must go beyond "the very encouraging level of what Dr. Hannah said this morning," into these political realities and mechanisms. "I know we won't be able to achieve consensus even in this very small room, but those are the questions which I think we have to solve."

6

Political Change and Religious Institutions

presented by Paul Moore

Bishop Moore followed immediately, taking Professor Avineri's emphasis on the political nature of the crisis and the basic malaise of western society to the next logical step. He spoke of the dynamics of national policies and of religious and pastoral impact upon political consciousness, almost entirely from the viewpoint of the American experience—yet his critique could be applied in many industrialized nations.

"Our job, as so-called religious leaders, is, in the Bellagio context, to do what we can in our own nations—and perhaps beyond them, if we have that kind of influence—through religious and ethical motivation, to influence the political will of our people."

U.S. POLICIES AND INFLUENCE

"The indirect causes of world hunger contributed by the United States are enormous. As I see it, our policy is completely inconsistent." With one hand our country gives "a few more million dollars to the World Food Council to feed a few people, or to help with agricultural expertise; with the other hand, we're doing much more harm—by false military and political support, by promoting the consumer lifestyle of urban America throughout the globe through magazines and television, and so on."

Ambassador Martin and Professor Avineri have shown us the

tremendous political complications of the food crisis. As Bishop Moore sees it, to help the food supply around the world, the first thing U.S. citizens have to do is try to change the foreign policy of our nation.

"This is not very easy. The United States often actively supports repressive regimes. Our government is working against the poor people of those nations by supporting regimes which—to put it mildly—do not have the feeding of poor citizens as their highest priority. The United States justifies such actions in the name of its short-term national security." Perhaps, the bishop speculated, it really has something to do with keeping the price of raw materials down. "But in the long term I think it is a very insecure thing for us to do.

"Another problem with American leadership is that one-third of the national budget goes to military expenditures. Since 1945, we have spent $1 trillion (a million millions) on armaments in our country. Some of these resources could have been better used. The problem is not only that we are a military nation, but that our whole economy is geared into that kind of expenditure.

"Our economy is also geared into a lifestyle which means that some 6 percent of the world's population are using about 40 percent of the world's resources. This is very embarrassing to confess before an interfaith body such as this. Our whole economy is keyed into that lifestyle, our whole advertising industry is geared into that level of high consumption. The priority given by developing countries to urban consumer wants rather than rural needs has to do with the exportation of American ideas across the world through magazines and television. But the possibility of our stopping the export of television programs and magazines which lift up the glories of the urban lifestyles is nil."

So when the religious institutions of the United States begin to concern themselves seriously with the politics of the world food situation, they find themselves in very deep political and economic water at home.

CREDIBILITY

Bishop Moore brought in the additional problem of the credibility gap. "The American people need to know the facts, they need to be able to believe what they are told by their government. But Watergate and all the revelations since that event have made it very hard for us to know whom to believe. In addition to this malicious attack on communication by some government officials, there is also the problem that you can read one thing in one newspaper and something else in another. So the person in the street and the person in the pew simply don't know the facts. And if they are told, they don't know whether to believe them or not."

Religious institutions, therefore, must insist that government reports provide higher credibility and assist people in learning the facts. "Also, religious bodies need to understand and agree upon the goals and priorities of our nation in order to help solve the hunger problem. Religious leadership must give more attention to developing national goals than we have in the past."

THE SOCIAL DYNAMIC OF POLITICAL CHANGE

Once the facts are understood, once some consensus on goals is reached, for Bishop Moore the next question is: "How to motivate political will? I'd like to talk about the relationship of religious institutions to the social dynamic of political change. I was fairly active in the civil rights movement and the peace movement, and I have been thinking about these experiences ever since because they were both microcosms of religious motivation in social change."

When movement and institution cooperate, they bring opposing qualities into their effort. A movement has tremendous dynamic but is usually short on lasting impetus. Institutions tend to be steadier, more objective, less emotional, more rational, even more pragmatic. But as soon as movements become institutions, they tend to become triumphalistic and also become covered with various mosses which impede their progress.

Bishop Moore recounted his own experience: "The civil rights movement began in a very idealistic fashion with people like Martin Luther King. It was a highly religious movement which created the great Selma event where thousands of religiously motivated people marched together with Dr. King. All of us were terribly keyed up about it. We felt we were making a great breakthrough in our country's consciousness. And I think we did. A lot of good things came out of the civil rights movement.

"But we did not take account of the anger which lay buried within many of the black people with whom we were walking. And because we were unrealistic and perhaps too idealistic in those early days, the civil rights movement fragmented into an explosion of enormous anger, very unlike what had happened in the United States before.

"Black Power was also a tremendous dynamic. But it was so totally fragmented and unchanneled that it became self-destructive. The cities were blown up, but in the ghettoes, not in the white communities. The anger became addressed at the people who did the destruction. And as the dynamism of the civil rights movement fragmented off into this angry phase, the old civil rights institutions became less and less dynamic. And so you had, on one hand, a destroyed movement and, on the other, institutions which had lost some of their power.

"The peace movement could be reviewed on the same lines."

From these experiences, Bishop Moore has come to believe that religious institutions, such as churches, synagogues, and more informal groups, can fill a twofold role. "They can at least touch some of the same dynamisms within the human spirit that movements touch, and they can temper dynamisms with theological discipline and institutional order." But the great dilemma is "to keep the balance between the fire of movement and the touching of the human spirit which really changes people, on the one hand, and enough institutional order and theological discipline to be consistent and sustaining, on the other."

PASTORAL MOTIVATION

Finally, as a pastor, he admitted that we who are religiously responsible "do not know how to motivate our people. We can go home highly informed from a conference like this but then what happens? The gap between motivated religious leaders and the person in the pew is wider than any other gap I know.

"What do we do when we get home? We will have to reach more and deeper levels than we ordinarily think we have to touch. As Rabbi Blank suggested this morning, we will have to rethink some very serious questions, such as: Are our theological rationales the result of deeper psychic realities? What are the psychic bounces from theology and worship?" (The bishop here was referring to Rabbi Blank's opening statement which gave reasons why the sponsoring group had convened us at Bellagio. The religious elements of Rabbi Blank's talk are incorporated below under Session Three.)

"Keep in mind," Bishop Moore concluded, "how difficult it will be when we get home to prevent ourselves from being too academic and perhaps too technical. But we must always be aware what facts can motivate the human spirit through its religious and ethical dimension."

7

Discussion: Intertwining Political and Economic Power

Chief Simeon Adebo, chairman for this session, grasped the mind of our gathering in his comments opening the discussion. He brought to the Colloquium his long experience at the United Nations and from his more recent responsibility as chairman of Nigeria's National Universities Commission. (I find it noteworthy that his native land is very mixed religiously: Of its sixty million people, about one-third are Muslims, one-third Christians, and one-third members of indigenous African religions.)

Because the chief's main points entwine with the themes which followed, I have grouped his comments with these. Economic, political, and ethical spheres are constantly interpenetrating. Changes are imperative in the structures of power, working toward a new world order. Religions must become more involved. Political and ethical dilemmas face aid-giving nations. Nuclear power threatens peace.

ECONOMICS, POLITICS, AND ETHICS

Chief Adebo asserted that everyone who has attempted to deal with the problems of food or energy in isolation has soon discovered that it simply cannot be done. "It cannot even be done aside from the political context. The trouble, of course, is that the world has changed. For example, we could have anticipated this so-called energy crisis, if we had known the true cost of oil. But even a few years ago we of the developing world were not told that we were selling our oil cheaper than we should have. Rather we were told that our oil receipts were in strict accord with the law of supply and demand. But, of course, the shortage showed up as soon as some of the supply was withdrawn. Now our world has become better informed. You see, many of the people of the developing countries themselves have now gone to college, so a new spirit must transform all negotiations. . . .

"I come from a country which is a member of the OPEC group; we used to be very short on money; now we get bountiful revenues. But we are also members of the Organization for African Unity, many members of which are suffering from shortages caused by the rise in oil prices. Remember, even among the developing countries there is great disparity. We have not solved that problem; we must not shut our eyes to it."

Professor Askari took up a note from the chief along with Dean Avineri's thesis about the erosion of the western socio-economic system. "Why did it take place so quickly? We are caught up in the diplomacies and the politics of the West projected this way or that way through blocs. Somehow the West's confidence in its socio-economic system was accepted in the East as well, even though that system rested on a conscious dislocation of the ethical and the political. Indeed, I know of only one person in the modern history of my country who insisted on a conscious linkage between politics and ethics. That was Mahatma Gandhi, and the linkage he tried to establish was based on the willingness of the people to accept others, in political partnership or confrontation, as human, as given, as authentic."

Professor Askari charged that western bloc politics hamper the potentiality of religious and spiritual groups, "including the Muslims in our subcontinent, Arabs and Jews in West Asia, the black and the white groups elsewhere." The projection of western political norms also adds confusion to the food and energy crises. "I take both these crises as symbols, as tokens of something more fundamental, more basic."

(I call westerners' attention to Askari's use of "West Asia," which is more accurate than our use of "Middle East." The latter term makes Europe the center of the world, as we westerners have thought it to be for many centuries. As Christians, we center our ecclesial awareness also in the West, in Rome, Geneva, Canterbury. Bellagio confronted this erroneous Euro-centrism among western Christians. Our Orthodox fellow faithful, and the other religions, will, I hope, redress our provincial borders of faith consciousness.)

Ambassador Sol Linowitz rejoiced "that in the last hour or so we have finally plunged into the real world. We are now confronting the fact that we can accept certain principles as valid and yet still have to decide how to use them in the world as it actually exists. It's very appealing for us to enunciate the principles that every human being has the right to life, the right to eat; that each of us has the responsibility to see that this principle is carried out; that nations are charged with the obligation to feed their own people; and that other nations with greater resources are called upon to share their resources with those who are less fortunate." But, he continued, acting on these principles entails an "intermingling of economic, political, and religious considerations."

He then focused specifically on the role of the United States. "If the United States sends food to a country which has a repressive regime so that the hungry may be fed, are we supporting repressive regimes?" (This reflected Ambassador Linowitz's personal concern for human rights, a concern which shows up in his work as chairman of the Commission on United States and Latin America Relations.)

In the ambassador's view, no nation in history has a better humanitarian record than the United States. "But precisely because we have performed so well, more is expected of us, and there, I think, is the heart of the matter. Little is expected of the communist countries because they do so little. But let me point out bluntly what a U.S. congressman sitting here would think: Governments are political entities. Political entities are run by politicians. Politicians are responsive to the will of the people, but politicians are also aware of what is said about them in other parts of the world. When the United States is criticized because it does not do enough, while other nations which have done nothing are left uncriticized, this does not set well with those who have the responsibility of making allocations of resources.

"In short," concluded Ambassador Linowitz, "I think it is incumbent upon other nations in the world that are benefiting from the generosity and the humanitarian instincts of the United States to acknowledge that the United States has made a contribution, and, therefore, is entitled to have that contribution recognized and applauded, perhaps even while the recipients insist that more can be done."

As a professional economist, S. L. Parmar charged that "modern economists have been guilty of emasculating the science of economics by making it nonpolitical. From its very inception, economics always was political economy; even the classical

economists talked about political economy. And certainly the
Marxist and other socialist economists always speak about political economy. If we talk about economic measures strictly as
economic measures and not in the framework of their political
implications, I think we are dealing with the surface expressions
of the problem, not with its fundamental expressions."

Professor Parmar found Ambassador Martin's view of the food
crisis too narrow. "To say we need food reserves, we need fertilizer, we need money, we need an extension of educational and
technical facilities which will reach the poor is again falling back
upon narrow techno-economic measures for the solution of fundamental structural problems." He charged that at the World
Food Conference "it almost appeared that a determined effort was
being made to avoid questions of structure which had political
implications. But here we, who are more free, must feel that
questions which have political implications are of the very heart
of our discussion."

Professor Parmar agreed with Ambassador Martin's analysis
that poverty is the underlying problem, more basic than production. However, he said, the fundamental causes of poverty are
structures based on injustice and inequality, within a nation and
in international relationships. "The popular term for that is exploitation. It has been mentioned that resources do not reach the
poorest and the needy. The reason for that is the existing pattern
of relationships which control economic power and which, therefore, control political power."

Fr. Hehir, responding to the defense of the U.S. role by Ambassador Linowitz, did agree "that in terms of humanitarian charity,
the U.S. record is something that I would be willing to stand up
and take a bow for." But charity implies an option, a choice to help
or not to help, whereas justice imposes an obligation. "The shift
from charity to justice is what is emerging in the international
debate today. . . .

"There has always been a question of sharing your extra goods
with others in our system." But, he pointed out, charity starts
with the assumption that a *surplus* is held by the generous donors
who *volunteer* to help the needy whom they choose to favor, and
when they so choose. Therefore, the charity motive provides no
"feedback mechanism" to decide among competing needs. "Now, if
the international economic and political system is to be reorganized on the basis of obligatory justice, how do you decide
among competing needs when resources are scarce?" Under op-
tional charity, the richer powerful "haves" usually choose to let

the poorer, weaker "have nots" stay that way. Justice could shift the balance.

In speaking to Professor Parmar's plea for the linkage of politics and economics, Fr. Hehir asserted that a shift is occurring in the international system toward giving greater weight to economic objectives. "Certainly during the period of the modern state, we have understood international politics in the terms of political and strategic questions. (Strategic here refers to the area of national defense and security.) In that definition of international politics, the use of force was linked rather precisely to certain political purposes." But during the past decade, political analysts tell us, "consideration of economics has been raised to the level that political and strategic questions used to hold. So now we have two agendas: the political and strategic, and the economic."

Commenting on this phase of the discussion, Ambassador Martin showed a strong distrust for donor nations intervening in the economies, politics, and structures of recipient nations. Over and above the ethical issue, he finds it "a bit presumptuous of the developed countries to think they know better than the developing countries what is the right step in their present stage of development. We have spent 200 or 300 years evolving our own present structures, with which we are all not entirely satisfied." Now we are learning that "we don't always know how to run the economies of other countries better than they do. It seems an even more ambitious boast to think that we know how to run their *societies and politics* in general better than they do."

Further, in the ambassador's experience, intervention sometimes has an effect opposite that desired. "If you put a country in a difficult situation economically, the political spectrum moves to the right, not to the left. And you get repressive or military regimes taking over to tighten the belt or introduce additional repression, rather than otherwise."

CHANGING THE STRUCTURES OF POWER

After this exchange on interpenetration of the economic, political, and ethical spheres, the participants centered on changes needed in the structures of power. Demand for a new world economic order came up repeatedly because the old order is not adequate to meet today's crises, much less those of the foreseeable future. "The trouble, of course," Chief Adebo began, "is that the world has changed. After the traumatic experiences of World War II, solutions were evolved that met some circumstances of that time but they could not be good for all time. The United Nations itself said in its Charter that it was to be reviewed after ten years. Well, it is more than thirty years since that organization was established. Why should we now complain that it is not doing its work very well? The world has changed a lot."

Chief Adebo regards the world monetary system devised after World War II at Bretton Woods as "a great classic, a fantastic achievement for that time, and it worked for quite a long while. But those who drew it up, including Maynard Keynes, could not have foreseen the tremendous changes—political, economic, and especially technological—that have taken place since that time. And although a lot of people pointed this out and asked that monetary units be looked at again, they were not heeded until there was a complete collapse of the system."

The entire international division of labor should be reviewed, Chief Adebo concluded. He noted that Dr. Hannah had proposed short-term and medium-term solutions for the food/energy crisis. But the long-term solution "must be dealt with on a more comprehensive basis, by the creating of a New International Economic Order. And that order cannot be dealt with outside its political context. The political alignment of peoples has changed."

Cardinal Arns was "very interested in Professor Avineri's points about the need for changing structures. During recent years, the economy of Brazil has grown by about 10 percent of the GNP annually. Specialists say that all Brazilians could eat very well from our harvests. But we still have some 70 percent who do not eat sufficiently." The pastor of São Paulo asked about the role of religion in changing structures in such a situation. Yet he does not think national or international structural changes offer "a complete solution. We must think about the education and participation of the people in their own development. I state this as a fact, not as a theological or philosophical reflection."

For Dr. Klompe, "the problem is that the political and economic structures in our world are wrong, and we have to do something." But no government is willing to negotiate with other governments "and make a treaty to change these things—which in many cases would ask sacrifices of its citizens, especially from the rich—if they do not know that their people are willing to make these sacrifices. Religious institutions, religious movements should have the influence to change the mentality of their own adherents, to help them understand that we have to change this world completely, that the structures in today's world do not work."

Some of Professor Parmar's views on structures and a new world order were reported above, especially his insistence on integrating the economic and political spheres. And during Session Four, he was to treat this "heart of the matter" head on. At this point, however, he focused on attempts to use aid for promoting justice within the receiving nation. "If those who are giving food assistance think they should also talk about the internal structures of the recipient country, I personally would have no objection. However, the debate must then be enlarged in a double sense, beyond the marginal factor of food, to embrace the justice of *all* international structures. If you want to say that food is to be used by recipient governments in a just way, and, therefore, they must have just structures, the same thing should be said about the multinational business, the same thing should be said about the pattern of international trade. Economically, food is the most marginal of all these things.

"And if we are prepared to look at a totality of the relationships between structures in the developed and developing countries, and at their bearing on the international structure, I think we would be moving ahead in this discussion."

Rabbi Henry Siegman said he looked forward to thorough pursuit during the later session of this basic issue of structures raised "forcefully and directly by Professor Parmar. But at this point, the question I would like to ask is whether the term 'change of structures' is really a euphemism, whether we need to confront very honestly the question of how one goes about changing existing structures. Obviously these structures exist because they are supported by very powerful interests, which will not simply fade away as a result of our analysis here.

"Structures are changed usually through violent revolutionary means. I raise this point with some trepidation because I know that is what divided the Aspen Consultation.* But I think this is a very basic question, a question posed to ethics and morals in its sharpest form when this issue of structures is confronted honestly. At some point we have to confront—and not in euphemistic terms—the very difficult, painful issues that arise out of such necessary changes of structures."

Professor Avineri turned to the philosophical concepts of the nineteenth century, specifically the philosophy of Hobbes, which begot the root concept of personal individualism. "It seems to be

*A seminar held June 1974 on the food crisis, attended by Jewish and Christian leaders of the United States. It was sponsored by the Overseas Development Council and hosted by the Aspen Institute for Humanistic Studies, Aspen, Colo.

that the same historical development which brought about the concept of personal individualism brought about the concept of national sovereignty." These twin concepts of the atomistic individual and of absolute sovereignty determined societal structures within each country, as well as among nations across the globe. "National sovereignty is really personal individualism enlarged in a Hobbesian way, and with the obsolescence of one, something is happening to the other as well."

For Professor Avineri, this has consequences on a number of levels, "including the move from individualism to social responsibility within each nation and the move from individual national sovereignty to global responsibility among nations." It also opens the way "for negative intervention: We withhold aid from a country, and obviously we intervene in the power structure of that society, because we may be helping one group against another, say an underground or resistance movement against an oppressive regime."

There are still more fundamental ways in which we are coming to think sovereignty is obsolescent, he continued. "We no longer consider a person's individual wealth to be totally his own possession. We believe that society can, under the rule of law within certain conditions, intervene in personal wealth. So it is becoming impossible to consider economic wealth, be it raw materials or industrial wealth, the sole property of the nation-state within whose boundaries it is concentrated because of historical consequences, past wars, good luck or bad luck."

Professor Avineri sees this evolution of concepts even among nonsocialists. "Modern views of socialism have helped us to evolve a concept of social responsibility that transcends individualism in the nineteenth-century atomistic sense." In the same way, on a number of levels we have to transcend our concept of national sovereignty, which emerged in the same period. So, in addition to new economic and political structures, "one of the things which needs restructuring is our conceptual framework, our rather naive nineteenth-century atomistic individualism."

Bishop James Rausch asked us to look at this move away from national sovereignty under two aspects: the grouping of several nations into "economic power blocs"—such as the half dozen nations that control food exports and the OPEC countries that control petroleum—and the psychology of power operative within these blocs.

While Professor Avineri discerned the intellectual evolution of concepts, Bishop Rausch stressed the role of the will—the will to power. "I find it somewhat frightening to think of the role which these economic power blocs can play in this whole issue of food. We should look profoundly at the psychology of power that is operative. I think it is also very interesting to examine the psychology of blocs like the OPEC nations as they begin to understand and utilize power. Above all, we must try to understand the meaning of powerlessness for the Third and Fourth World and what that does to people, particularly in the Fourth World. All this ties in with our talk about structural change and examining the structures which presently determine the distribution of goods. On this subject, it seems to me that we are being very cautious."

With change at the center of the stage, scenarios for the future entered on cue. Dean Stendahl found Ambassador Martin's idea of making only short-range and medium-range projections inadequate. Theologians need long-range thinking: "We, after all, are specialists on the very long perspective. Such projections contribute to the needed climate and enthusiasm, to conviction, zeal, and zest. And this affects motive, the will to act, political will—the psychology of commitment, as well as that of power."

Fr. Spae recalled the scenario presented by a meeting on "Trends in Mathematical Modeling" in Venice in 1971. UNESCO had asked twenty-five well-known experts "what they saw as the imminent possibilities and forms of economic and cultural life on earth in the year 2000." Four of their ten conclusions "related immediately to our colloquium here and I state them in increasing order of certainty: (1) Zero population growth will be attained in the entire world by the year 2000; (2) Controlled thermonuclear power will become available very much as electricity is now; (3) An economically accepted means of producing artificial protein will be discovered; (4) The economic gap between the developed world and the Third World will continue to increase." Fr. Spae agreed with Dean Stendahl that we theologians by definition must project our thinking into the longer-range future also.

Ambassador Martin repeated his diffidence toward long-term predictions. Even ten years seems very far away. "I would be astonished if the food situation in 1985 turns out in any way as we now think it will. I suspect the same is true of energy."

Fr. Spae's fourth point about the increasing gap between North and South did need attention, the ambassador thought. "One of the central issues that we face with developing countries in the New International Economic Order is this dependence of their growth on our growth." He doubted that we can completely break this dependence, but returned to this earlier statement that "to weaken that link is a critical matter. We provide their markets and unless our GNP goes up rapidly, their export earnings will not go up rapidly. Then they will not be able to expand economic development with any great rapidity. The longer this goes on and the tighter resources get, the more critical it becomes.

"I once made a calculation that if the GNP of the poorer countries grew 4 percent a year per capita—which will not be feasible for a long time—and rich nation GNP grew only 2 percent annually per capita, the numerical gap in per capita dollar income would start narrowing after something like 88 years, and might become even in about 128 years. So the gap issue is not within the realm of early solution."

For the third time, Ambassador Martin expressed lively interest in the newly formed Third World Forum. "This is a group of very able, brilliant economists and social scientists from developing countries who decided that they should no longer be—as they have been in the past—dependent on economic and social scientists and institutions from developed countries to do the work on development. They decided that they had better start thinking for themselves." This Forum will have its own staff "to work with national institutions in the developing countries. Their goal is to deal with poverty—not with the power struggle, which tends to be the main interest of some developing countries. Poverty is really the central issue."

Ambassador Martin also admires the Third World Forum because its members are interested primarily in equality of opportunity, not in equality of income. "In other words, they are not going down the path of 'gap-ology.' Rather, they are searching for: 'How can we get a real opportunity for ourselves as individuals, for our people, for all humanity to get someplace?' These are people whom I think have a future in trying to work out the content that can be put into a New International Economic Order. They are capable of drawing up a new set of economic rules of the game—rules which are not dictated by the West, but which have the interest of the world as a whole at heart. This is important because up to now the New International Economic Order has been more rhetoric than substance. We urgently need brain power to find answers to the kinds of questions its necessity presents."

Ambassador Martin closed his remarks and this part of the discussion by a sudden reference to distributive justice within nations: "I forgot to answer one question on distribution. I think the communist countries have done a superior job, in general, with a smaller pie."

THE INVOLVEMENT OF ORGANIZED RELIGION

Several speakers expressed their conviction that religions should become more involved in the food/energy crisis and in the promotion of more just structures, worldwide and within each nation. However, the papers and discussions for the rest of the week centered on this subject, the very raison d'être of this Colloquium, so I shall keep the comments here brief.

Chief Adebo introduced this theme into the discussion. In his opening remarks, he said that religious leaders have the duty first to inform themselves on the nature and complexity of the problems that face the world, "and then, having learned this, to help their congregation participate in these affairs on the basis of their religious beliefs and convictions. Indeed, in many parts of the world today, notably Latin America, priests and bishops are finding themselves as leaders of social change. . . ."

The layman also "must not run away from involvement. He must involve himself in a spirit that you would expect of a Christian. The same goes for a good Moslem, a good Hindu, a good Buddhist, a good Jew. Speaking for laymen, of whom I am one, an experience like this Colloquium is of great value. When I go back, I am not going to keep the lessons I have learned here to myself; I am going to try to project them to my fellow laymen. Therefore, what we are doing here is very important for both laymen and religious officials."

The views of Bishop Moore, Dr. Klompe, and Cardinal Arns on the role of religious bodies in changing structures have already been noted. Professor Parmar warned religious leaders against the error made by many economists who divorce the economic sphere from the political: "I hope that religious bodies, which many people here represent, will not fall into the old trap which has caught religious leaders like social scientists so many times—the idea that discussion of political questions is outside their jurisdiction."

DILEMMAS OF DEVELOPMENT AID

The theme of dilemmas in development aid policy and practice reappeared and received more attention than I have space to report here. As already noted, Dr. Klompe, Ambassador Linowitz, and Professor Parmar spoke of the dilemma of external intervention into a nation's internal affairs through the giving or withholding of aid—or through tying it with conditions in order to optimize results for the needy.

Rabbi Norman Lamm also spoke to this question. "One side of the dilemma is that you are immediately accused of neo-colonialism or paternalism, of giving with strings. That is a bad thing for the prestige and the national psychology of the receiving nation. But on the other side, not only is your philanthropic endeavor—philanthropic in its highest sense, as love of humanity—being frustrated. Even worse, the limited resources misused by one country are not going to another country, to the people who most desperately need it."

In the judgment of Rabbi Lamm, "a moral choice of this kind would come down more on the side of withholding food and risking insults to the national dignity of a government, rather than denying the food to the poor, to the children who are not interested in national dignity but simply in survival."

But Rabbi Lamm does not see tied aid as "a novel dilemma. A similar dilemma has already been solved with regard to nuclear arms." Assistance to build nuclear power plants is not given without the right to inspection, on the principle "that we are not going to give it to you unless you do with it what we want, for the protection of the world. Now that principle has already been established and seems to be working, so why cannot the same political stance be taken with regard to food aid and the priorities for using it?"

Dr. Al-Nowaihi believes that in this matter we should distinguish between government and the people. "Would a starving Indian really resent being given U.S. food? I do not know. But I think I know about Egypt. It depends upon how the aid is given. It is true that the ugly American sometimes was really ugly and gave aid in an ugly way. But that ugly way was the reason for the resentment, not hurt pride, not the fact of aid itself."

Chief Adebo is "prepared to accept what I call 'equitable strings' to aid. Some of them may not be agreeable to my country, but you have a remedy. If you give us money for the next five years, and you look us over after four months and see our bureaucrats are using it only to advance the interests of their relatives, then all you have to say is, 'We think we might help Tanzania next time.' If Tanzania's policies are more agreeable, if they look after their masses better, then naturally you talk to them. I myself am prepared to acknowledge that the developing countries are not a group of angels, and that we are guilty, from time to time, of inequities which we have to remove if this world is to be reorganized on a viable basis."

Ambassador Martin had already commented on his suspicions of intervention in general, both for political and for economic reasons. Again he insisted on the complexities involved in all aid and the differences in concrete cases: "It is very hard to say how aid does or does not help the poor. People have talked about withholding food aid if it wasn't given to the poor. But there are cases in India where the best way to help the poor is to have our food aid used by the middle classes in the cities. Then you can leave locally produced grain out there in the rural areas where it is produced, not sending it into the cities. Then it's used out where the really poor people are. In other words, you can't identify a particular bag of wheat and say this one has to go to a poor family, who may live five hundred miles inland from the port, and then have to bring the goods the poor produce themselves down to the rich people living in the city. That is ridiculous."

The ambassador also stated that he finds the interconnections of aid and its development very difficult to identify and grasp in their totality. However, he does believe "the trickle-down theory* has been grossly exaggerated. . . . But development itself, as it educates people and raises their level of living does give them new ideas of the kind of society they want. In other words, it creates motors for change. So if what you are looking for is change, then develpment tends to break up structures of a rigid society, and it may produce its own results."

THE ENERGY CRISIS AND PEACE

Whether and how the energy crisis is a direct threat to peace was little discussed, but strong concern was expressed for the magnified menace of war through proliferation of nuclear power plants and technology. Dean Stendahl, Dr. Klompe, and Rabbi Lamm all raised this fear.

Asked why he did not suggest nuclear energy as an alternate to petroleum in his paper, Ambassador Martin readily admitted: "I

---

*"Trickle-down" is a theory in development economics which states that if the GNP of a country as a whole is increased by any means (usually by increasing the incomes of the upper strata which control its society) the benefits naturally will "trickle down" to all levels. This should result in a general rise of living standards throughout the nation, whether or not there is any change in societal structure and power balance. Not all economists accept the theory.

am worried about our ability to control it. It may even be, as some have suggested, beyond our control already. Someone who has two pounds of plutonium and a little bit of ability to read scientific articles can make a bomb. Perhaps there are some chances of getting the problem under control, but I am worried about it."

However, aside from worrying about the dangers of using nuclear sources, he is optimistic about the energy situation. "We have a coal supply of three hundred to five hundred years of energy needs, as now predicted, and much of that is in developing countries. There is enormous potential in solar energy, again best available in the developing countries. They say that on a flourishing wheat field we now use only one percent of the solar energy that hits it. There are a lot of things like this that may be used as research goes on. So I still feel that energy is not apt to be a long-term problem, if we handle our business anything like reasonably."

Session Two thus placed the facts of the food/energy crisis in the context of economic and political structures, within each nation and among all nations forming the world community. This transnational community is becoming interdependent to an increasing degree; many spoke of the need for a new international economic order. But there were some basic ethical and pragmatic disagreements about how to accomplish this with peace and justice.

SESSION THREE

THE ROLE OF RELIGION IN
POLITICS AND SOCIETY

The first two sessions provided premise and background. Their papers and discussions aimed at giving the Colloquium sufficient facts, theories, and stances in the economic, technical, and political spheres to prepare the participants as a group to address the main issue of the meeting: the role of the major faiths in responding to the great social issues of the day—as epitomized by the food/energy crisis—in the course of their joint search for world peace and justice.

The third session got down to this central focus with Wilfred Cantwell Smith's scholarly paper on "The Role of Religion in Politics and Society," followed by responses from representatives of each faith community.

The Colloquium, by its very nature, assumed that religion does fill a significant role in society in general and in politics in particular. This was its working hypothesis, to be supported or disproved by the witness and experience brought into our exchange. But a role can be positive or negative. Does religion advance human betterment in this world? Does religion today promote that human progress whose secular version is envisioned today as social justice, civil rights, political freedom and participation, development and peace? Or does religion, as movement and/or as institution, ignore or even impede these aspirations that have so marked humankind during our age? (Modern western origins of

views of the person and society greatly complicate these exchanges, particularly now when the West's values and aspirations
are undergoing such criticism. Still we make the effort, aware of
this parochialism.)

All ramifications of this key question could not be pursued during one conference. We entered the issue by looking at religion's
role in promoting divisiveness and/or unity within and among
nations and societies. Dr. Smith drew from his lifelong study and
experience to provide seeds and savor for our discussion. Buddhist, Hindu, Jewish, Muslim, and Christian representatives responded.

Dr. Smith had prepared a carefully written and original paper
which was circulated beforehand. It showed the breadth of this
scholar's vision of the major religions he has studied all his life—of
Islam, which he studied during his first years; of the eastern
faiths, which occupied his middle period; and of western religious
thought, now his central concern.

I have reproduced this paper in its entirety because it was a key
element of our Colloquium, and because it is a contribution to
scholarship in religious, philosophical, and social studies. But
nonacademics, even ecclesiastical bureaucrats like myself, should
not be frightened by Dr. Smith's scholarship. We may easily dip
into his deep thought with great profit. He writes with the wide
knowledge of a man whose thought makes connections between
diverse disciplines and cultures—and with the simplicity of the
very wise.

8

Divisiveness and Unity

by *Wilfred Cantwell Smith*

RELIGION'S MULTIPLE ROLES
IN TODAY'S CRISES

It is manifest that religious faith in its many forms has been both a divisive and a cohesive force. This has been so throughout history; it is so today. The divisiveness, the cohesion, and the force of faith continue major. In an age such as ours, not conspicuously religious, the activating forcefulness of faith is at times obscured. In an age such as ours, in which other forms of social and political ordering dominate, the cohesive quality of the religious may not come to the fore. Yet however one may rejoice in or deplore a waning of faith in our era (or discern or minimize a rewaxing of it), the divisive potential of religious loyalties stands, it would seem, ever clear and firm.

Even those who might belittle the positive capacity of traditional religious motifs today to galvanize individual action, or to generate corporate unity, or otherwise to matter very much, are yet reminded by Northern Ireland, Pakistan-India, and the Middle East, that negatively in any case religious differences can and do still disrupt. In the complicated problem of world community and concord, even of world viability, the religious is hardly to be gainsaid.

Recently prevalent, especially among operative groups in Western society and highly popular with them, was a "piecemeal" view of human affairs, dividing life up into parts and then settling down to dealing with problems one at a time. This outlook presup-

71

posed that in principle one had plenty of time: that the sytem in general was stable enough to allow for the solving of one difficulty after another; that although it might be a pity to have to await the resoiution of some problems, yet this was merely unfortunate and required patience. Or, if not the system, at least the planet, the human race, were stable enough for such procedure.

This outlook, moreover, presupposed that, in principle, the various "parts" of life were independent and separate. The economic, the philosophic, the political, and, alongside the other categories, also the religious, were conceived as each discrete or at least distinguishable realities, complicating life no doubt by influencing each other in surreptitious and admittedly intricate ways, yet ultimately distinct—at least in the sense that problems in social life are technical and difficulties in any sector can be treated technically.

These objectificationist trends also meant that the fundamentally human questions as to what sort of person one is or shall become, and what overall vision deserves one's loyalty, were hardly incorporated into the model. In this scheme, the religious tended to be seen as just one more factor in the social complex, although it was tacitly recognized as being different from the others at least by the consensus that it was to be left alone —whether because it did not really matter any more, or because it was too unmanageable.

One reason why the food and enery crises of today are crises is that these presuppositions are seen no longer to hold true. The threat of large-scale starvation is so massive and so multifaceted that we may not have time to deal with its "causes" *seriatim*. The energy crisis is so involuted that it calls in question the very foundation of the theory that human problems are technical and can be solved technically—which has regularly meant solution by the application of more industrial energy.

Given problems of this magnitude and of this multidimensionality, one begins to think about bringing all resources, from whatever source, to bear upon their solution. Maybe even religion can be used to help deal with these threats?

The idea is attractive because of the potential activating forcefulness of religious faith. Since heroic measures, on a wide base, seem requisite and since faith, apparently, even and perhaps especially among the rank-and-file of society, can call forth concern, dedication, hard work, stamina, then might religion not be enlisted in the service of this goal?

Caveats: Divisiveness and Being "Used." Two caveats, however, present themselves. One is the divisiveness matter. Responsible world leaders are given pause by their sense that once religious feelings are aroused, even in a good cause, who knows but what they may eventuate in internecine conflict. Each religious community is committed, within its own terms of reference, to the problem of hunger, presumably, if not necessarily to that of energy.

Yet, given the fact that today, for the first time, hunger is a global problem, clearly requiring the cooperation of all humankind, can the disparate religious communities be counted upon to work together? Even if they avoid mutual bickering, rivalry, or at least embattled collision, can they be expected to know how to collaborate positively? Or even to learn how to do so, in time? Is secularity, whatever deficiencies it may have, the only practical basis for world order, and secular language, whatever its other limitations, the only one in which men and women of diverse forms of faith can speak to each other?

The second *caveat* is that religion must not be "used," not even for a good cause. Faith is our relation to ultimates, to absolutes. To subordinate faith, or to try to subordinate it, to any practical purpose, however worthy, is explosively distorting. Even those who may not be too concerned over the possible distortions must be cautious about the possible explosions.

Corporate Guilt and Repentance. Persons of religious faith are particulary sensitive to the problem of distortion, more so than socio-political leaders. Both groups are alert to the former problem, the fissiparous quality of religious life. Men and women of faith within each community, and not only secular observers on the outside of all, take note of and weep over the deep divisions that scar the religious history of our planet, the scars not yet healed, the scarring itself not yet over.

We are haunted by an awareness of the devastation that we human beings have wrought in the name of God, the gulfs that we have dug among people, and the woes that we have inflicted. At least, we *should* be haunted, the awareness *should* be stark, although self-righteousness has also been a besetting sin of the religious person or group, and each of us has often written and read a history that justifies our own community and is blind to its treatment of others.

As a Christian, I am very conscious that the Christian church has been exceptionally guilty in this matter. I wonder if any other religious group on earth has such a sorry record of internal strife and external negativity as we do. Yet none is fully innocent. I still remember the sharp sorrow with which I first learned of the violent destruction in 1465 of the Honganji Temple in Kyoto at the hands of armed monks from Mt. Hiei, members of the rival Buddhist sect, the Tendai. My sorrow was due to finding thus shattered my earlier impression that in one instance at least—the Buddhist—we human beings had been peaceful not only in our visions but also in our religious practice. Buddhists and Taoists have a far better record than others of us no doubt; and other communities will, I hope and advocate, be able to learn from them in this matter.

Yet all humankind has yet to learn to be one community. Twentieth-century life has juxtaposed us, intermingled us, but our becoming a community is still a general religious aspiration to which specific religious aspirations and traditions are still an obstacle.

This is painfully obvious in the Christian case, especially to non-Christians. It is fairly obvious in the Islamic case, especially to non-Muslims. It is obvious, alas, in the Hindu case, despite disclaimers, for along with that faith's admirable conceptual universalism go fierce sociological rigidities and rejections. As for Jews—a small group and in the past harmless and only the victims of excluding communal solidarity by others—their cohesion in the state of Israel has become a divisive matter today. But Christians must never forget that the implacable extrusions of Christendom into that part of the world lie, in significant part, behind the situation there. Through Shinto, the Japanese people have been welded into a community, from which fact outsiders have sometimes not profited. Christians may lead in the need for repentance in this realm, but we are not alone.

Repentance, however, is a proper yet not adequate response. For the problem is not an aberration from religious ideals and faith; it is inherent in them, a function of them, central to them. Divisiveness is not a failure of the religious (as we have inherited our traditions), but an ingredient of its success. It is for this reason, I take it, that a conference of this sort wrestles with such an issue and requests among its agenda items a paper such as this, addressed specifically to it. It is demanded of us not only that we bewail our sins but that we reconceive our virtue; for a virtue of our religious faith is that it binds persons together into partial wholes.

Two Secularist Fallacies. One solution to interreligious strife, the one that the modern West has tried most seriously (and recently has insistently pressed on others), is to play down the religious dimension of life, or at least religious loyalties, especially in social ordering. Two dramatic fallacies in this position have shown up to wide dismay. One is that secular substitutions of other forms of community—most conspicuously, nationalism and the nation-state—have proved a deceptive solution. Nationalist wars in the twentieth century have been unprecedentedly violent. The United States approaches its two-hundredth anniversary less confident of its nationalist dream than it has been for long. Nor has any nationalism clearly worked where there have been serious religious differences.

The Soviet Union and other ideological states seem to combine the failings of both the secular and religious orders. Moreover, it was the secular nation-state of Hitler's Germany that perpetrated the holocaust. The Christian church's treatment of Jews has been horrendous, but even at its worst never went so far.

The second sorry disillusionment with the irreligious outlook has lain in the discovery that it is not enough to get rid of obstacles to unity (such as religions and their divisiveness) for community—global or other—to emerge. The process is not so automatic; on the contrary, unity is a positive thing. It has to be attained and sustained.

Religious faith, even if at times only within certain boundaries, has turned societies into communities. Remove it, and there is danger of atomism, isolation, the juxtaposition of lonely individuals. A congeries of those alienated from both the universe and each other is a high price to pay for the dream of "Let's get rid of religion"—or even, "Let's make it an individual matter."

Community Requires Transcendence. The only way to transcend the limited loyalties of extant traditions in societies is through a transcendence greater and more serious, not less.

Durkheim is of central importance here. He saw religion as the expression, the symbolization, of community. Our problem will be more intractable, not less, if we ignore or endeavor to gainsay his powerful point. Is it not feasible, however, and truer and more helpful to accept his position, but to turn it upside down, seeing community, perhaps all society, as the expression, even the symbolization, of faith (although not necessarily of explicit religious faith).

Durkheim was Jewish, which accounts in part for his sensitivity to this particular aspect of the sacred; he took community for granted. The fact that he lived at the turn of the century also accounts in part for his attitude; today we, alas, are sadder and wiser. We know about *anomie* and the potential of disintegration in place of community. Society, in Durkheim's cohesive meaning, is not "natural" in the sense of being able to give a naturalistic explanation for faith. Rather, vice versa. Faith is (in part!) the capacity that persons have to enter into, and to sustain, and to let themselves be sustained by, a group. (I say "that persons have," but one may rather insist, "may have." Theists, by their phrasing about faith being a gift from God, remind us that it, too, is not to be taken for granted.) Faith, I may repeat, is what turns a society into a community. And I would urge this sociological reality on Durkheim's modern successors.

Faith is personal, but not in the sense of "individual." Indeed, an individual becomes a person only in community, and the degree to which a society is personal or impersonal varies. It becomes impersonal, as ours are visibly doing, through lack of faith.

From World Society to World Community. In the twentieth century, one of our most challenging tasks is the requirement of turning our world society into a world community. As a juxtaposition or congeries of individuals, nations, or religious systems, our planet flounders. To the extent that each individual, nation, and religious community does not learn to think, to feel, and to act as a participant in and a loyal member of humankind in our global context (that is, humankind as transcending each individual's own limits), the floundering will only get worse. To that extent also, each of our separate loyalties and visions and faiths will be less than truly fulfilled.

For example, Canada's ability to serve its national interests by protecting the fishing rights of Canadians in offshore waters will probably fail, even as a selfish aspiration, insofar as, at the Law of the Sea Conference, it and other nations each pursue only the rights of its own citizens, rather than striving toward a rational law of the sea for the whole human community. Somewhat similarly, Christian theology will fail so long as it thinks of itself as merely Christian theology.

My own view is that religious faith is probably the only force capable of engendering and sustaining the larger vision, allegiance, and activity requisite to the building of the new world community. Yet whether I be right or wrong on this point need not be an issue, so long as we in this room feel religious faith to be at least *a* force germane to this task. If others can arrive by other routes, splendid, but let us push ahead on ours. We, at least, must recognize, and act on the recognition, that community means faith; and that world community involves faith, both our own and our neighbors'.

I would argue, and would expect this conference to agree, that no viable human world order is theoretically conceivable other than one that the faith of each of us will inspire us to build, and that, once achieved, that faith will find worthwhile sustaining. The world's corporate goal must be one that not only we jointly approve, but toward which also we are severally impelled.

The Faith Community, Both Closed and Open. Throughout human history, the relation between community and faith has been close and dynamic. It is also dialectical: Faith generates community, and vice versa. Each conditions the pattern and process of the other, in unending turn. The relation has also been uneven, often far from smooth; each not only posits but, in part, criticizes the other. The degree of tension between the two varies, as does the effectiveness of the criticism—in other words, the destructiveness or creativity of the tension.

Furthermore, the community to which faith pertains may be closed or open. More accurately, it is both closed and open, in sharply varying proportions. We have said that every faith system—in ways and to an extent that differ from system to system, from century to century, from village to city, from class to class, from particular case to particular case—has been related to a social grouping that is internally coherent, cohesive, and at times closed against outsiders. And we have said that this is both a virtue and a vice. In addition, all faith, in ways and to an extent that differ even more markedly, aspires to a community open to all—at the least, to all humankind.

To take one example, the Christian tradition has dug deep gulfs and bred chronic or strident hostilities in its metaphysical teaching (e.g., "the saved and the damned"), its liturgical procedures (e.g., the denial of intercommunion among Christian churches), and its social behavior (e.g., the scandal of anti-Semitism, the Crusades, and other doleful treatments of outsiders). On the other hand, in its moral imperatives, in its universal vision, and even in some of its behavior, both internal and outward-oriented, it has striven, sometimes mightily, to bridge gulfs, to seek reconciliation, to generate peace and harmony. Moreover, the strength of the two forces, the closed and the open, and the ratio between them have varied historically—in part, with the varying visions of leaders.

Something of the sort has been also true for the other traditions. The historian may trace the varying forces and study the varying ratios.

We are back, then, to my opening sentence, "... religious faith ... has been both a divisive and a cohesive force." In the light of where we have come, however, we are now ready to deal with this double truth, and not simply to be teased by it. We need not adjudicate the formidable question of whether the cohesive outweighs the divisive, or vice versa, in general or in any given case. Recognizing the dynamic quality of this ineluctably historical problem, analytical observers may address themselves to the more crucial question: Whether the movement of religion in our day—in general or of any particular religious group or school of thought—is toward or away from a higher ratio of the force for unity to that for divisiveness. And we men and women of faith, members of this group or that subgroup, may each try to see to it that our contribution be toward raising that ratio.

It would be hypocritical not to recognize the problem, and irresponsible not to recognize that what we do can affect the ratio: the strengthening of the one force and the weakening of the other. As intellectuals, our business is to discern, to understand, and to clarify the forces at work. But as leaders or participants, our business is to fortify those processes that are headed in the direction of community (which today must mean both partial and global community) and to illuminate and to attenuate those making for narrowness and discord.

The problem is not so much the academic question of whether we are more unifying than divisive, as the moral and trenchantly practical one of whether we shall be more unifying tomorrow than we are today.

This view goes with my general interpretation (observation) of the history of religion, whereby each tradition is seen as historical, as constantly in process, each generation being entrusted *sub specie aeternitatis* with the ongoing and not unmalleable process during that phase of the development in which it itself participates. One prays, of course, that this participation is responsible: to the inheritance from the past, to the contemporary community and its environing problems, to generations yet to come, and above all to that timeless truth (whom those of us who are theists call God, although not those of us who are Buddhists, and so I leave the term as "timeless truth," *paramartha saddharma*) in the vision of and commitment to and apprehension by which faith consists, and in which the forms of the tradition are the mundane and historically changing expressions of that faith.

This thesis presumes that in our day truth or God is calling us to the construction of world community, that our faith also involves many other things, but also this. We must so move as not to endanger the islands (or continents!) of community already attained over the centuries, and not to jeopardize those nurturing sources of faith committed to us from the past—lest both community and faith be dissipated. Yet, in this late twentieth century, the vision of faith, nurtured by those very sources, is, I am contending, of a convergence of community such as to embrace all inherited communities in mutual trust and loyalty: the emergence, if one will, of a new, humanity-wide community, pluralist in form but true in substance, pluralist in religion but one through faith—and the last phrase is what true community means.

RELIGIOUS INTERDEPENDENCE

With this vision some may not agree. In particular, the most ardent universalist must treat with respect a thesis that this vision of global harmony and transcending loyalty is too utopian, too liberal-humanist; that it does not reckon with the negativities of history, with sin, with the possibility of failure.

It is possible to argue that the task of faith in our era of formidable crisis is not to modify inherited forms in the direction of a deceptive romanticism, fallaciously thinking to bring in the millennium by human contrivance. It is possible to claim rather that the task of faith is to steel men and women against the impending doom, giving them, in terms of the traditional forms however tightly preserved, the courage to face the coming catastrophe in the conviction that humanity's true home and faith's true focus is not this crumbling earth but a transcendent realm. A quiet but firm orientation to that realm endue them with serenity and transcendent hope, stable against all mundane disaster.

Expressing Transcendence Through Human Community. My answer is first to honor this view, but secondly to suggest that a deep sense of faith sees the two as not incompatible. In perhaps all our religious traditions individuals can, and indeed must, stand responsible for their own actions without being responsible for the whole course of history or the fate of the world. The *Bhagavada Gita* makes the point unusually explicit. The person of faith, and he or she alone, can strive with might and main for world peace, for an end to world hunger, for harmony and love among all religious communities, knowing that one may fail (*aphala*). This dedication and perseverance require no assurance of success —only assurance that the objective is right, that it is the will of God, that it is part of the inherent and final truth of that person's faith.

I am arguing that in our day an interpretation—in theory and practice—of religious faith and of one's own forms that will conduce to the community of all people (and not only to that of one's own group) is the interpretation most closely approximating the transcendent truth historically enshrined in our separate traditions. I am saying that for this reason (in addition to or over against any utilitarian goal) it is incumbent upon each community among us to work toward this, attempting to carry our own groups with us. (I am not saying it is the only incumbency—not even in the matter of interpersonal solidarity.)

This is not the occasion to argue my point with my fellow Christian theologians and church leaders. I can do so effectively, I realize (or at least, I hope), only if it can be shown that the move ahead in this realm can and must be accomplished without prejudicing the other truths vouchsafed in our tradition; indeed, only by more truly apprehending them. This task I and others pursue elsewhere. This *is* the occasion, however, to suggest that this very task can best be achieved through collaboration among faith communities. One could go further and aver that it can be achieved no other way.

No religious community can learn to be less offensive and damaging (or at least less irrelevant or unintelligible) to others unless it learns to listen to those others. There are also more positive aspects. For instance, I have already suggested that Buddhists have much to teach the rest of us about living in peace religiously. Certainly the Jews might teach the rest of us how to combine deep internal conviction with a contentment in outsiders' having other convictions. And if I turn out to have anything at all significant to say as a Christian theologian, it will be, in large part, because I have directly and indirectly learned much (about God, man, the world, Christ, faith, and religious history) from Muslims and my study of Islam, and more recently also from Hindus and my study of things Hindu.

We Need Each Other's Help. As I often stress, however, it will not be easy for any of our communities to move from our present inadequacies in the realm of human mutuality toward something more pragmatically genuine. We need each other's help. We must collaborate not only in treating problems of world hunger; we must collaborate also in learning how to collaborate. No one of us can learn on our own how to be able to work together. In our day, a new demand is laid upon every religious and social system: the demand of becoming compatible with alternative systems. The incompatible will perish. (Also it will be immoral.) Most of us do not even know how incompatible we currently are, let alone how to change this sorry state. And we can find out only in concert.

Some would call off in our day the missionary movement. Anyone who has not felt the enormous force of this argument is sadly insensitive. Nonetheless, I would transform that movement—rather drastically: I would insist that we must learn to invite missionaries to come to us, as well as to send, on invitation, a radically new type to others. Theists who feel that God has spoken, and speaks today, only to or through their own group, or through theism, or nontheists who feel that they have nothing to learn from theism, are both surely misinformed and unimaginative.

Again, of course, I realize that in recent centuries the West and the Christian Church have been the most arrogant and the most at fault in this area; but they (we) are learning. (The institutional Church is learning perhaps more slowly and more painfully than other sectors of the membership at large; but it is learning.) The movement toward religion's (and religions') becoming a unifying more than a divisive force is, in significant part, a process of learning about those on the other side of each divide. That process is under way, partly inescapably, and now increasingly by deliberate resolve.

Faith, classical thinkers have long seen, is partly inscrutable ("the free gift of God"), and is partly a matter of the will, partly of the intellect. We may say that it arises in part from outside oneself, but insofar as the person is himself of herself involved, both will and mind play a part. The faith that may constitute the foundation for a global community is coming and will come through all three considerations. (Those modern Westerners who add feeling to will and intellect as three "parts" of the person should say: "through all four considerations.")

HUMANKIND AND THE OTHER CONTINUUMS

So much for the general level. We move on to a specific point, one that will illustrate, in a concrete and rather different way, some of the larger issues that are, subtly, involved. The illustration still has to do with humankind-as-a-whole, as a total community, and still has to do with religious sensibilities; but it presents the point in another fashion.

Subject/Object Polarity. A traditional teaching in many religious systems (explicit in many, perhaps implicit in all) has been that finally the subject/object polarity is misleading (and mis-led). A traditional religious aspiration has been to transcend it. The significance of this seemingly remote idea impinges on our world at the present time sharply. Some of us are beginning to see that the current disillusionment with scientific objectivity and technological impersonalism results from an inchoate restlessness at precisely this point. Blindly but increasingly, humankind is resentful of the sharp disjunction between man and nature, between knower and known, that science has been fundamentally errant in setting up. Science has been intellectually and practically wrong in this, despite its spectacular intellectual and practical success in limited areas.

Humankind is beginning to recognize that this disjunction is potentially disastrous in its treatment both of object and of subject—its treatment of the natural world (thus the ecology crisis) and its dreary relegating of man to nihilistic impersonalism. This split between subject and object has led to the widespread, but again disastrous, view that the only alternative to objectivity is subjectivity. (Insofar as the young believe this much-preached fallacy, they are tempted to choose subjectivity, even through drugs or self-assertive violence, revolutionary or aimless.)

To reconstruct a vision of man and nature in mutual relationship, to achieve an understanding of truth that correlates knower and known, is perhaps the greatest challenge to thought (and faith) today. Traditional religious orientations encourage us to recognize the possibility of this, and its value, even its obligatoriness. Faith has traditionally been this. Yet traditional forms of faith have collapsed in our time partly because they correlate the knower not with what today is known. (Quite apart from the vast new knowledge provided by science, the awareness of even explicitly religious matters with which most traditional forms of faith integrated man was much more restricted than the knowledge we now have, especially of each other's faith, and of our own and others' histories.)

I will certainly not develop this matter here. The relation

between religion and science is a vast question. It remains so even when narrowed to the particular question of science's tendency, thus far, to eliminate all human community, to isolate individuals into meaningless atomistic "subjects," over against religion's tendency thus far to weld persons into partial communities.

The Population Problem as Example. One particular issue I will raise, however, in the religion/science question to illustrate the point: the outlook whereby one perceives the population problem.

Because of the subject/object orientation of science and technology and, by transference, then, even of social or behavioral science and policy planning, this and other questions have been conceived in "we/they" terms. (This scientific objectivity reinforces the traditional religious propensity to regard outsiders as "they.") Basically this particular problem has been posed as "population control"—an inherently immoral concept—in the form of "What can *we* do so that *they* will have fewer children?" The Ford Foundation, governments (whether in Washington or New Delhi), and research organizations proceed fundamentally within such a framework.

Some years ago, Harvard University's Center for the Study of World Religions, of which I was then director, was approached in connection with a "population control" program for India. I responded that the "we/they" conceptualization was in our Center's judgment wrong; and I proposed instead that a joint Western-Christian-Hindu team aim at reformulating the question in terms that would be simultaneously intelligible and cogent within the ongoing Hindu moral tradition (*dharma*) and to outsiders. (One goal was to touch on the rather novel question within the Christian community of the ethical problem of Christians' and other Westerners' participating in moral choices of Indians, and vice versa.)

In other words, I was striving to concoct a program that would enable the issue to be seen and dealt with as a joint world issue, whereby "we" human beings, *some of us* being Hindus in India and *some of us* being Christians or humanists in the West, could intelligibly and jointly articulate what in the matter before us was possible and what desirable. Specifically, we wished to generate terms of reference that would elucidate the population problem in India, seen from within as a moral matter of choices *by* Indians (and not a policy *for* Indians implemented either by the West or by the New Delhi government).

I have since learned to conceptualize this sort of goal as "corporate critical self-consciousness." Probably at the time my formal submission was inadequately worked out. In any case, the Ford Foundation dismissed it as of no significance, my concern with ethical and religious and human-community issues striking them as a distraction, irrelevant to an urgent practical task.

It has since turned out that in "population control" programs the operationalist, not to say manipulative, approach of the foundations, research centers, and governments, based as it is on a we/they polarity and secularistic view, has been proving ineffective, and not merely immoral. No population "policy" can be wise that is not correlated with, even rooted in, people's faith, or that is not correlated with or rooted in religious faith that is particularist without yet being global. Population is a problem of the worldwide society of our day, which can be dealt with only by and for a worldwide human community not yet attained. (It may help us to attain it; but it takes more than problems to turn a society into a community.)

Faith and the New "We" of Humankind. I mention this point as I said, illustratively. The population problem is simply one instance of a general point: If we human beings are to confront modern world problems adequately, our most important move is that we should become a new type of person.

Requisite in all realms are not merely new programs for these problems, but new persons to draft them: persons who have the sophisticated expertise to be technically proficient, but who also see and feel those whom their programs will affect not as those "others," those people over there whose behavior is to be controlled or who are to be persuaded, but rather as drafters who constitute, along with themselves, a corporate community, a "we" whose future is at issue, and whose free and now newly informed moral choices will conduce to that joint future.

Our modern world has hardly yet come to recognize that practical matters, involving many millions of dollars of expenditure and several years of valuable and nowadays crucial time, may turn on the issue of religion as a cohesive and divisive social force. (Operationalist programs have begun to recognize, of course, that religion cannot be ignored, as used to be imagined or hoped; but those who run them tend to consider religion a "factor" in the total complex, something that "they" have and whose objections to what "we" propose may be overcome, or whose potential contribution to our goals may prove serviceable.)

Yet those of us of faith must not simply berate the secularists for their blindness. The point of my paper is that the task ahead of us, religiously, is indeed important to all humankind, but has as yet to be discharged, and it is we, in a conference like this, who must tackle it.

My submission may be summed up in three sentences. One of the most important facts about any human being is whom he or she means when saying "we." One of the most important facts about any social group (such as the whole of humanity or any of its parts) is what each person within that group means when using that word. One of the most important religious imperatives of our day is that faith must, and probably alone can, lead us to mean by "we" all humankind.

9

Distinction, Identity, and Community

a Hindu response presented by K. Sivaraman

(Spokesmen from the five faiths represented in our Colloquium
had been asked in advance to respond to Professor Smith's paper.
Dr. K. Sivaraman, Rabbi Norman Lamm, Professor Hasan Askari,
and Monsignor Charles Moeller came prepared to speak briefly to
the subject, each from the viewpoint of his faith—Hindu, Jewish,
Muslim, and Roman Catholic Christian, respectively. The Venerable W. Ananda Thera had been asked to do the same from the
Buddhist viewpoint; instead, he generously prepared an exten-
sive statement of Buddhist teaching on the role of religion in
politics and society. To give the many westerners at the meeting
further insight into the less familiar viewpoints, Professor M.
Palihawadana and Dr. Mohammed Al-Nowaihi asked to add un-
scheduled remarks from their Buddhist and Islamic perspectives.
Additionally, the session was chaired by Professor K. Satchidananda Murty, who interspersed observations from his own
Hindu tradition throughout the discussion.)

For twenty years, Dr. K. Sivaraman taught philosophy at the
Hindu University in Banaras, the Holy City of India; he now
teaches at McMaster University, Ontario, Canada. He has been a
student under Dr. Smith at Harvard.

Dr. Sivaraman's remarks were largely extemporaneous, his

notes scanty, and his words far more provocative of new ideas than I can hope to capture on the printed page.

Dr. Sivaraman expressly assumed "the posture of a Hindu who is contemporary and is also involved in the quest for meaning within his traditional past. From this point of view, I can have no hesitation to acclaim with zest the central thrust of Professor Smith's paper, to share without reserve his profound concern." We must think of these problems with a primary focus, not only peripherally, "as implying a call and a challenge to faith. . . . We shall be talking with each other about ourselves religiously speaking, even when we discuss energy or ecology or population."

So Dr. Sivaraman is willing "to dream with Professor Smith of the viability of a world order, undistracted by actualities."

RESPONSIBILITY TO REFLECT

It is this primacy of reflection, and the duty to do so, which Dr. Sivaraman wanted above all to communicate. "At a time when we are inescapably confronted by competing ideologies of action, all alike imposing on us, in the name of industrial growth and development, the urgency of immediate action unimpeded by ideas, at a time when ideals and values are considered simply distractions, it is perhaps a useful service to remind ourselves of the never-ending responsibility of reflecting, thinking, discerning, understanding, clarifying. At any rate, as a Hindu, I have nothing better to bring to this conference."

The Hindu philosopher cautioned, "Maybe more issues are at stake than meet our eye in this whole business of adapting to a new view of growth, progress, and communal living—issues connected with human autonomy, freedom, man as the maker of his own law." In sum, for Dr. Sivaraman, these are expressed in "the drive toward homogenization of the state, rancorous, cruel statism which homogenizes all heterogeneous elements, mastering objective human and nonhuman nature alike. All of these seem to me part of the package of technological civilization. And all these things raise profound religious issues."

That is why Dr. Sivaraman urged that we "sometimes include storms of pause, to renew our 'corporate critical self-consciousness,' to use one of Professor Smith's beautiful conceptualizations." These "storms of pause" would help "in the pursuit of values and ideals which direct our creating of history. I submit this as a Hindu who has no theological obsession for a directional world history as entailed by acceptance of God's reality, as a Hindu who is at the same time no stranger to the zeal of making the social environment accord with the demands of the time."

COMMUNITY AND FAITH

Dr. Sivaraman desired to "start with the positive side. What can be more positive than the vision of a new world community —refreshing contrast to the dismal picture of our universal homogenized state? This vision of global harmony, of convergence, of community, is not the vision of an idealist, of a utopian, but of a religious historian. For Professor Smith, the historian, what seems eternal in a religious tradition is ... the fact that it is a constant, ongoing process, and more precisely and significantly, the fact that each generation is interested in the ongoing process during that phase of development in which it itself participates. The present phase of development of every faith witnesses special responsibility toward the contemporary community and toward generations yet to come. All this sounds like music to my Hindu ears."

Before making critical remarks, Dr. Sivaraman praised "Professor Smith's revolutionary proposals for changes in comparative religious studies: renouncing the misleading label of 'religion' in favor of 'Faith'; renouncing the commonplace assumption that truth resides in religions in favor of the view that it resides in the attitudes of faith in which it is received by persons."

HINDU RIGIDITIES

Dr. Sivaraman urged meditation on Professor Smith's proposition that in our day every religious and social system should become compatible with alternative systems, lest it perish. It is not that simple. "The Hindu is theologically exercised by a constant vision of life that is compatible with alternative systems. I do not pretend that, in practice, Hindus have always been models of tolerance, or, for that matter, that, even in theory, their openness to alternative systems has meant a self-critical awareness of how significantly incompatible the systems are.... Their tolerance, indeed, becomes notoriously limited under the actual exigency of historical encounters with systems that are structured differently—or, more often, by their lack of encounter of them.

"Professor Smith referred to the 'sociological rigidities' of Hinduism, existing side by side with its glorious universalism. . . . If by 'sociological rigidities' he meant the system of caste, let me hasten to say Hindus themselves do not look at it as incompatible with the goal of universalism. The law of spiritual hierarchies in life stations is pursued by Hindus as structural to life as it is. It is marked by heterogeneity, variety, plurality, and an essential absence of parity.

"But the goal of spiritual freedom in this age," in Dr. Sivaraman's view, "demands transcending the conditions under which the hierarchical structuring of life obtains—not that Hindu men and women of faith have less reason to be haunted by their awareness of humanity, by what they as human beings have wrought in the very name of this insight. They have only to recall Gandhi's struggle with this problem. . . . The point I want to make here is not to defend the caste system, but to isolate what I consider the harder lessons of Hindu experience." At the sociological level, a non-equalitarian outlook is incommensurable with "a universalism which goes so far as to deny theologically the very validity of the contrast of self and other."

Dr. Sivaraman wholly endorsed "Professor Smith's idea of cohesiveness superseding the divisive element, but I have difficulty with the terminology. . . . Divisiveness has been equated, it seems to me, with difference or distinction—which to me is another name for identity." The Hindu scholar sees distinction and identity as having quite opposite meanings in the proselytizing religions of Christianity, Islam, and even Buddhism, as compared with the nonproselytizing religions. "In other words, if I may generalize, for one family of religions, distinction is division. But for the family of religions typified in the Hindu orientation of spirit, distinction comes with the demand that it not only be tolerated, but be acknowledged as incommensurably valid and, therefore, as compatible."

SECULARISM AND BELIEF

"I have only one more point—about secularism. Professor Smith is acutely sensitive to the multicultural atmosphere in which modern man lives and faces the crisis of life today. But the modern world includes many men and women of faith that express themselves through rejection of faith. In his scheme, what is the place of a faith that is no faith? . . . Do we not find elements of faith in the structure of the secular mind itself? Is there not that inscrutable element of faith, as well as those elements of will, intellect, and feeling, which comes to the fore when traditional religions lose their power and meaning?

"Speaking from the side of modern Hinduism, I cite again the instance of Gandhi, whose relevance to Hinduism's encounter with growing secularization is a case in point. Gandhi's passion for justice, honesty, and truthfulness, his total dedication to a more fully developed humanity, his call for liberation from bondage to authority of every kind—all these religious elements pointed back to the roots of Hindu religious tradition, but assumed the form of protest and even a rejection of traditional religious forms. Gandhi's was a clear case of protest from within the framework of Faith, as a proper name.

"For Hinduism," Dr. Sivaraman concluded, "one of the positive virtues of secular encounter is a great promise of a new orientation of non-Hindu religions and a new vision of religious unity, consequent of a new self-understanding of Hinduism."

10

Buddhist Social and Political Thought

by W. Ananda Thera

(Two spokesmen for Buddhism presented their perspective to the symposium. One was the Venerable W. Ananda Thera, who had generously prepared an essay on the social teachings of Buddha; this was circulated among the participants beforehand. The other was Professor M. Palihawadana, who added extemporaneous remarks on the position of nontheists in interreligious encounters and on Dr. Smith's thought in particular. Dr. Ananda is head of the Department of Buddhist Studies, International Buddhist Center, Colombo, Sri Lanka. He is also professor of Buddhist philosophy, College of Oriental Studies, Graduate School, Los Angeles, Calif. Dr. Ananda's paper did not respond directly to Professor Smith; rather, it surveyed the social and political teaching of the Buddha and gave examples of how this has been applied in Asian society. Much of this is new to my western ears, so I have reproduced the paper almost in its entirety, with only slight abbreviation and editing, and no space-saving paraphrasing.)

*　　*　　*

Religion and politics are two terms that have been so variously defined (and ill-defined) that to recount even a few of the attempts here would be to put ourselves into a web of confusion. To one person, "Religion is the opium of the masses"; to another, "Politics is the last refuge of the scoundrels." Because opinions are so numerous and conflicting, I shall proceed without attempting exact definitions, with the caveat that my own opinions do not reach either extreme of the spectrum.

Using certain definitions of religion and politics (perhaps because of using them), some people believe that religion has no place in government, that the two are diametrically opposite to one another and should be in two separate, watertight compartments. In other words, they proceed on the premise that "religion is religion" and "politics is politics" and never the twain shall meet. The purpose of this paper is to examine this hypothesis and its opposite from the Buddhist perspective, both in theory and practice. Can religion and politics be harmonized and synthesized? Do religion and politics subscribe to divisiveness or unity?

In dealing with this subject, I have divided it into four main parts. In the first, I broadly outline what constitutes religion and politics. In the second, I examine the political thought found interspersed throughout the teachings of the Buddha. In the third, I deal with the interaction of religion and politics in the light of Buddhism, especially that of the Theravada countries,* and examine to what extent the elements of divisiveness and unity come into play there. And finally, I look to what the Buddhist ethic might provide for the future.

Editor's note: The Theravada school of Buddhism is dominant in South Asia, in Sri Lanka, Burma, Thailand, Laos, and Cambodia. The very word *Theravada* means "the Teaching of the Elders." This indicates that the school falls within the older, more conservative wing of Buddhism, called collectively *Hinayana*, literally "small" (*Hina*) "means or way of salvation" (*yana*). The younger, more reformist wing is called *Mahayana*, literally "great" (*Maha*) "means of salvation" (*yana*) (i.e., more universalist and wider than "the small way").

Hinayana is sometimes used by westerners as synonymous with Theravada; that is incorrect, since Theravada is only one of a dozen or more Hinayana schools, albeit one of the most important. Theravadins claim theirs to be the authentic and original form of the Buddha's teaching, as contained in the scriptural canon received immediately after the death of the Buddha, at the First Buddhist Council at Rajagaha. Consequently, Theravada is among the most venerable faith traditions, some twenty-four centuries old.

Mahayana emerged during the period between the birth of Christ and A.D. 100 (about five centuries after the Buddha lived). It became the prevalent form of Buddhism in North Asia, in China, Japan, Korea, and Taiwan. The two schools combined in Vietnam. Mahayana gave greater place to the virtue of compassion than had been the case of the traditional Hinayana, which placed heavier emphasis on wisdom. Mahayana valued compassion and wisdom equally. It also urged *bodhisattva* as the ideal or goal of human life which all people could and should strive for; by this, Mahayana democratized the availability of enlightenment and a possible savior role (the qualities of *bodhisattva*), even the attainment of deity, for Buddhists generally. Mahayana disciples also engaged wholeheartedly in intellectual debates of the time and began using Sanskrit, the language of the Brahmans, who were contemporary Indian intellectuals. (See S.G.F. Brandon, ed., *A Dictionary of Comparative Religion* [New York: Scribners, 1970].)

WHAT CONSTITUTES RELIGION AND POLITICS?

It has often been said that Buddhism is not a religion because it has no definite belief in a personal God or in an undying human personality (soul) and has a consequent absence of any worship and prayer. Some have, therefore, called it a philosophical system; others, an ethico-religious social philosophy; still others, a Way of Life. If religion can mean only a "binding or abiding relationship between man and his God," then certainly Buddhism does not fall into the category of a religion.

Max Müller, in *Lectures on the Science of Religion,* talks of "the broad foundations on which all religions are built up—the belief in a divine power, the acknowledgement of sin, the habit of prayer, the desire to offer sacrifice, and the hope of a future eternal life." But popular usage has been too strong for him. Not one of these five are found in pure Buddhism, yet he does call Buddhism a religion. And most of the world—Buddhists and non-Buddhists alike—seem to agree with him.

The Ideal of Harmony in Life. To Buddhists, religion is a Way of Life by means of which human beings may train themselves to make desirable changes in their own personalities through an inner revolution (thereby establishing more adequate relations between themselves and the universe of which they are a part).

The Buddhist ideal is to set up an equilibrium between the inside and the outside, between the externals of nature and the world of human beings—in other words, to realize and establish the fundamental unity of humankind, irrespective of caste, color, race, or other physiological characteristics.

Broadly speaking, Buddhists regard politics as concerned with the governance of communities in themselves and among themselves—that is, with the laying down of definite rules or laws for human conduct individually and in groups, and for determining the general conditions under which people live. Politicians will inevitably differ as to the best kinds of laws and regulations to achieve this end. But among the great variety of individual opinions, there should undoubtedly appear a basic law acceptable to the lawmakers *and* in harmony with religion.

One Goal for Religion and Government. In India's ancient past, religion and politics were combined to further the advancement of civilization; indeed, politics was actively sustained by religion. As such, the guiding principle and ultimate motive of statecraft were how to make the subjects morally and spiritually better, in addition to making them materially better off. (The combination is not unique. For example, the Greeks, too, saw ethics and politics as two aspects of a single inquiry. The function of their ethics was to prescribe the good life for the individual; the business of politics was to determine the nature of the community in which that good life could be lived.)

Thus, Buddhists have believed throughout their history that if religion exists to inspire human beings, enrich personality, stimulate action, and ennoble thought and motive, then governments exist to create, secure, and preserve such conditions as are consistent with the attainment of this end. Indeed, since both politics and religion are concerned with the provision of conditions most favorable for the perfection of the citizens, in their material and spiritual aspects respectively, the perfection of ideal citizens may be the goal of religion and politics combined. And, in fact, religion and politics at their best are but the obverse and reverse of the same force making for righteousness in the state. Religion does this by trying to destroy all wickedness through changing human nature by teaching and preaching; politics does it by trying to change the environment and eliminate all wickedness by legislation. When these two processes are harmonized, we have the ideal state.

Buddhism came into existence in the sixth century before Christ, a time when India had a very highly organized society. It was primarily a Way of Life designed to show the individual the path of emancipation and liberation. But, although the Buddha's primary concern was the problem of suffering, he was a teacher of foresight, farsight, and insight too, and did not totally ignore the material side of life. Thus, Buddhism is by no means a world-denying religion. Indeed, the Buddha described his teaching as being primarily concerned with *this* life and with *this* world (*Sanditthika*). The Way of Life he taught was a harmonious synthesis of the material and spiritual aspects of life. He was concerned with human happiness, and he believed happiness was not possible without leading a noble and pure life based on moral and spiritual principles. But he was aware that leading such a life was difficult in unfavorable material and social conditions.

The Buddha did not consider material welfare as an end in itself—only a means to a higher and nobler end, but a means which is indispensable. In other words, he recognized that certain minimum material conditions are required even for the spiritual happiness which is the ultimate goal of life. As a result, he did not

take life out of its social, economic, and political context, but
looked at it as a whole.

The Buddha in the India of His Time. The Buddha did not concern himself with active politics, but he was very clear on his
political views and on good government.

When Buddhism arose, North India was broken up into several
monarchies, varying in size and power. There were republics and
confederacies, there were democracies with elected monarchs,
and there were kingdoms with hereditary kings. The Buddha
himself grew up in one of the democratic republican clans (the
Sakyas); he not only imbibed high ideals of democracy but became
well aware of the existence of different types of political administration. However, he did not speak of the relative superiority of one
type over the other. To the Buddha, the success of any system
depended on the extent to which the ruler or the government
followed the norm of good polity (*saddhamma*), as implied in
socio-ethical concepts. But from the admonition he gave the Vaj-
jians (the most powerful republican state of his time) about guard-
ing their independence and solidarity, it can be inferred that he
favored the democratic form and had even expressed the view
that democratic government was the form most conducive to the
stability of society.

In the days of the Buddha, as today, there were rulers who
governed unjustly, oppressing and exploiting the people, imposing excessive taxes, inflicting cruel punishments. The Buddha
was deeply moved by these inhumanities of people to people.
Whenever ruling kings (some of whom were his great patrons)
came to him for counsel, the Buddha spoke to them of the art of
good governing. He showed them, as he wrote in the *Cakkavatti
Sihanada Sutta*, how a whole country could become corrupt, de-
generate, and unhappy when the king and his ministers became
corrupt and unjust.

Both religion and politics are fundamental necessities of life;
they have a common goal—the good and welfare of humanity
—and the Buddha showed a way by which they could be harmonized. The task he left to his followers was to create a workable
polity in accordance with his teaching, a polity where people could
live in harmony and peace by performing both their duty to themselves and their duty to others; this harmony will eventually lead
to contentment and happiness in society, which constitutes the
ultimate aim of both religion and politics.

In the view of the Buddha, the end and object of life is to perfect human nature in all aspects. This cannot be achieved merely by teaching or preaching or calling on people to be better. The social and political structures in which people are formed and live must also be changed, improved, adjusted, and made consistent with realities. Therefore, in any country where the population is predominantly Buddhist, the task of good government has been and should be to bring the everyday life of the community in all its social, economic, and political aspects into harmony with the Buddha's Way of Life—in other words, to bring the functions of the state into harmony with the spiritual (and prerequisite material) needs of humankind.

POLITICAL AND SOCIAL THOUGHT
IN THE BUDDHA'S TEACHING

Some scholars have erroneously asserted that Buddhism is a mere individualistic doctrine of salvation and that early Buddhism had no political or social philosophy. Max Weber goes to the extent of calling Buddhism "un-political and anti-political." Nothing could be further from the truth. Political wisdom is scattered throughout the teachings of the Buddha.

The Common Good: Citizen and King. In the Buddha's very first sermon, "Establishment of the Rule of Righteousness," he developed the concept of the welfare and happiness of all beings, without any discrimination whatsoever "out of compassion for the world" (*bahujana hitaya bahujana sukhaya*). It was the first time in human history that there was envisaged a common good which affected not only all the people of one nation, but all the peoples of the world.

In this message, the Buddha demanded an ever-widening fellowship for each human being and called upon the state to protect the citizens from exploitation, to secure justice for them, and to give them equality of opportunity. The Buddha greatly valued the liberty of the individual, freedom of thought and expression, and the ideals of democracy. His goal for society was the creation of a happy, content (*Sanutthi*) community of all human beings, irrespective of caste, class, color, or race.

Regarding the origin and establishment of political authority, the *Agganna Sutta* mentions a socio-compact theory for society and a correlative governmental-contract theory for kingship; within this relationship, it discusses the establishment and protection of property rights. As for the nature of political authority, the *Maha Parinibbana Sutta* presents a juridical conception of kingship as a necessary political institution; the principle of collective or representative political authority is also mentioned. Later, however, the Buddha substituted a theory of kingship glorified and personified in the ideal Buddhist ruler (the *Cakkavatti*).

In the Buddhist texts, the ideal ruler is pictured as one who sets rolling the wheel of human prosperity under the superior power of righteousness (*Dhamma*). They list certain characteristics of a successful king, including: belief in the power of righteousness; the generosity of a benefactor who keeps open house to all without the slightest discrimination; intelligence, wisdom, and the capacity to think out matters relating to the past and the future. In fact, the good king or ruler is defined as one who delights his subjects in accordance with righteousness, in other words, one who rules righteously, judiciously, and in accord with the law of piety. Moreover, he must not be an autocrat but must follow the advice of his competent ministers and counselors. The king who selfishly sits on his throne, yielding indulgence only to sensual pleasures, intoxicated with his authority, is openly condemned. The righteous king, while retaining the exalted state of the ruler, must consider himself in no way superior to his subject, must dispense justice to his subjects without fear or favor, must learn to treat everyone equally.

As far as possible, he must also attempt to rule without the use of cruel punishment and weapons, regarding his subjects with the loving kindness of a mother to her children (*mata yatha niyam puttam*—the analogy from the parent-child relationship is typically Buddhistic). Additionally, the law cannot act as an automaton because all administration has to deal with individuals who are primarily psychological units. (According to the Buddha, the conditions to which people are subject as social beings are to a large extent psychological.)

Finally, the Buddha's good king or ruler, as the constitutional head of state, should consult the people's wishes on all important matters. This respect for a constitutional procedure whereby the king consults the wishes of all his subjects—from the highest aristocrat down to the lowliest peasant—is one of the Buddha's original conceptions and can be seen to advantage in the working of his monastic order (*Sangha*), which is designed to be a self-governing institution. Indeed, the monastic order of the Buddha, which is considered the oldest democratic institution in the world, was set up as a model for lay organizations, including political institutions.

The influence of the Buddha's democratic ideas on India's government institutions is attested to by Lord Marquess Zetland, in *Legacy of India*, who says that Buddhist writings give early examples of representative self-governing institutions, and that in these Buddhist assemblies in India over two thousand years ago are to be found rudiments of British parliamentary practice. He cites the appointment by the assembly of a special officer who foreshadows "Mr. Speaker" in the House of Commons, and another officer who had to assure the presence of a quorum, prototype perhaps of today's party whip. A member initiated business in the form of a motion, which was then open for discussion. In some cases, this was done three times, a practice comparable to the Commonwealth parliamentary requirement that a bill be read and discussed three times before it becomes law. If discussion disclosed differences of opinion, the matter was decided by the vote of the majority.

Royal Virtues and Economic Welfare. The Buddhist ideal of kingship was further elaborated upon in *Dasa Raja Dhamma*, the ten royal virtues. This emphasized that the evil or good behavior of the people depends on the behavior of their rulers; if they give themselves to vice, their subjects will follow suit. Therefore, for the good and welfare of the people, the Buddha set out these virtues to be practiced by rulers. The ideal set before the king is one of energetic beneficence. The ten royal virtues are:

Generosity (*dana*): the king should not be greedily attached to his wealth but give it for the welfare of his people.

Morality (*sila*): he should be a person of high moral character.

Munificence (*parriccaga*): he should cultivate the spirit of sacrifice for the good of the people.

Honesty and integrity (*ajjava*): he should be free from fear and favor in the discharge of his duties.

Impartiality (*maddava*): he must possess a genial temperament.

Restraint (*tapa*): he should live a simple life of self-control.

Freedom from hatred (*akkodha*): he should bear no grudge against anybody.

Nonviolence (*avihinsa*): he should prevent anything that involves violence and destruction of life.

Patience (*khanti*): he should be able to bear hardships and criticism.

Friendliness and amity (*advirodha*): he should not oppose the will of the people, but rule in harmony.

In all these Buddhist conceptions of social, political, and juristic ethics, the underlying principle is clearly one of loving kindness (*metta*) to all.

The same principle manifests itself in Buddhism's concept of the proper economic policy for the ruler or government. To the Buddha, economic advancement depended on a sense of proportion in the meaningful acquisition of wealth and the spending thereof. Planning for economic welfare was clearly emphasized as a function of the king or state. When it is well executed, said the Buddha, the people "following each his own mission, will no longer harass the realm, the state revenue will increase, the country will be quiet and at peace and the populace, pleased with one another and happy, will dwell with open doors." (Note the cause-and-effect linkage of economic welfare with peace.)

In the *Cakkavattisihanada Sutta*, the Buddha stated that poverty is a cause of immorality and crime, but he expressed the firm belief that these problems could be adequately controlled, not by punishment, but by providing the people with opportunities to engage themselves meaningfully and profitably in other occupations so that they could lead happy and contented lives.

The best charity, according to Buddhism, is to help people to positions where they will never need charity. Economic security, the enjoyment of wealth, and freedom from debts were some of the factors listed by the Buddha as essential for a happy and contented material life. In times of disaster, such as the failure of crops, it was the bounden duty of the king or the state to provide grain and other facilities for the redevelopment of agriculture, financial assistance from the state coffers for those engaged in business, and adequate wages for those who were unemployed. When the people were thus provided for, they would have no fear or anxiety.

Applying Religion: Emperor Asoka. The great test of a religion is how far its philosophy can be applied to human problems in the work-a-day world. While satisfying profound and lofty aspirations, it should still be able to bear the strain of everyday life and help harmonize relationships among people. The Buddha was convinced that society, in the ultimate sense, was a collection of individuals, and therefore he lay emphasis on the part to be played by individuals in matters of social value. His concept of society included all the beings living at a given time; in this society the fundamental moral basis of people's relationship to others must be based on the virtues of *metta* (loving kindness) and *karuna* (compassion).

This social ethic does not differentiate between people's attitude to their own kith and kin and to their fellow beings in the outside world; however, in fulfilling their duties as social beings, people must first consider those nearest to them. In the *Singalovada Sutta*, the Buddha set out in detail the reciprocal duties between parent and children, husband and wife, master and servant, friends and relations, monk and laymen, and teacher and pupil.

Further, the Buddha enunciated numerous teachings for the well-being of the individual and society, such as the practice of generosity, kind speech, service for the benefit of others, equality, indomitable effort and skill in one's occupation, wariness in protecting the righteously earned income, association with good, faithful, learned, virtuous friends, maintaining one's expenses in proportion to one's income, and leading a faultless life without resort to trickery or cunning.

If a country is ruled by people endowed with such qualities and the people adhere to the social ethic outlined, needless to say all will be well with that state and its people. This is no utopian dream; there were kings in the past, such as the illustrious Emperor Asoka, whose rule was based on these ideas.

Asoka (273–232 B.C.) was the first to translate the Buddha's way of life into a polity. After the Kalinga war, which was the turning point in his life, he concentrated on moral and spiritual conquest (*dhammavijaya*). He showed, both in his personal life and in his administration, that the Buddha's doctrine was not merely a philosophy, but a Way of Life to be cultivated within his whole domain.

Asoka's vast empire contained people of many castes and creeds. He not only found that Buddhism, with its tolerant attitude and its social, economical, political, and juridical ethics, was accommodating of this variety, but that by putting the polity of the Buddha into effect, he was able to bring unity into this mass of diversity. The Rock and Pillar Edicts he left are evidence of the transformation that came over his land through using the social ethic of the Buddhist *Saddhamma*.

Under Emperor Asoka, the entire Buddhist concept of the righteous king ruling righteously (*dhammiko dhammaraja*) was put into practical use; a conscious effort was made to influence society through the political principles of Buddhism. Asoka developed a paternal concept of kingship and believed that his subjects were wronged if the king failed to provide them with the conditions of virtuous living. He declared that all people were his children, and more than once reproved his provincial governors for not applying this precept thoroughly: "Just as I desire on behalf of my own children that they should be provided with all kinds of comfort and enjoyment in this as well as in the other world, similarly, I desire the same on behalf of all my people."

Asoka believed in a positive obligation to his subjects and wanted the people to be free from fear; they were to receive only happiness, not sorrow, from him. He was not even satisfied with the welfare of his own subjects only; he extended his attention to lands outside his empire. From this day onward, Buddhist political thought found a firm foothold, and many rulers came to look upon Asoka as a model, embodying the Buddhist concept of kingship.

BUDDHIST POLITICAL THOUGHT IN ASIAN COUNTRIES

After this brief survey of the nature and scope of Buddhist political thought, it is possible to examine how that thought has influenced specific countries: the role it has played and to what extent it has been divisive or cohesive. However, in view of the varied nature of Buddhist political thought and the number of Asian societies to which it must be related, space permits only a cursory glance at some important features of a few of them.

State Religion and Nationhood. Today Buddhism continues to mold the values and concepts of Asians while retaining its monastic ideal. During the course of its historical development, it rescued itself from its social irrelevance and, by adapting itself to the social and political environments, showed itself to be a practical religion. In many countries to which Buddhism spread, it profoundly influenced cultural development. Additionally, the way it reacted to the socio-political milieu caused radical change within Buddhism itself. In many countries, the relation between Buddhism and the state became so intimate that religious customs and practices decreed by the king in council became recognized as part of the law of the land. In other words, Buddhism became the established or state religion. Thereafter, in the development of these Asian countries, Buddhism and political authority were correlated in prosperity and adversity.

From the time that Buddhism was adopted as a state religion, less emphasis began to be placed on its original spirit of renunciation, and it gradually developed into an ecclesiastical organization with numerous duties in the social, political, and religious spheres. After Buddhism became the state religion, it not only validated and complemented the institution of kingship but had a very close and intimate relationship with it, as has been evident in the history of Sri Lanka, Burma, Thailand, and other Theravada countries. And it was in these countries that Buddhism had its first real opportunity to demonstrate its religio-political potential since the time of Emperor Asoka.

Even in the present day, the dominant political ideologies and movements of Southeast Asia, such as nationalism, democracy, and socialism, have been reconciled with Buddhism. In these countries, the blending of religion and politics has demonstrated deeply and clearly Buddhism's usefulness, more than its limitations, in relation to providing the legitimacy of the political system, effective political leadership, national integration, economic development, and democratic process.

Throughout its history as a political norm, Buddhism has demonstrated itself to be an element of unity rather than of divisiveness. Buddhism, it must be understood, is not an ethnocentric religion. It goes beyond all ethnic, racial, tribal, and national boundaries. Even in a country such as Burma, where there are diverse ethnic groups, Buddhism has played an important role in bringing and binding together the diverse ethnic groups.

In traditional societies such as Sri Lanka, Burma, Thailand, and Laos, the people did not think of nationality apart from the religion they professed. Indeed, it was Buddhism as a religion that had united them; the very idea of nationhood among these people owes its origin to Buddhism. And for the majority of Buddhists in these countries, it would be difficult to tear themselves away from the idea of state association with religion.

Legitimating Political Authority. In the Asian countries mentioned above, the relationship between religion and political authority has generally been one of interdependence. The quest for political legitimacy has always been through Buddhism as a religion. The rather close association of religion with the governmental system has constituted an invaluable means to maximize the legitimacy of political authority. In general, kings, rulers, and political leaders have striven to maximize the legitimacy of their political power since it permits them to govern their subjects day to day without resort to coercive power. And throughout the his-

tory of Sri Lanka, Burma, Thailand, and Laos, religious values
have ranked—and still do—highest among the "primary values"
of the ordinary people.

In most Buddhist countries, this quest for political legitimacy
through the popular religion has been highly successful. In Sri
Lanka, for instance, from the third century before Christ to the
end of the Sinhala rule in the nineteenth century, only a Buddhist
had the right to be king. The coronation of kings, which was
originally the secular business of the state, assumed the garb of a
religious ceremony of sacred significance and had to be performed
in the monastery in the presence of monks. The king was also
considered to be a *boddhisattva*,* and by virtue of his being a
boddhisattva could do no wrong to his people nor his country. His
rule was assumed to be tempered with mercy and justice. Such
legitimacy was reciprocal. It was the primary duty of the king or
ruler as "defender of faith" to promote religion, to build places of
worship, to support and maintain the monks, and to enforce regulations that would not be oppressive.

The Role of the Monks. Some argue that, according to *Vinaya*
rules, Buddhist monks are expected to eschew all involvement in
politics and even interest in mundane activities. But note what
Edmund F. Perry, an orthodox Christian, has to say on this point:
"The image of the Buddhist monk as a public leader engaging in
social and political activities had been obscured, deliberately so,
by Western colonialists and their accompanying Christian missionaries. By imposing a particular type of Christian monasticism
upon the Buddhist clergy, restricting the clergy's activity to individual purification and temple ministries, the colonial adminis-
trators dispossessed the *bhikkhus* of their influence on the public
life of their people."†

In the course of history, the pace of monastic life changed with
changing conditions in society. In Sri Lanka, for example, the
monks started taking an active interest in political matters within
two centuries of the introduction of Buddhism. It became the
practice for monks, as religious functionaries, to advise, support,
and help the king legitimize his temporal power. The monas-

Editor's note: A *boddhisattva* is a being who, having himself attained enlightenment and salvation, still foregoes the final happiness until all beings are saved.

†*Editor's note:* Perry was a Fulbright professor of comparative religion at Vid-
yodaya University, Sri Lanka in 1967–68. Dr. Ananda did not give the source of this
quotation; perhaps he personally heard Perry say it.

tic community (the *Sangha*) provided an organization for the religious implementation of the king's administration and political authority. Buddhism became intimately related to political authority on the one hand and to society and ethnic culture on the other. The dispensation of the Buddha (*Buddha Sasana*) and the Sinhala race became inextricably bound and identified with each other until Buddhism was the guiding force in the formation and development of national life and gave rise to what could be called "Buddhist nationalism."

Much the same happened in Burma, Thailand, Laos, and Cambodia. In these countries, too, Buddhism has developed as a religion of socio-political involvement, and the people cannot think of their nationality apart from the religion they profess.

In all these countries, the king or ruler had to lean heavily on the support of the monks to retain his legitimacy because the *Sangha* constituted an effective check on the exercise of the king's absolute power. Indeed, the influence of the monastic community over the masses was so great that the rulers were usually careful to win over the monks for the sake of successful and peaceful government; the approval of the *Sangha* on all significant matters was absolutely essential if the king was to establish social stability. The monks could provide popular support to the ruler because the *Sangha* hierarchy provided an integrated structure with a relatively effective chain of command.

The monks' high social prestige and their traditional role in society as teachers, friends, advisors, philosophers, and mentors placed them in a uniquely advantageous position to participate in nationalist politics. To them, politics connoted all spheres of human activity directed toward the public weal. Except in very rare cases, however, the monks wielded their political power not for personal benefit, but for the greater good of society, for the welfare of the people. As religious functionaries and guardians of the people, they saw to it that the government existed for the good and welfare of all the people—not only for those who professed Buddhism, but for each individual.

On occasions when kings acted as tyrants, the monks were swift to act; they would even go so far as to depose the king and appoint another who would have the happiness of the people at heart. Although there were occasional disagreements between the *Sangha* and the state regarding spiritual and religious matters, there was evidently no friction between the two on political or mundane matters.

This strong partnership of king (ruler) and *Sangha* undoubtedly worked for the prosperity of both the nation and religion. The monks never seem to have attempted to wield political power directly, but they always used their influence to support kings whom they could persuade to carry out their wishes. With such a relationship, neither the king nor the *Sangha* could afford to ignore the traditional prerogatives of the other.

That the state economic policy of these societies was guided by considerations of equity can be inferred from considering the qualifications of a king who was considered righteous and impartial. Thus, in the matter of levying taxes, the good ruler not only had to impose taxes sufficient to run the state; he also had to take into consideration the plight of the people who were being taxed. Giving to the needy (*dana*) was considered part of righteous administration. Organized distribution of wealth (*dana samvibhaga*) was typical of the Buddhist king's policy; in practice it amounted to an equitable distribution of wealth among the subjects in his domain. Capitalists (the *dhanapati*) were tolerated to the extent that they were also generous donors (*danapati*).

The greatness of this socio-political ethic lay in the fact that it did not differentiate between a person's own kith and kin and fellow beings in the outside world. No stranger was considered a rank outsider to be treated differently from one's own family. Historically, Buddhists treat others not as apart, but as *a part* of themselves. There are recorded instances of Buddhist kings supporting Christian missionaries, and of Buddhist temples providing for the maintenance of Mohammedan rights among their tenants. Additionally, the Buddhists' proud boast was that they never employed force in those fields where reason alone should prevail. This liberal ethic has made the people more accommodating and generous.

Contacts with Foreign Groups. Successive waves of foreigners seeking to obtain a foothold and to establish their political and religious control over the people have swept these Buddhist Asian countries from time to time. In accord with the Buddhist ethic, their ambitions were never suspect and their alien ways never resisted unless they came in actual conflict with the even tenor of national life. One result is that the people have become accustomed to much that is quite different from their original way of thinking.

Another result, however, is that foreign invasions, the infiltration of foreigners who formed their own separate ethnic groups, and the conversion of native groups to various other religions have posed many problems to the peaceful and contented life that had prevailed in these lands.

During the last four or five centuries, Buddhist countries have suffered from western colonialism and the deliberate attempts of other religions to weaken and destroy the prevailing religio-political system. The invading colonists divorced religion from the nation, a very astute policy that enabled them to keep the people in subjugation. The result has been that in those countries where there had been one established religion and one or more groups who identified themselves with that established religion, we are now presented with multiracial, multireligious, and multilingual groups.

BUDDHIST SOCIAL TEACHING
AND HUMANKIND'S PRESENT PROBLEMS

The modern question then is whether or not the Buddhist principles outlined can act as a cohesive force in a multireligious, multilingual, and multiracial society faced with the many problems of today—the population explosion, the food crisis, rising unemployment, inequality of opportunity, the gap between the haves and have-nots, to mention but a few.

Ideas, Power, and Human Development. Amid all conflicts, people throughout the ages have searched for and looked to certain ideas as guiding lights, within the evolutionary process of ideas. Simple as these ideas may seem, their infective power, their modes of transmission, and the magnetic spells they cast are astounding and marvelous. This revolution through and of ideas is forever surging forward. The human mind is never content. The whole gamut of history shows that people have learned, by slow and painful degrees in the school of experience, modes of conduct that are ever more beneficial in private, social, political, religious, national, and international life. The lesson is still unfinished.

The eternal human quest has been the search for peace and happiness, but how far have we succeeded in finding it? Everywhere we find profound dissatisfaction with the present order. We find chaos everywhere: in our social life, in the economic sphere, in the political field, and in religion. New problems keep on cropping up, and we find it difficult to grapple with or find satisfactory solutions to them.

Today the climate of opinion is very different from that when the Wellsian faith was widely held, when most thinking people believed that the march of science would automatically insure a brave new world of plenty and happiness. Science has failed to find the secret of happiness; the conquest of nature has not succeeded in achieving plenty or peace.

This is not surprising to us Buddhists because, according to our belief, happiness is to be found living in harmony with righteousness or justice (the *Dhamma*). Today's real problem lies in the fact that there has been a vast increase in human power and consequently a vast release of human energy, but no proportionate increase in ethical insight. Lessons of the past point to the fact that no amount of change in political machinery or social institutions will lead to stability and happiness on the part of the individual unless the moral feelings of the community are adapted to the new changes. We cannot convert people by coercion. There were such periods in history, but they have had their day. Today we live in a more enlightened age.

What human nature is really trying to find in its eternal quest for happiness is some system of government that will give all individuals a full, fair chance of developing their personalities to the utmost. It must do this by insuring security and justice to all people and their families, by delivering a decent minimum of comfort to each individual, and by giving each person a liberty of thought and action that is restricted only by a code of honor forbidding hurt to others.

Change and Harmony. The distinctive feature of the modern world is the acceleration and magnitude of the process of change. There is almost unbelievably drastic and revolutionary transformation of all institutions in every field of human activity. The world is changing so fast that it is going beyond recognition, and human survival is tied up with this change.

This is where modern people may find Buddhism to be particularly relevant to this age. To the Buddhist, change is the fundamental fact of life. Buddhism accepts change; in fact, it is built on the truth of constant flux and change. As such, in the predicament that humankind is facing at present and may have to face in the future, the Buddhist Way of Life and concept of integrated development offers a plausible solution that could help to emphasize the element of unity, rather than divisiveness.

A fundamental doctrine of Buddhism is that all human misery proceeds from human ignorance. We are prone to be unhappy because we have looked for happiness in the wrong place. Part of the tragedy lies in the belief that happiness can be found only in material welfare. Yet is it not a truism that even the world's highest standard of living has not produced the highest standard of happiness? The cure lies in achieving a spiritual balance in our minds. The problem we all have to solve is how to secure our own ends, expand and realize our innermost and profoundest needs, without interfering with lives and purposes no less justifiable than our own, without injuring them, without treading on the rights of others.

People should sooner or later understand that harmony is the keynote of the universe. It is in people's minds that conflicting ideologies, resulting in tension and problems, are born; therefore, it is from people's minds that these conflicts should be eradicated so that each individual can be filled with thoughts of love, harmony, and peace. It is worth noting that the Buddha anticipated the United Nations Charter by twenty-five centuries when he declared that the mind is the forerunner of all things good and bad, that when the mind is cleansed of evil, then peace, harmony, and happiness will be the order of the day.

The Whole Person and All People. The world today is a disunion indivisible. It is true that the idea of world unity in diversity —rather than our present divisiveness in diversity—must be the goal of the human race at all levels, national or international. This goal, however, cannot be reached by a fanatic leap over Himalayan-like obstacles. And the mass of humankind cannot be made into angels in the course of a few years or a few generations by any natural process. Therefore, we must seek to find an ethical and political system that will effectively harmonize, for social ends, those energies of human nature common to the whole race.

Religion has far too long been concerned almost solely with moral and ethical systems, leaving social problems in the hands of economists and politicians. But religion, if it is true religion, must take as its province *the whole person*—not merely certain aspects of the person's life. In other words, the person who follows religion knows that there can be no happiness or peace on earth as long as there are poverty and starvation, injustice and oppression, social disabilities, mutual distrust and suspicion, racial segregation, and discriminative legislation.

Modern thought has begun to realize that the most developed personality is the integrated person. Hence, the future of humankind—if this future is to be progress and not stagnation or degeneration—must be guided by a sound religio-political system. And if that is to be a firm cohesion, rather than a divisive element, it may not be based on a single religion, but the highest ethical good of all religions (*Saddhama*).

11

Faith and Ideology

a Buddhist response presented by
M. Palihawadana

Dr. M. Palihawadana, of the University of Sri Lanka, in
Maharogama, asked to insert a few extemporaneous remarks
from his own Buddhist viewpoint. This seemed very appropriate,
not so much because Dr. Ananda had made no direct response to
Professor Smith's paper, but because the more we westerners,
who dominated the Colloquium, heard from representatives of the
eastern faiths, the better.

PROBLEMS OF COMMUNICATION

Dr. Palihawadana admitted to feeling somewhat out of place in
the discussion thus far because the technical and western theological approach differs so greatly from his own. He felt humbled,
saddened, chastened, but did not find it strange that in such
exchanges "the Buddhist would be the odd man out. The reasons
are too obvious to mention. I even feel that this kind of Colloquium
may be out of place and may not be required for many decades to
come, because the problems that crop up between us are enormous.

"But we should overlook all this, and address ourselves to the
task. I do hope a way out of the impasse is possible. Only let me say
that those of us who are Buddhist must exercise extreme patience, and those who are not must also show extreme patience."

The Buddhist professor asked then: "How can those of disparate traditions address these problems? One way is in person-to-person encounter. This I began to understand personally when my relationship with Professor Smith began two years ago. I began to admire and even to understand him, to such extent that I had probably misunderstood him. But upon checking the point with him, I found that here indeed was a case of *understanding*. My warm regard for him makes me feel that whatever our separate traditions, it is possible for us to come together and to understand each other in a superlative way.

"This certainly points to a way to proceed. Ultimately our different theologies may not matter that much; it is the human touch that makes contact possible."

THE IDEOLOGICAL ASPECT OF FAITH

Dr. Palihawadana then addressed the topic, "The Role of Religion in Politics and Society," via "the sphere of the historical and factual." He attempted to draw for the Buddhist situation a "historical parallel to what Professor Smith observed regarding the situation of Christianity and Christendom." In this context, the Buddhist professor concentrated on a most substantial point that no one else had so emphasized: the Buddhist faith, like all faiths, operates "in the life of people at two different levels—the ideological aspect, and the transcendental aspect.... Although it is not true to say that the religious equals the ideological, it does seem permissible to say that religion has provided the basis for ideology since most ancient times."

He cited three applications of this religious basis for ideology from history. "My own research in Vedic studies has convinced me that Aryan racialism vis-à-vis the people in ancient India was nurtured by the Aryan cult. This cult sanctioned their presence and their violent program." Similarly, Singhalese racialism took root in Sri Lanka during the third century B.C. under religious impetus. "It was proclaimed that the safety of the island and of the Singhalese race was entrusted to the God Vishnu by the Buddha himself. When the Tamils of South India invaded Sri Lanka, a conspicuously violent campaign was organized against the indigenous people on the ground of protecting the Buddhist dispensation." Coming close to our own day, "the sociologist Francois Houtart has argued convincingly that right down to the end of the nineteenth century the entire feudal system in Sri Lanka was ideologically served by the hierarchic mythology developed by popular Buddhist teachings."

As the Sri Lanka scholar saw it, "In these three examples, religion has been internally unifying, but externally divisive. And it has blessed an obsolete social system. But it was only by historical development that the oppressive, divisive character was brought into the Buddhist system; the original Buddhist teaching of compassion for all beings is too well-known to be repeated."

He added the less-known fact that "the Buddha also preached religious concord." His disciples were not to exalt themselves because of their virtuous mode of living nor disparage others who followed another way. "These nobler aspects of his teaching were not, in fact, discarded when the Buddhist system was partly reduced—I emphasize partly—into an ideology. But this reduction, by many changes in the spirit of the old teaching, served to hold a socio-economic system in place for well over two thousand years."

BUDDHISM AND MARXISM TODAY

Dr. Palihawadana pointed to the significant lesson that, as a matter of documented history, Buddhism has been simultaneously involved at two levels of life. Nevertheless, "the fact that the Buddhist system was partially used to serve a feudal system has not been reckoned as an argument against the system as such. Even Marxists have not deemed it necessary to regard the Buddhist system as their implacable aggressor. On the contrary, it has been argued that social and economic structures of a Marxist kind, or at least of a socialist kind, are the structures most compatible with the Buddhist society."

He recalled that in the Colloquium's previous discussions questions had come up as to what elements for change the old religious systems could offer developing societies which are dominantly religious, especially elements for generating "political will." He judged it not wrong to say that in his country "the ideological basis of the chief constituent of the coalition government, the Sri Lanka Freedom Party, is Marxist-Buddhist, rather than purely Marxist. For example, in our period of change, this party has rejected violence and has pledged democratic elections.... Its democratic and human welfare aims have sought inspiration from the characteristic Buddhist tradition, such as the ideal of nonviolence, recognition of acquisitiveness as a source of human misery and discontent, rejection of extremes of luxury and poverty, and democratic conduct following the procedures of the monastic orders."

Dr. Palihawadana's conclusion was that a new ideological development is taking place, "seeking to implement an ideology of socialist development, but inspired on one hand by the Theravada Buddhist vision, and the Marxist economic vision on the other." This gives new relevance to the important question raised by Professor Smith. Since religion here is actually operating in the life of the people at both the ideological and the transcendental levels, it seems that the Buddhist could proceed further, could go beyond his tradition and respond in this way as a multifaceted response to other religious traditions.

"Therefore, the Buddhist need not consider himself as the odd man out, though for important theological reasons he might consider himself to be such. There is a way out. And it is for those of us who are Buddhist to seek how to proceed that way and how to come to a greater understanding with the great religious traditions of humankind."

12

A Strategy of Ideological Self-Restraint

a Jewish response presented by Norman Lamm

Rabbi Norman Lamm, who teaches philosophy at Yeshiva University, New York, had been asked to give the Jewish response to Professor Smith's paper. He made, however, creative proposals which went beyond Smith's thought; these I highlight here.

In addition, several of Rabbi Irwin Blank's prepared remarks for the Colloquium's opening session directly pertained to some of Professor Smith's ideas, so I have also presented them in this section.

Insisting that his is not "the," but only "a" Jewish response, Rabbi Lamm's head-on focus was "on what I consider Professor Smith's main point: the distinction between society and community, and the assertion of a moral imperative to all faith communities to use religion in order to turn what is merely world society into what should be world community."

From the philosopher-rabbi's carefully written paper I have extracted six major points converging on this focus and its dangers. Note that by the title he gave his paper, "A Strategy of Ideological Self-Restraint," Rabbi Lamm deliberately raised caution flags.

SOCIETY AND COMMUNITY

"The society/community distinction seems to me both valid and valuable as a tool for formulating the main purpose of the paper.

113

... In the Hebrew Bible, there are two words generally used for a collectivity: *Kahal* and *Edah*. The first term denotes a conglomeration of individuals who happen to be assembled in one area at one time. It accords with a nominalist conception and implies nothing more than a group of people gathered together, no matter the level or efficiency of organization. The second word, *Edah*, is organismic and implies a metaphysical dimension. . . . It denotes a group that feels itself called to some transcendent purpose. The biblical terms thus seem to parallel Professor Smith's use of the words 'society' and 'community.'

"Moreover, the question of whether the calling or the community comes first, or which is the cause and which is the effect, has already been discussed in a somewhat different context by two of the most important Jewish philosophers of the Middle Ages. Saadia Gaon (tenth century) saw the people of Israel as coming into being as a nation only because of its spiritual vocation. R. Yehudah Halevi (twelfth century) would have it the other way around: the people of Israel began as a 'natural' people, and its spiritual dimension is superadded to it."

In Rabbi Lamm's view, the fact that Professor Smith's ideas are implicit in scriptural terminology and were already discussed almost a thousand years ago "may not prove anything, but they certainly lend credibility to the raising of the question."

THREE DANGERS IN WORLD COMMUNITY

"I turn now to the main thrust of Professor Smith's paper. At the expense of being a spoil-sport, let me adumbrate some dangers of the concept of 'world community,' including, more explicitly, some of the caveats Professor Smith himself has hinted at.

"The whole enterprise is not without considerable risk, despite the obvious desirability of achieving world community, especially by the inspiration and motivation of religious faith. . . . I hope my comments will not be misconstrued as further evidence of Professor Smith's reiteration of the unhappy history of religion as a source of divisiveness. . . . On the contrary, it is because the goal is precious that every precaution must be taken to avoid three fundamental errors or misinterpretations.

"The first of these is the possibility that 'world community' will become a euphemism for what can only be called religious homogenization or ideological imperialism, whether conscious or unconscious." (I recall Dr. Sivaraman's fear of state homogenization.) "Every great idea is in some ways a dangerous idea, and the more valuable the idea the more potentially disastrous can be its consequences; in the language of the Kabbalah, 'the side of holiness' always has its concomitant 'other side,' that of impurity and evil. 'The other side' of universalism, as sublime and even sacred as that may be in its conception, is totalitarianism. Universalism, lofty as it is, may create a climate of contempt for those who do not share its basic ideological and theological presuppositions, may forget that universalism can be as narrow and idiosyncratic as particularisms."

Rabbi Lamm thinks many universalisms based on election are "riddled through with the hubris of self-righteousness," just as a particularist doctrine of chosenness might be. He made the point that only "particularism" is usually used in a pejorative sense, but universalism can also bring harm. "This kind of universalism may well be conceived as the only legitimate means toward the salvation of all humankind—*nulla salus extra ecclesiam*—with results too dreary and too well-known to bear repetition now. The tendency of universalist religions toward self-identification with Hegel's 'absolute religion' has littered the road to salvation with countless corpses of stubborn dissidents.

"The second error against which we must guard is the imposition of a kind of apologetic strait jacket on individual theologies, frequently distorting them in the course of striving for preconceived conclusions acceptable to others." Rabbi Lamm fears that advocates of specific religious traditions, sometimes unintentionally, become "so enamored of the goal of world community that they are ready to 'prove' that their traditions always entertained such notions, or, at the very least, that such ambitions flow naturally from the historic principles of their faith. . . . Jewish thought in particular has often suffered from this willful, if well meant, distortion.

"Third, one must beware of falling into the trap of theological indifferentism, which regards any form of theological and cultic exclusiveness as necessarily retrograde and reactionary. This has occasionally happened to more liberal theologians, particularly to those who were receptive to secularizing tendencies."

THE FAILURE OF SECULARISM

"Does this mean that, despite my personal faith commitments, I prefer an exclusively secular effort at achieving world community?

"Absolutely not. I quite agree with Professor Smith that secular motivations for human unity have proved to be abysmal failures—at least as unsuccessful as religion, and frequently more cataclysmic in their consequences.... The road to utopia is frequently far from utopian."

The rabbi recalled the generation that built the Tower of Babel and the Bible's sarcastic comment on this early example of human pretentiousness derived from technological capacity: " 'The whole earth was of one language and of one speech,' and people, thus united, sought technological expressions of their combined powers, in utter disregard of all humankind. The result, of course, was catastrophic. Our linguistic and cultural divisiveness today is, according to Scripture, the heritage of that primal act of universalist hubris."

A COMMUNITY OF COMMUNITIES

But Rabbi Lamm assured his listeners that, despite his apprehensions about secularist and religious aspirations, he is not ready to abandon the human quest for world community. "No, not at all, now when the very survival of the species may be at stake. The caution that I am proposing is for the sake of promoting, not undermining, a cause the urgency of which becomes more evident with each passing week." He offered, however, "a slight but possibly significant modification in nomenclature.... In order that world community not be thought of as an imposed uniformity throughout the world, the concept needs to be restated as a 'community of communities.' The term suggests that the identity of each group must have its integrity utterly respected." Its substitution also gives an implicit warning against universalist excesses.

He quoted from the Joint Proposals of the Jewish-Christian Consultation, held in Geneva, April 1972, on which occasion he had first suggested the term "community of communities."

World community is not only the sum of individual human beings; it is composed of communities of diverse kinds and of a variety of societal structures, some natural, some historically and culturally determined, some freely contracted (e.g., ethnic, linguistic, religious, political). Individuality can be expressed through membership in various communities. World community must recognize the value of such communities as they provide human life with identity and meaning and work toward overcoming the threats of loneliness and anonymity and uniformity.

(I recall Professor Avineri's earlier reference to the common parentage of exaggerated individualism and absolute state sovereignity derived from the philosophy of Hobbes. I also note the similarity of Rabbi Lamm's position to the principle of subsidiarity within Catholic social teaching—that the larger, wider social grouping must not take over the functions of the smaller, narrower grouping. These are areas to explore together.)

PROXIMATE AND ULTIMATE GOALS

Rabbi Lamm then offered "community of communities" as a proximate, intermediate goal, not as an ultimate one. Some religious traditions have ultimate goals for "the end of days" (*eschaton*), and these goals are not identical. But these "must be scrupulously excluded in the endeavor to establish a peaceful and just 'community of communities.'

"The term, in other words, represents a conscious de-eschatologization of the concept of world community. It obligates all participants to a form of collective self-restraint. Many religions entertain dreams or visions of universal acceptance, in one way or another. Many of the major faiths of humankind today, especially those of the West, envision the ideal state of humankind as one in which all humans will embrace their respective prophets or dogma."

What Rabbi Lamm proposed is "a strategy of ideological self-restraint." By using the term "community of communities" our ambitions are narrowed for the sake of ultimate success in the quest for true world community. He kept insisting that "world community" must not be confused with "the end of days" (*eschaton*), because such confusion would invite a clash among religions, "each propounding a different universal goal, that could only result in realizing the full potential of religion for divisiveness and fragmentation and, perhaps worse, for triumph and domination."

To avoid this clash, he urged that each religion and ideology first openly acknowledge its eschatological goals. Having done this, "each group must affirm that our contemporary mutual quest for a world community of communities is non-eschatological or, at the very most, pre-eschatological." And each must resolve that such world community must never become the instrument "for activistic eschatological realization, and the proselytization that it implies." The rabbi admitted that this is "asking a great deal from those communities for whom the achievement of the eschaton is an essential doctrine and an effective motivation of conduct. But unless such self-restraint is forthcoming, and unless it is forthcoming in a manner that will inspire trust by others, the quest for world community will be bedevilled by mutual suspicion and will die aborning."

MOTIVATIONS FOR SUCCESS

Finally Rabbi Lamm admitted he feels "uneasy about the possibilities of success. . . . Can the magnetic pole of the Transcendent, as each of us conceives it, really evoke from among us, among all the disparate members of the human race, those sublime elements from within each tradition and ideology that together can weld us into a world community, or community of communities?" Experience and intuition—perhaps, too, a dash of quietism insinuated into his Jewish tradition, which is largely activist—make him pessimistic: "The spiritual temperature of humankind is simply not high enough."

What then? He invoked here an important Talmudic principle that concerns motivation: "Not only must praxis be in conformity with the divine will, but inwardly people must be motivated by a selfless submission to the divine moral order." Yet the sages of the Talmud acknowledged that few humans are capable of such immediate high-mindedness. Consequently, they advised beginning on the right path "even for reasons of self-interest (within certain limits) and not for the purest of motives." The Talmudic sages were confident that in the course of acting properly for improper reasons, one will eventually come to do so for the right reasons.

"It is this principle I would apply to our quest for a universal 'community of communities.' Initially, the appeal to men and women and to the various communities—ethnic, religious, national, political—must be on the basis of shared perceptions of danger, rather than the promise of mutual uplifting." Before we can achieve the new definition of "we" of the entire family of humankind, as Professor Smith dreams, "we must clearly perceive that all the lesser 'we's' must work together or perish together. Religious and secular leadership alike must arouse the world to the awareness that our self-interest demands a new level of international and intercommunal collaboration. The religious principle is simple enough: Life is sacred, and further lack of cooperation across political, national, ethnic, and religious boundaries pose a clear and present danger to the continuation of life on this troubled planet."

He recalled the Orson Welles radio program of the 1930s which "reported" the invasion of earth by spacemen. Perhaps another such experience would shock and arouse us. "Or if our governments were strong and brave enough to impress upon the world population the frightening facts . . . and if all of us would learn that our smaller collectivities, all of them no more than partial wholes, are simply inadequate to the task of solving such overarching problems, then, the very process of collaboration, not because of ultimate idealistic reasons, but specifically because of global mutual self-interest, might teach us the practical techniques of worldwide cooperation."

Rabbi Lamm concluded, "So my 'strategy of ideological self-restraint' is one whereby spiritual leadership will bring to bear upon the crises of our times a religious principle common to all: the sacredness of life. There is enough self-interest in this concern to arouse the most indifferent, and enough religious value in the survival of the species to elicit a genuine faith-motivation. Meanwhile, we shall continue to keep and nurture our great 'secret'—the ultimate unit of 'we,' the entire human family, which will be attained because of love and not because of fear, because of faith and the Voice, not because of floods of fire or water—or the lack of food and energy."

13

Food, Faith, and the
Political Process

from comments by Irwin Blank

Rabbi Irwin Blank, president of the Synagogue Council of America, had given us his thoughts at our opening session, but I have kept for now those portions of his talk which referred to his own faith, especially as it relates to other communities. In addition to his national position, Irwin Blank is rabbi of a local congregation, Temple Ohabei Shalom, Brookline, Mass.

Rabbi Blank stressed the differing faith approaches to the very fact of food and hunger. "We may not assume that the question of hunger occupies the same place on all our agendas or that we invest it with the same meaning. Since our various understandings of revelation, salvation, and redemption do not coincide, why should our theologies of food and hunger?"

He suggested some thoughts on the subject that his own faith leads to. Besides the fast days and forbidden foods of the Hebrew tradition, the rabbi cited the Talmud volume *Nedarim*, which treats the making and abrogation of vows. "Vows which restrict one's relationship to the material world, which go beyond the simple fear of gourmandizing, do suggest an essential uneasiness with the material world."

In fact, God seemed to use hunger to test the faith of the children of Israel during their sojourn in the desert on their way to the holy land. The tone of the biblical text "suggests that they were an unworthy people because they permit hunger to weaken their sense of purpose. When God did provide the manna, it was with the overtone that having made Israel hungry in the first place, then listening to the supplications of Moses on their behalf, he used the situation as an opportunity to work yet another miracle which would demonstrate his goodness. . . . It is these concepts of testing, of the mysterious ways of God, and of the unknowable divine plan that foster ambiguity within us. Within my own commitment, we speak of ourselves as partners of God in creation. But our role in creation, given these other concepts, is not clear."

Rabbi Blank sees the relationship of church and state as especially troublesome when members of different faiths tackle problems, such as the food crisis, that are partly political. "The state, the political system, is a metaphor for materialism. The church is a metaphor for spirituality. History is crowded with examples in which the state used the church for its own ends in return for granting the church special authority. The reverse, in which the church controlled the state and was corrupted by it, has also been known.

"In our Colloquium these difficulties are compounded by the different ways in which we experience government, and surely by our different perceptions of the nature of government. Our postures toward secularism and pluralism do most certainly affect our stance vis-à-vis the state and the political process. Theocracy is not dead, nor is triumphalism. As one whose ordination and rabbinic decision have no authority in the state of Israel, I speak from firsthand knowledge."

Despite these differences, Rabbi Blank is hopeful. Since the Colloquium participants have shown willingness to confront together the urgent concern for hunger, "we shall find in one another soulmates prepared to share in the embarrassment which accompanies faith in the possibility of the redemptive act. . . . But every journey of faith involves overcoming the sense of hopelessness and preparedness to be embarrassed. So we have learned from Sarah and Abraham. So let us begin our journey from here to where God will lead us."

14

The Religious Reply to World Crisis: Islamic Potentiality

presented by Hasan Askari

Professor Hasan Askari and Dr. Mohammed Al-Nowaihi responded from the Muslim perspective, the first with a prepared paper bearing the title given above, the second with informal comments he asked to introduce as a "modern Muslim."

Professor Askari heads the Department of Sociology, Aligarh Muslim University, Aligarh, India. His paper had four major divisions, to which I have added headings.

TRANSCENDENCE, SOCIETAL STRUCTURES, AND IDEOLOGIES

Professor Askari opened with the assertion that "human survival seems to be tied up with three questions:

1. Whether national and religious communities, as they are constituted in our times, possess any transcendental commitments.
2. Whether these communities, in case they do possess one or another transcendental commitment, are disposed toward activating it today.
3. And whether such self-transcendence admits of translation into concern for justice and peace.

"In other words, self-transcendence, as it takes the form of concern for justice and peace between communities, becomes inter-transcendence. This is perhaps what is aspired for in the norm of interdependence."

But as Professor Askari sees it, human communities, while claiming transcendental values, actually institutionalize whatever faith they hold. By doing this they develop superstructures which tend to de-transcendentalize human thought and work. "Transcendence, therefore, is not a function of social structure but more its antithesis. . . . Transcendence is more a form in which we reject the closed equation, as Durkheim entertains, between transcendence and society."

Because of this tendency, he warned "of the danger of our tremendous capacity to set ourselves against our own great possibilities, against our own freedom and salvation.... Communities may believe that they possess transcendence, and yet they may not have it at all."

In our times, this brought about the the interplay of certain extraordinary developments. He cited five of these present-day dangers and obstacles to true transcendence: (1) freedom; (2) western nationalism; (3) western rationality; (4) modern technology; (5) politicization.

Freedom. If a community takes its freedom for granted, it risks the danger of falling into pseudo-transcendence. "This situation can be redeemed if the free people are perpetually alert lest their freedom be lost or undermined at their own hands." The potential for this exists because free communities are capable of deriving "finite absolutes" from their own self-righteousness; examples of such self-imposed traps are race, nation, money, land, ancestry, and sanctuary. Other peoples are not free because of barriers imposed from outside themselves, barriers not of their own creation. But once a people becomes aware of what oppresses them —from within or without—its usual response to the barriers is to struggle for liberation.

Professor Askari cited the transcendental effects in human history of three great revelatory acts of God, through three prophetic personalities—Moses, Jesus, and Muhammad. Each came as a liberator in his society and era, with far-reaching consequences thereafter.

"Moses, for the Bani Israel and symbolically for all humanity, is a sign of struggle against barriers to freedom. He is thereby a liberator.

"Jesus, for the Jews of Jerusalem and thereby for all humanity, is a sign to undo the trap of self-righteousness into which only the free are tempted to enter. He is therefore a savior. Again, only the free are capable of producing the finite absolutes of race, nation, money, land, ancestry, and sanctuary.

"Muhammad, for the free clans of Hijaz and thereby for all humanity, stands as a sign of people's capacity to say 'no' to the finite absolutes and of their courage to bear testimony to the only Absolute of God."

Summarizing this insight, already so packed with meaning, Professor Askari repeated that liberation from "the barrier of slavery is not enough: one may be entrapped in freedom. Freedom by itself is not enough; one may be tempted to absolutize the finite. To this process in human affairs is addressed the revelatory act of God reflected in another movement which constitutes the unity of Moses, Jesus, and Muhammad. The more the unity of this movement is in world history, the less is the danger that people become slaves of their self-made absolutes."

(Throughout the Colloquium—in informal conversation and table talk, as well as during the formal discussion—Professor Askari repeatedly stressed this substantial unity and capacity for community shared by the Peoples of the Book—Jews, Muslims, and Christians. I must express personal gratitude to him for deepening my own grasp of this substantial commonality of our three faiths in their sources and in their content. Through his words I perceived anew our particular call to work and witness together in face of the dangerous issues our three faith communities confront, especially in the Middle East, Western Europe, and North America. I also recalled the situation in the Philippines and Indonesia, where, a month before the Bellagio meeting, I had discussed with local religious and government leaders ways of reconciling the Muslim and Christian communities in that region.

(On the other hand, I do not wish—and much less does Hasan Askari, a Muslim of India, wish—to advance among us monotheists, Jews, Muslims, and Christians, a movement that would place us outside the larger community of our fellow believers in the Transcendental—the Hindus and the Buddhists.)

Western Nationalism. Professor Askari thinks that acceptance of the western model of the nation-state is increasingly entrapping the vast world of the Orient, "supposed to be the home of the religious and spiritual traditions.... And its potential for self-transcendence seems to be increasingly forced into the service of nation building.... The phenomenon of curbing and eliminating political dissidents implies an ever-growing qualification to freedom for all groups and institutions.... The nation-state ultimately sets itself as a rival individual wholeness. As people give up a part of their totality, they give it up more and more, each time more unconsciously."

Western Rationality. "Another important factor blocking self-transcendence is the very structure of western rationality and its growing supremacy on a world scale." This mode of thinking rests on the power of the negative, "of making distinctions, of dividing and separating, and also of seeking new unities. . . ." This gives "a mastery over nature and society through objectification, abstraction, and conceptualization."

Professor Askari recalled that, as Hegel insisted, nothing can offer itself to this western spirit as a barrier that cannot be surmounted. "It is by virtue of this great power of objectification that the western mind appropriates every other to itself. The 'other' may be a different culture, a different religion, and also the transcendental.... With such a mind set, rationality, as such, loses its critical self-awareness, and turns into dogmatic and monstrous wisdom.... It thrives on a permanent gap between the cognitive and the emotive, ethics and metaphysics, and allocates to itself the authority of final judgment. It puts other rationalities, within the western tradition and in the Orient, on a defensive and apologetic level. It is one of the basic structures opposed to self-transcendence."

Modern Technology. One embodiment of western rationality is modern technology, which poses a still more serious challenge to all promises of self-transcendence in our age. Drawing from the views of John Francis, of the Church of Scotland, Professor Askari described the situation as a maze in which "there are no prophets and no utopias. All the visions of transcendence take the maze for granted. The maze is indifferent to ideology. The ideology is again one of the attempts to reach to the center of the maze. The maze is co-terminous with human beings."

The technological worldview is so invidious that the Muslim thinker even questioned the impact of the counterculture response. "Theodore Roszak believes that, though technology cannot be overthrown, it can be displaced, 'inch by living inch.' But this hope may also be another illusion. Modern spiritualism, modern art, and modern technology are actually a unity, and from within this unity, each viewpoint appears as a liberation from the other. There are, however, no exits and no entrances."

   Politicization. In Professor Askari's judgment, politicization seems to be the "only transcendence available to communities caught up between the objectifying rationality of the West and the technology that such a rationality engenders.... Politicization today is a process in which everybody is enveloped: the Communists who conveniently forget the Marxist critique of politics and state, and the Muslims who, in spite of upholding the unity of the religious and the political for the last thirteen centuries, still grope for a political theory to guide their modern governments."

   Having sketched the universal reach of political power, Professor Askari launched into a fundamental analysis of its all-embracing nature: "The political, though a part of the social, assumes the role of the totality, and demands allegiance from all other social institutions, creating its own system of command indifferent to all ethical and spiritual norms. It reduces the individual to the level of an abstraction made concrete only in the act of service and sacrifice at the altar of the state....

   "For this reason, it is in the nature of the political solution that it rests on the fear that it can be undone. Hence, it has to be enforced by diplomatic alertness; by preparation for self-defense and even the capacity to take the offensive in the very interest of self-defense; by control and even suppression of opposition from within, again in order to protect the primary structure of political solutions; and by subordination of all the civil and economic needs of the people to the overall fulfillment of the paramount political interest." One example of these relentless requirements is the phenomenon of famine and large-scale starvation, which is largely the derivative of one or another political policy.

   The Indian professor next raised a threefold critique of the political solution: It demands uniformity, it is incapable of dialogue, and it becomes an end in itself. Consequently it shuts out the "other," erodes transcendence, and becomes closed to true community.

   Uniformity marks the political solution. It aims at reducing to uniformity the human, real-life situation of *multi*formal and *multi*lateral reactions. Political solutions perpetuate this kind of reduction. Consequently, the political solution is always an escape from a real solution. "It is a confession of refusal to understand one who differs on fundamental issues. It is why religious communities always ask for separate states so that they can obtain a political situation of more or less uniformity."

Political people therefore are capable only of monologue; they cannot enter into true dialogue. They become "monological persons who must oppose all dialectical and dialogical views of reality. The 'other' is always to be appropriated. The 'other' is not an opportunity for transcendence, but an obstacle to be leveled and removed. The political brings under its vigilance and control family and religion, art and science, philosophy and mysticism."

The political also becomes an end in itself, "and thereby antitranscendental through and through. Whichever institution comes into contact with this charisma of the political loses its potentiality for self-transcendence."

Because the political is so invidiously all-embracing, Professor Askari judges that religion suffers harm to the degree that it is conjoined with the political. Paradoxically, he agreed, "it is sometimes correctly held that every religious proposition is a political proposition, that to bear witness to God as the only authority is a challenge to every other authority." This challenging witness is tenable only at the prophetic level. "As soon as the prophetic moment is embodied into a historical community, its disposition to equate its religious vocation with its political destiny creates divisiveness and conflict."

Professor Askari closed this section on the relation of transcendence to societal structures and ideologies by identifying three clusters of modern development which are highly unsettling:

1. The total helplessness of the intellectual culture before the political culture; an increasing irrelevance of our knowledge to the reality we live in; and the total subordination of the thinker and the teacher to the authority of the politician and the warrior;
2. the appropriation of the religious culture to the needs of history; the re-emergence of ideological and religious triumphalism; rationalization of the imbalance in the possession and distribution of resources and opportunities in the name of such triumphalism; and the abolition of the transcendental from within religion itself;
3. the triumph of collectivism, the emergence of mass societies without spiritual basis, leaving privatized and alienated individuals exposed to the pseudo-transcendental therapy of national, racial, and communal calls to self-glory.

Because of these unsettling developments, the Muslim professor admitted to being gloomy about the human prospect. He sees such trends "right in the center of the ruins of five thousand years of human civilization. Intranational and international conflicts should then be the order of the day. Famine and mass starvation should not surprise us."

(Neither then should we be surprised that within his own Muslim community, Professor Askari has raised warnings against a resurgence of triumphalism, fueled perhaps to fresh flammability by recent liberation from western imperial power and by the petroleum power now possessed by several Islamic nations. He touched this delicate issue later, but without indicating the implications of a Muslim triumphal springtide for relations with other religions (especially with Judaism and Christianity) and with other regions of the world. I encourage him to write more on this subject. I hope he will also expand on western and Judeo-Christian triumphalisms, past and present; perhaps, too, on whatever Hindu triumphalisms he has encountered or might encounter because of his Muslim minority status in today's India.)

RELIGIOUS AFFIRMATION OF THE NEW

Professor Askari then recalled a statement of Julian Huxley: " 'What the world now needs is not merely a rationalist denial of the old, but a religious affirmation of the new.' " This call was the keystone of the next section of his paper.

Before entering into "the Islamic mode of affirmation of the new in the world around us," he introduced three principles which govern any true religious affirmation: (1) It must involve "the entire world community, as Professor Smith observed, comprehensive of faith, both our own and our neighbors'; (2) it must follow the rejection of idolatry in all its forms, the rejection of what is not God; (3) it must be a declaration and celebration of the freedom of God in an act of praise for him who is unrestricted by what he revealed in the past to humankind and what he differently reveals in different religions."

(I pause before the profundity of this statement, its fecundity, its openness. It suggests an openness among the faiths because it specifies that God remains unrestricted by his one revelation which engendered *my* faith; he is free to make other revelations which engender religions differing from my own. It also suggests an openness toward the future because it states that God's freedom to make further revelations is not limited by those he has made in the past.

(A little later Monsignor Charles Moeller took a similar tack, giving a Christian view—more precisely, a post-Vatican-Council-II Catholic view—of God's freedom to reveal in and through other faiths, and to continue revelation through "the signs of the times," which are perceived in the secular world as it unfolds in history today, yesterday, and tomorrow.

(Such sovereign freedom of God would seem fully compatible with those faiths that believe in the almighty God of Abraham and Moses, Jesus and Muhammad, and in God's historic revelations. So here, Jews, Muslims, and Christians, at least, find additional roots for religious interdependence. How Hindus and Buddhists react to these beliefs, I do not know; regrettably our discussion did not enter this seminal area.

(But the question should be pursued. How far might we of the five transnational faiths agree, or at least discuss and understand our differences, concerning these primordial sources of our belief? The prospect of addressing the food/energy crisis (and others) in our world "community of communities" through serious, long-term cooperation among our faiths and cultural regions, will be largely decided by our response to this religious question.)

Professor Askari continued along the thrust of interdependence among our faiths. "It is only by a general* religious affirmation that each religion becomes a revelation. In order to be a theology, a given theology cannot be a theology of just one religion. Unless such a general affirmation takes place in every religious faith, no singular faith, with all its claims to universality and validity, can be a source of regeneration for humankind. As I noted earlier we stand today amidst great crisis. We cannot just afford to repeat the communal religious history of mutual distrust and hate. Human history can begin again only if our religious situation is generally and fundamentally restated. Let us turn to the Islamic potentiality for such a general, fundamental restatement."

ISLAMIC POTENTIALITY FOR GENERAL RESTATEMENT

Affirmation of monotheism is the hallmark of Islam. In its very nature the monotheist claim "overflows the boundaries of com-

---

*Professor Askari's key word "general" was clearly used throughout this statement in the sense of "universal."

munities and traditions. Monotheism presupposes the unity of humankind, and, by virtue of this presupposition, it makes all religious boundaries tentative. It is this tentativeness of one's own religious identity that monotheism turns into the servant-ship of God. Religious community is not the expression but the end of monotheism.

"By the Islamic emphasis on the monotheistic orientation, human civilization obtains its highest moment of liberation from its self-made absolutes. Here, we start recognizing the enormous power of the Muslim testimony of the negative: 'There is no God but....' " (With great delicacy, Professor Askari cut the quote at this point.) However, "only if Islam presupposes the unity of reve-lation of God in history," can the negative and positive assertions of Islamic monotheism become universal terms of reference. So the Islamic potential for a general religious affirmation is un-questionable in principle. "Its concepts of monotheism, its unity of revelation, and its power to say 'no' to the self-made absolutes are undoubtedly the solid foundations on which humanity today can build its religious destiny.

"But there are facets of historical Islam which qualify this hope."

THE QURAN* AND HISTORICAL ISLAM

What are these "facets of historical Islam which qualify this hope?" In answer, the Muslim scholar began by quoting Reinhold Niebuhr, the Christian theologian of ambivalence and ambiguity: " 'No cause on earth can be trusted utterly.' As a Muslim, I should say that the Quran should be trusted utterly. But this very faith in the Quran makes me remember that the Muslim worldview and behavior is one of many historical and relative phenomena in the life of this earth. Hence, I do not equate the Quran with the actual life of the Muslim *Umma* (people, community). The Quran, rather, remains a permanent critique of Muslim history and community, as well as a critique of the history of the world as a whole."

In fact, Professor Askari asserted, much Islamic historical de-

---

*Throughout the Colloquium, Muslim participants used this spelling for their sacred Book. *Webster's New Collegiate Dictionary*, 1973 edition, gives "Quran" as a variant of "Koran," which is more familiar to westerners. Webster also gives another spelling which places an aspirate sign before the last syllable, "Qur'an," and it was pronounced thus by Professor Askari and the other Muslims.

velopment has run directly counter to "the Islamic potentiality for a general religious affirmation," which, as he had demonstrated, rests on three basic concepts: "the negation of false absolutes, the monotheist commitment, and the unity of revelation in history. . . ." This counterproductivity began early in Islam's history when three developments "arrested from within" fulfillment of that potentiality. These were "the equation of the political with the religious, the choice of violence to curb and eliminate opposition, and the measurement of faith's validity in terms of triumphalism in history."

Then Professor Askari followed with a critique of historical Islam which was so profound and self-effacing that I felt humbled by its courage. I gladly add, at the risk of eroding my humility by the backhanded boast, that he reminds me of current Roman Catholic critics of historical Christendom.

1. Equation of the political and the religious "has not yet settled the question of authority in Islam. Contradictory formulations of authority can be equally defended by the principle of religio-political unity. More important for us, this unity disconnects the religious content of Islam from the general religious consciousness and development of the world. The general religious testimony of Islam became a specific and closed testimony on account of the unity it sought—and still seeks—with the political."
2. "The choice of violence to curb and eliminate opposition ultimately qualifies the potential of the community to say 'no' to the false absolutes engendered by the very unity of the religious and the political."
3. "The equation of faith with triumphalism in history is the most crucial transformation of Islam into a worldly and historical system. From the beginning every failure in history was written off as an aberration, as *fitna*, or as a conspiracy of the enemies of Islam. This triumphalism perpetuates the mood of resentment at all critical evaluations of systems and history."

Therefore, Professor Askari concluded, "historical Islam seems to block the development of all tragic consciousness, of suffering, of the power of humility. Triumphalistic orientation incapacitates the group to identify itself with the vanquished. It creates a permanent rupture between humanity. It absolutized the *Umma* and places it on par with the Quran. It blinds Muslims to other people of other 'books'; it destroys the unity of revelation of God's Word in history.

"The culmination of historical Islam is the emergence, in our times, of an ideological systematization of beliefs and practices. It is in the structure of ideological dogmatism that it eliminates from within itself all such categories as lead to ambivalence and uncertainty. The most ambivalent category for religious ideology is that of God, and the most unsettling is his universal act of revelation. So, one should not be surprised to notice that all religious ideologies tend to abolish God and refuse to deduce their commitment to humanity from God's universal act of revelation." Following this general tendency, "ideological Islam has become a total antithesis to the general religious affirmation of the world, an affirmation which is revealed in the Quran.

"Ideological Islam must then be anti-dialogical (i.e., against dialogue). It must be suspicious of intercultural contact. It translates itself into backward-looking transcendence. Ideological religion and self-transcendence cannot, therefore, be brought together."

Professor Askari's far-reaching critique of historical Islam led him back to the roots and founts of his faith: God's continuing act of revelation. "But God's revelatory act continues in history. God took upon himself the responsibility of preserving the Quran until the last day of this world. To preserve the Quran is to preserve within humankind and history the potentiality and courage to remember the liberating grace of God. The Quran is as liberating at the close of the twentieth century as it was in the beginning of the seventh century.

"The Muslim commitment to justice and peace in the world is possible to the extent that the Quran is not equated with *Umma*, and that God takes precedence over ideology."

15

Comments from a Modern Muslim

presented by Mohammed Al-Nowaihi

(Professor Askari's profound and seminal paper was followed by comments from another Muslim scholar, Mohammed Al-Nowaihi, chairman and director of the Department and Center of Arabic Studies, American University, Cairo.

(Dr. Al-Nowaihi had not been scheduled to give a formal response to Dr. Smith's paper, but after the Colloquium began, he asked to comment on the role of religion and on the population problem. While waiting his turn, the Cairo scholar was listening to Dr. Palihawadana's presentation and was so disturbed by the latter's statement, "the Buddhist seems the odd man out," that he hurriedly scribbled a response, from the viewpoint of a modern Muslim.

(I found Dr. Al-Nowaihi's observations so striking in both content and expression that I have taken his handwritten notes and reproduced them here in their entirety. They convey something of the spontaneity, the give-and-take, the human feeling, and the highly personal statements which suffused our Bellagio "community of friends."

(In all fairness, I must stress that Dr. Al-Nowaihi jotted down these thoughts during the actual session, so other scholars and his fellow Muslims should not regard his remarks as a definitive statement of his positions. On the other hand, I felt the extemporaneous, even tentative, character of his comments added to the feeling of authenticity. This was clearly a case of heart talking

133

to heart, as well as mind to mind, better still, friend talking to friend in open trust. I will not interrupt his outpouring of ideas and feelings by quotation marks.)

*   *   *

Are we all sure that we fully realize the importance of this Colloquium? A number of religious people, both lay and clergy, have met to concern themselves with problems of food and energy, hunger and disease, the inequitable distribution of power and of wealth, neocolonialism, political and racial exploitation, and the like.

For a long time now religion has been accused of being little more than "the opium of the masses," tricks perpetrated by the rich and mighty to induce the destitute and downtrodden to accept their miserable lot on this earth as the ordained will of God, the scheme of things divinely sanctioned. And it has to be admitted that this accusation was no mere defamation by atheists and materialists.

All too often through history, established churches and official custodians of religion have entered into an unholy alliance with the powers that be, using religion as an argument to secure the resignation of the have-nots. Under the pretext of transcendence and the evanescence of this world, leaders of religion have directed the hopes of the people to the world-to-come, where justice will be done by God and where they will be rewarded for putting up with the inequities of this world by being granted eternal bliss and the salvation of their souls.

This Colloquium then—especially since it follows the Roman Catholic church's recent Synod (held in the Vatican no less!) during which the clergyman's duty to engage in the battle against economic, social, and racial injustices was asserted by several delegates—marks a momentous historic occasion. On the first page of his paper Professor Smith remarked on the "piecemeal view of human affairs that has been prevalent among operative groups in western society, dividing life up into parts. . . ." To this we must add the piecemeal view of human nature itself, splitting it into two separate entities—the body and the soul—so that an individual could be seen as having a starved, diseased, and dwarfed body, and yet possessing a fine, contented, serene, and uplifted soul. But during this Colloquium men and women of religion have concerned themselves with mundane problems; they have thus recorded their abjuring of that false and vicious view of human nature and declared their belief in the monistic, integrated, indivisible human entity. If the lead they have given is followed, religion should no longer be abused in the way it has long been.

The central theme of Professor Smith's paper is religion as both a cohesive and a divisive social force. He sees this apparent contradiction as natural but not insoluble; he believes, in fact, that the two aspects, though paradoxical, are reconcilable and that religion's great value lies in its very ability to effect a reconciliation. How he himself has been able to achieve this reconciliation—remaining a fully convinced Christian and yet accepting the essential truth of Islam and other major religions—without falling into the real dangers against which Rabbi Lamm has wisely warned, can be discovered from reading his many books and articles.

Professor Smith and a few other Christian thinkers point the way to a genuine rapprochement among the major religions of the world. And I believe this is important to remember here in this Colloquium because, although the chosen topic for its first meeting is the food/energy crisis, its long-term goal, stated and implicit, is to get people "from different faiths and from all parts of the world to face the great issues of human survival in the closing decades of the twentieth century."*

Now Professor Smith believes that these great issues cannot be tackled while the operative groups in western society continue to believe that the problems are technical and can be solved technically, while they continue to ignore or belittle the contribution that religion can offer. And he does not view this contribution as merely one among several solutions. Even though he is ready to tolerate such a view for the sake of argument and in order to get these operative groups to pay more attention to the role of religion, he actually believes the religious solution to be much more. He believes it to be the pervasive, integrative, sine qua non of all solutions. To this belief of his, all religious men and women will surely agree.

POPULATION

Arguing against the polarization of secular versus religious

---

*The quotation is taken from the letter of invitation to the Colloquium.

approaches, Professor Smith declares: "No population 'policy' can
be wise that is not correlated with, even rooted in, people's faith."
The same is true for other great social issues. If we ignore Professor Smith's reminder, then all the energy we are expending in
studying the food crisis and in thinking up ways to solve it will just
be wasted.

Let me give two crude examples. We cannot solve the starvation
problem in India by telling Hindus to eat beef. Neither can we
solve the same problem in Pakistan and the Middle East by telling
Muslims how cheap it is to raise pigs and how nutritious pork is.
Nobody will gainsay these obvious examples, yet we may fall all
too easily into more subtle absurdities and impossibilities if we do
not learn the lesson Professor Smith is teaching us.

Here I shall mention the problem of family planning, or, less
euphemistically, birth control. All the facts and opinions I have so
far heard during this Colloquium have convinced me that without
solving this problem the food crisis will not be solved. And yet the
problem of birth control has not really been raised; it has scarcely
even been mentioned. I do not know whether this lack has been
deliberate or accidental, but, in either case, we are not facing up to
our full responsibility.

I know it is a thorny problem; I know the heated debates and
agonized heart searching that it has been causing many religious
people, and I deeply respect the tremendous moral scruples of
those who oppose birth control because they believe it to be crimi-
nal slaughter of possible or nascent human beings. But all the
same, the problem must be faced.

In saying this, I do not mean to suggest that we should change
this present meeting into a polemical theological contest. But we
must at least admit the existence of the problem, probe its dilemmas, and see if we cannot reach a minimal common ground. It is a
sensitive, possibly divisive question, but we must face it coura-
geously, as a test of how much mutual good will we can muster
among ourselves and of how far we can rise above our denomina-
tional differences in planning a solution to which all peoples, no
matter what their faiths, may agree without compromising their
basic convictions. If we cannot do this, all our technical discussions and proposed solutions will come to nothing.

As Professor Smith has been at pains to advise us, we must be
aware of peoples' religious and social mores. And we must attempt
to discover plans that can best take these mores into account.

The description of this Colloquium that was sent out to us said that it would not be its business "to make hortatory proclamations for the public consumption." Agreed. But what I ask for is not a hortatory proclamation. What I ask for is sensitive, sympathetic consideration of the different values and assumptions of different religions and peoples, and an attempt at reaching what I called the minimal common ground. I ask for this when we face the issues of survival which this Colloquium wishes us to face, now and in sessions to come.

If we do not do this, this Colloquium has no right to call itself "The Interreligious Peace Colloquium."

THE BUDDHIST: ODD MAN OUT?

There is one other caveat that I feel any true "Interreligious Peace Colloquium" must keep in mind—that the nontheists among us must not be made to feel out of place. Frankly, this had not occurred to me as a potentially serious problem until I heard Dr. Palihawadana suggest today that he felt somewhat out of place in these discussions, that it was natural that "the Buddhist would be the odd man out."

This feeling is, of course, the antithesis of the rapprochement among the major faiths that Professor Smith—and the rest of us—seek, and I was delighted to hear Dr. Palihawadana conclude that the Buddhists themselves can transcend their own traditional ideology and come to a greater understanding with the other world religions, particularly through re-examining the teachings of the Buddha and further developing their new socially oriented ideology.

However, it seems to me that the journey toward reconciliation cannot be entirely one-sided. What can Islam's attitude be toward nontheistic religion? I would like to present my personal view as a "modern" Muslim—a view which I must admit is not in full accord with the traditional stance.

In his presentation, Professor Askari stressed the Islamic concept of the unity of God's revelation in history, yet he admitted that the Quran talks only of the Jewish and Christian religions—the "People of the Book." However, by inference, he claimed that this applies to other religions. But I do not think it is merely a matter of inference.

A statement in the Quran, repeated in two different verses, affirms that God sent many messengers to humankind, and goes on to say: "Some of them we have told thee about, and others we have not told thee about." ("Thee" is Muhammad.) I personally have no doubt whatsoever that Zoroaster and Gautama Buddha —to name only two—were among those messengers whom God did not tell Muhammad about in the Quran. Other modern Muslim thinkers, more authoritative than myself, though still unconventional, have expressed a similar view.

Now Zoroaster did believe in a personal God, so the problem regarding his followers is not too difficult. But what about Buddha, who did not?

Islam, it must be conceded, insists on the existence of the theistic God. But in addition to its concept of the unity of revelation, which Professor Askari explained, Islam also includes the further concept of the gradualness of the revelation. In the successive religions, God reveals more and more of the divine truth, until it reaches the complete and absolute theistic truth of the Quran. But in coming toward that complete truth, God may have sanctioned graduating steps.

Furthermore, the Quran states that God never left a nation without sending them some messenger of their own kind, speaking to them in their own language.

The Quran also distinguishes between *nabi* and *rasul*, rather inadequately translated as "prophet" and "apostle" respectively. Although there is much controversy in classical Islamic theology about the definition of each category and which is more inclusive or higher, there is general agreement that some of these teachers come with a "book" and some without, and that some speak from direct revelation and others from indirect inspiration as well as through the examples of their lives set before their peoples.

In addition to the *nabi* and the *rasul*, Islamic tradition includes the *wali* (the "client of God," roughly equivalent to the saint in Christianity). Both the *Shi'ites* (partisans of Ali and his progeny or relatives) and the *Sufis* (Muslim mystics) stress the holiness and importance of the *wali*. Indeed, some go so far as to claim that the *wali* is higher than the *nabi*. But this is not accepted by the *Sunnites*, the so-called orthodox majority.

The verse in the Quran stating that Muhammad was "the seal of the prophets" has been interpreted to mean that he is the last to come with direct verbal revelation (*wahy*), but he is by no means the last to come with inspiration (*ilham*). The *Sufis* especially stress this idea and insist inspiration is not even limited to *walis* but may be made to quite ordinary human beings to help them in some great personal stress, be it mental or practical.

As to Buddhists in particular, I have heard three different Azharite learned men (*ulema*) from the great seminary of Al-Azhar, in Cairo, say that although Buddhists are wrong in not believing in the personal God, yet they have two great religious truths which are in accord with Islam.

The first of these truths is the Buddhist stress on the importance of action and the insufficiency of mere faith. Islam, too, stresses the duty to lead a good and virtuous life and the right to enjoy happiness and obtain redress in this life, rather than being asked to wait for it in the life to come. Islam, like Buddhism, teaches that this present life is to be enjoyed, made use of, and lived properly for its own sake.

The second great truth on which Islam and Buddhism are in accord is their refusal of priesthood. Our *ulema* are just learned men (as the very word means), without any special sanctity or immunity or infallibility or power to dispense grace, without any right to set themselves up as the only legitimate pronouncers on religion.

In other words, Islam's recognition of religions is not limited to People of the Book, nor to recognition of the religious truths that were pronounced before Muhammad. So, as far as my humble self and some other modern Muslim thinkers believe, a Buddhist need not feel himself "the odd man out" in interreligious searching, as far as Islam is concerned.

16

Faith, Church, and World

a Christian response by Charles Moeller

Monsignor Charles Moeller is secretary of the Secretariat for Promoting Christian Unity, Vatican City; he also occupies the same post for the Holy See's section on Jewish Relations. My friend Charles (we have worked together closely in the Vatican Curia since 1966) spoke as a Catholic theologian and ecumenical leader.

As was true of all the Colloquium participants, Msgr. Moeller's comments were personal; they did not constitute a formal statement from the office he occupies or the faith he holds. But he carries unique personal authority because of his wide experience representing the Roman Catholic church in ecumenical and inter-religious relations. He was among the dozen most prominent theologians of the Second Vatican Council, particularly distinguished for his work on "The Pastoral Constitution on the Church in the Modern World." In 1966, Pope Paul VI named him under-secretary of the Congregation for the Doctrine of the Faith; then, in 1972, to the positions he now holds.

Besides these Vatican posts, Msgr. Moeller has served as professor of theology and of literature at Louvain University, Belgium, and as dean of studies of the Ecumenical Institute for Advanced Theological Studies,* at Tantur, on the road from Jerusalem to Bethlehem.

*This research center was built by and is operated as part of the University of Notre Dame. Pope Paul VI personally requested the university's president, Theodore Hesburgh, to take this initiative as a living memorial of the first papal visit to the Holy Land since Peter's departure, a visit made by Paul VI in 1963.

(. . .Tantur, on the road from Jerusalem to Bethlehem! I pause, dear friends, as I write this sentence, because it embodies so perfectly that massive roadblock to Jewish-Muslim-Christian cooperation, community, and friendship: the political, nationalist, and military struggle in the Middle East. How should I identify this bend-in-the-road, so near paths trod by David, by Jesus, probably by Abraham and Moses, perhaps even by Muhammad—some ten miles south of Jerusalem? Is it in today's Israel? Jordan? Palestine? "Occupied-territory-since-1967" would probably fit the resolutions of the United Nations. Each possible phrase could offend so many and not only for nationalist reasons. Even as I write, I find myself diplomatically listing Israel, Jordan, and Palestine in alphabetical order. But many of my Bellagio friends could cite historical facts, divine events, prophetic promises, and realpolitik against my compromise. Few will, I wager, because we have all become imbued with the larger call of human suffering and the response of God—our one God: Yahweh, Adonai, Allah, Father—in and through the larger "us" of Jew-Muslim-Christian, all People of the Book, amid the still larger community of the living world faiths.)

Back to Msgr. Moeller's paper. Since it came from such a source, the Bellagio participants found it a creditable account of the opening to "the signs of the times" begun by Pope John XXIII in that portion of the Christian faith community which is Roman Catholic. (It was written and distributed at the conference in French, then professionally translated for this report by Linda Graham-Maingot. I have slightly shortened and edited Moeller's text, but have made no attempt to paraphrase any of it and have retained the first person singular pronoun.) Moeller's paper follows.

*   *   *

I quite agree with Professor Smith that religion has been and still is a factor of unity and of division. I also concur with his observation that we no longer live in a stable world in which problems can be solved in succession one by one. The issues are global and interconnected.

Each religion no doubt addresses itself to the human person under the sign of salvation, either along theistic or impersonal but transcendent lines. At the same time we are confronted with a universal and urgent call: How can we survive in a world of dangerously decreasing resources, in which forms of violence would appear to have the upper hand? *The Limits to Growth,* the well-known report of the Club of Rome, has revealed the seriousness of the issue—although perhaps with exaggeration.

Religions must be forced to confront their collective responsibilities in these issues, which surpass the immediate imperatives of each religion without excluding them. This should be one of the conclusions of this Colloquium.

When the faiths confront these global social issues, the interreligious approach is necessary and urgent. Fortunately something has been done in this respect; side by side with strictly theological issues, the ecumenical movement has been emphasizing the need for collaboration among all Christians in the field of justice and peace. For example, the SODEPAX Committee,* linking the Roman Catholic Church and the World Council of Churches, is a sign of progress along the road to peace for humanity. However, we Christians must listen also to what other faith communities have to say to us. Such listening to each other is indeed rare, particularly in religious matters, but, in respect to the global social issues joint study by the world faiths is essential.

It is necessary also to reach out beyond the opposing factors of the subjective and the objective. For example, it is impossible to treat the population issue while considering the countries involved as the object of a technique. It is together with them, as Professor Smith said, that we must seek a solution. The first step in this direction is to give life to that "we." What meaning do we attach to this word "we"? Religion is probably the only force which can lead us to visualize the whole of humanity in this word "we."

Has Christianity then failed in this aspect of religion? Certainly the Christian religion has not succeeded in overcoming division and war. There are, indeed, instances when wars have been fought in the name of Christianity. The Crusades were, no doubt, a very complex phenomenon and not without positive aspects, but their military aspect constituted a strange paradox in relation to the gospel. And what can be said about the wars of religion in Europe during the sixteenth and seventeenth centuries? The St. Batholomew Massacre fills us with horror. Religious schisms

*Editor's note: The Committee on Society, Development and Peace —SODEPAX—was constituted in 1968 by the Holy See, Vatican City, and the World Council of Churches, Geneva. Its purpose is to promote cooperation among the Christian churches in the fields of social justice, human rights, development, and peace. Its secretariat is in the Ecumenical Center at Geneva. I served as Co-Chairman of this unique body, named by Pope Paul, 1968–75. Since 1972 we have focused on cooperation among the world faiths.

have been involved in political divisions, thus strengthening both politics and religion under the sign of conflict.

One must remember also the phenomenon of sects. The turning of groups in upon themselves seems to be a recurrent phenomenon, constantly taking on new forms. Nonreligious factors play a considerable role in the formation of sects; they interfere with religious factors proper here as well as elsewhere.

Finally, I must mention "renouncing the world." Today it is difficult for us to understand the attitude of those Christian ascetics whose activities were designed solely to pass away the time. In fact, their renouncement of the "world" for life in the desert was not a condemnation of earthly realities; it was only a desire to manifest the existence of values other than purely temporal ones, to stress contemplation and disinterestedness. But it is certain that, at times, a kind of a-cosmism, a denial of the goodness of creation, has actually been connected with some forms of Christian life.

These are all historical facts about Christianity. However, without much attempt at system, I would like to put forward a few points of Christian doctrine that ought to animate our collective responsibility toward global peace and justice.

THE PHENOMENOLOGICAL APPROACH

Henri Bergson, in *The Two Sources of Morality and Religion*, shows that it is not "natural" to love the whole of humanity. It is easy to love one's neighbor in an abstract manner. What is difficult is to love those who confront us from the other side of the fence and who do not think as we do. Neither is it natural to listen to others. There is a tendency in human nature, particularly when it acts as a part of society, to lock itself in. This is a biological instinct of defense, expressed at all levels within the human person. The collective fear of a group paralyzes every form of opening toward those who are "the others."

Particularly well-ordered societies are often dictatorial; they eliminate all ideologies barring one. These societies do not feel kindly toward "modern man," as seen, for example, by Paul Valery: On a terrace which stretches from Elsinore to the Straits of Gibraltar, from Ireland to the Urals, the modern Hamlet has in his mind *simultaneously* all the visions of the world, all different and often contradictory. His brain is a "universal exposition of thought." How can this modern diversity be integrated into society? There is a great temptation to eliminate all visions barring one by creating a void around the others.

Bergson distinguishes between "closed" morality and "open" morality. The first is based on coercion, threats, and an order imposed from outside; it implies fear and awe. Conversely, "open" morality is based on the manifestation of an ideal that attracts by the force of its own beauty.

Likewise, religion can act by sociological pressure or by attraction. The mystic and the hero impose themselves on others not by force and fear, nor by any other form of coercion, but by the contagion of admiration. Their presence rallies human beings onto the road of forgetting self. While the instinct of defense induces people to withdraw into groups confronting the others, heroes and saints help these same people strike out beyond the limits of biological fear. This permits them to be open to the whole human experience under the sign of community and religious values. In that case, religion is no longer a means to make one forget the void, nothingness, and death. It becomes a call to forget self in the gift of oneself to others.

According to Bergson, Christian mystics do not depart from the world. They return to it in order to contribute that "supplement of soul" that makes for effective universality, for outdistancing the forces of separation that would turn upon themselves, which forces are forever at work within society.

Individuals, as well as social groups, are constantly torn between fear of others and the desire to be open. One mediation which makes it possible to overcome this fear is that of the heroes and saints. It suffices to mention Dom Helder Camara and Albert Schweitzer.

TRANSCENDENCE AND IMMANENCE

The Second Vatican Council spoke of Christian presence in the world and eschatological meaning in "The Pastoral Constitution on the Church in the Modern World":

Christians, on pilgrimage toward the heavenly city, should seek and savor the things which are above (Col. 3, 1-2). This duty in no way decreases, but rather increases, the weight of their obligation to work with all men in constructing a more human world. In fact, the mystery of the Christian faith furnishes them with excellent incentives and helps toward discharging this duty more energetically and especially toward uncovering the full meaning of this activity, a meaning which gives human culture its eminent place in the integral vocation of man.

For when, by the work of his hands or with the aid of technology, man develops the earth so that it can bear fruit and become a dwelling worthy of the whole human family, and when he consciously takes part in the life of social groups, he carries out the design of God. Manifested at the beginning of time, the divine plan is that man should subdue (Gen. 1, 28) the earth, bring creation to perfection, and develop himself. When a man so acts he simultaneously obeys the great Christian commandment that he place himself at the service of his brother men (57).*

A comparable idea, advanced by Yves Congar, can be applied likewise to the kingdom of God, of justice and of peace. This kingdom is not *of* this world but must be realized more and more *in* this world. People always need to experience the transcendent and eternal aspect of the kingdom of God, which is total justice and love, although this experience is inaccessible to purely human energies. Humans need to know that there is an ultimate meaning to the adventure of human history—this kingdom of justice and peace which God is preparing. At the same time they discover that this kingdom of God must be more and more in this world—less of the world and far more to the world.

The grace of God which is given to Christians, the experience of Jesus Christ which is theirs, the comfort of the Holy Spirit with which they are filled must help them to commit themselves to justice and peace in this world, rather than to flee the world.

The word "world" has several meanings, as is stated in "The Church in the Modern World":

. . . . the Council focuses its attention on the world of men, the whole human family along with the sum of those realities in the midst of which that family lives. It gazes upon that world which is the theater of man's history, and carries the marks of his energies, his tragedies and his triumphs; that world which the Christian sees as created and sustained by its Master's love, fallen indeed into the bondage of sin, yet emancipated now by Christ. He was crucified and rose again to break the stranglehold of personified Evil, so that this world might be fashioned anew according to God's design and reach fulfillment (2).

The "world" which one must flee is that of evil, hate, division,

---

*This and later quotes from this Pastoral Constitution of Vatican Council II are taken from *The Documents of Vatican II*, ed. Walter Abbott (New York: America Press, and London: Geoffrey Chapman, 1966). This constitution and other recent Catholic social documents are also to be found in Joseph Gremillion, *The Gospel of Peace and Justice* (Maryknoll, New York: Orbis Books, 1976). The number refers to the constitution paragraph quoted.

separation, the spirit of destruction and violence. But the "world" is equally the theater of human activity; it is in this "world" that the Son of God became incarnate, and it is to save this "world" that Christ died on the cross and rose again.

In this "world" of human activity, Bergson explains, the love of others must not be motivated out of love of God. Such a formula, which can have a very precise and correct sense, could also signify the slighting of the concrete person in favor of an abstract reality. We must love others *"with* the love with which God loves them," that is, with a disinterested and creative love which restores life to those who despair, which is full of creativity, which is present in history as a leaven that can never be suppressed.

The purpose of Christianity is, of course, not primarily political or cultural. As stated by Pius XI, "the aim of the Church is not to civilize but to evangelize." However, by evangelizing it does contribute to civilizing. Thus Vatican II could say, in "The Church in the Modern World":

Christ, to be sure, gave his Church no proper mission in the political, economic, or social order. The purpose which he set before her is a religious one. But out of this religious mission itself comes a function, a light, and an energy which can serve to structure and consolidate the human community according to the divine law (42).

By evangelizing, Christianity has introduced or deepened the meaning of some specific values—for example, the value of the person; progress in the christological doctrine has emphasized the absolute, immovable reality of the human person, who must always be respected and can never be merely used as a means. Christianity has introduced a universal appeal for solidarity. We cannot maintain that only Christianity has done this, but its very dynamism resides in the power to transform fear into joy and coercion into love.

There is a difference between faith, which is a personal act (even though expressed in a community), and ideology, which is a kind of sociological cement and often part of a lived faith. In the Middle Ages the Christian republic constituted one means of introducing the faith in Jesus Christ. But the church was always conscious of the distinction existing between the ideology of the Christian republic and the so-called Christian Roman Empire on the one hand, and faith in the living God on the other. However, the articulation which both united and drew a distinction between faith and ideology often became a paralyzing arthritis. As Joseph Leclerc shows in *L'histoire de la tolérance au XVI siècle*, the policy "the religion of the king is the religion of the kingdom" (*cuius regio illius religio*) closely knit religion and nation in an ideology that had its greatness. However, the sociological survival of this ideology explains the violence with which the contemporary world broke away from the Christian republic in order to attain its autonomy as secular reality.

THEOLOGICAL FACTORS FAVORING UNITY AND PEACE

A most important factor is the Christian view of person. The concepts of person and of community are not conflicting. It is not a question of choosing the person *or* the community, but, on the contrary, of seeing the person in the community and the community in the person. There is a dialectic link between the two.

"Person" has two classical definitions. First, the person can be defined as the individualized subsistence of a rational nature (*rationalis naturae individua substantia*). These words of Boethius stress the person's spiritual character, the primary element which justifies the inviolability of the human person. But this notion of individualized substance can easily become one of individual substance, turned in upon "that which is self," separated from others, somewhat in the manner of the windowless monads of Liebnitz.

Another definition of "person" is that the person is essentially an opening to "the other." This idea has often been taken up by modern psychology and philosophy. This image also ties in with the theology of the triune life of God. In the Trinity, the three persons are the relationships that distinguish and unite them. The Trinity is as much the basic unity of divine life, as it is participation of the three persons in that divine life. This ideal of participation and communion is the magnetic North, inaccessible but present in the quest for harmony between the person and society. One must even say that Christ, through his incarnation, introduces us into this triune mystery. When Jesus demands that all his disciples be one as the Father is with him and he with the Father, he gives us the model of that community among themselves of persons who are divine—an inaccessible model, to be sure, but nevertheless ever-present, ever-active, and ever-endowed with a driving force and progressive movement.

Here one thinks of Teilhard de Chardin. For him, the more unity and union develop, the greater becomes the difference between the beings who are united. The contrary of unity is, in fact, uniformity. True unity, on the other hand, diversifies.

An element common to Judaism and Christianity—one could cite many more—is the doctrine that the person was created to the image of God. It is useful to recall the description of this in the Council document, "The Church in the Modern World":

> For sacred Scripture teaches that man was created to the image of God, is capable of knowing and loving his Creator, and was appointed by him as master of all earthly creatures (Gen. 1:26; Wis. 2:23) that he might subdue them, and use them to God's glory (Eccl. 17:3–10). "What is man that thou art mindful of him or the son of man that thou visitest him? Thou hast made him a little less than the angels, thou hast crowned him with glory and honor; thou hast set him over the works of thy hands, thou hast subjected all things under his feet" (Ps. 8:5–6) (12).

These texts signify the task of dominating the world which the human family is called by the Creator to perform. Here is a radical justification of what has been called Christian humanism, which aims at building the temporal city or, at least, contributing to its construction.

Another essential element of the Judeo-Christian tradition is that of giving value to time. In the face of myths about the eternal return, a circle closed upon itself, or in the face of a linear image directed downward toward a kind of chaos, time for Jewish-Christian thought is the place of a possible genesis. Oscar Cullmann's *Christ and Time* remains fully valid today. A series of studies by Wolfhart Pannenberg and by Jürgen Moltmann have stressed the importance of history. It becomes the history of salvation through the intervention of the God of Christians, in Jesus Christ, not by disguising history or by creating a sacred history alongside a profane history, but by becoming part of the very dynamism of temporal history. What Christians call the Old Testament shows how God, while respecting that dynamism or "determinism" of human history, somehow subsumes history and becomes part of it by giving it a meaning which only the prophets can reveal to us.

Christianity is not a non-temporality or an "a-cosmism," outside of history and the created universe.

Also important to world peace and unity is the fact that Christian revelation, precisely because it is transcendent, but also because it must become incarnate, is not tied in an indissoluble and exclusive manner to a given form of culture. Such a situation would be paralyzing in all cases. Here again "The Church in the Modern World" offers material for reflection:

> There are many links between the message of salvation and human culture. For God, revealing himself to his people to the extent of a full manifestation of himself in his Incarnate Son, has spoken according to the culture proper to different ages.
>
> Living in various circumstances during the course of time, the Church, too, has used in her preaching the discoveries of different cultures to spread and explain the message of Christ to all nations, to probe it and more deeply understand it, and to give it better expression in liturgical celebrations and in the life of the diversified community of the faithful.
>
> But at the same time, the Church, sent to all peoples of every time and place, is not bound exclusively and indissolubly to any race or nation, nor to any particular way of life or any customary pattern of living, ancient or recent. Faithful to her own tradition and at the same time conscious of her universal mission, she can enter into communion with various cultural modes, to her own enrichment and theirs too (58).

Another text of the same document makes the point even more explicitly:

> Moreover, in virtue of her mission and nature, she is bound to no particular form of human culture, nor to any political, economic, or social system. Hence the Church by her very universality can be a very close bond between diverse human communities and nations, provided these trust her and truly acknowledge her right to true freedom in fulfilling her mission. For this reason, the Church admonishes her own sons, but also humanity as a whole, to overcome all strife between nations and races in this family spirit of God's children and in the same way, to give internal strength to human associations which are just (42).

The church is now at the beginning of a new period. Her success in baptizing Greco-Latin culture during the first two millennia of her history was but a beginning. She now stands before the immense and wonderful task of introducing Christian inspiration into various other cultures—for example, those of Africa and Asia.

So far the church's understanding of the concept of unity has not been sufficiently flexible and deep. Its inspiration has been geometrical or mathematical models, whereas it should have been that of unity in diversity. Many Christian schisms can be partially explained as cases when a new cultural expression of the basic Christian faith was not recognized by respective churches as the multiple splendor, the manifold colors of the prism of the one faith in Jesus Christ incarnate.

A very firmly established doctrine of the early church fathers, particularly those of the East, reminds us of the presence in the world of the Word as creator and giver of light. He who created the world, more precisely he in whom the world was created—as John says at the beginning of his Gospel—is and remains present in this world and lights it with his hidden presence.

Non-Christian religions pose a very fundamental question for us. Traditional Christian revelation does not tell us anything about the ways in which God reveals himself to those who do not explicitly know Jesus Christ. The purpose of the revelation we have received is not to teach us this, only to indicate the normal road of salvation for those who do hear the word of Jesus Christ. But there is scope for important research here, tying in with the theme of evangelical preparation in studying Christianity by starting with the world faiths.

Perhaps I can venture still further and, with Paul Tillich, speak not only of the Word incognito but of Christ incognito. The motto of the Tantur Ecumenical Institute, near Jerusalem, originates from an inscription on an ancient lamp found nearby: "The Light of Christ shines everywhere." An echo of this vision is found in "The Church in the Modern World":

All this holds true not only for Christians, but for all men of good will in whose hearts grace works in an unseen way. For, since Christ died for all men (Rom. 8:32), and since the ultimate vocation of man is in fact one and divine, we ought to believe that the Holy Spirit in a manner known only to God offers to every man the possibility of being associated with this paschal mystery (22).

Sometimes it would seem that Christianity always arrives too late and has, therefore, remained ineffective. This is what François Mauriac has called "the failure of Christ to sanctify history." History remains that monster of forces which, alas, we know too well, and which Nietzsche perceived with bewilderment and terror during his last year.

Hence, there is, at times, the impression that Christianity has "failed." In the measure that we have wanted to live it in total freedom of belonging, without any sociological coercion whatever, in the same measure it would have been almost impossible for Christianity to realize itself, at least at the level of society. A few heroes and saints can remain "alone," but most people need an ideology through which authentic religious values may reach them.

Finally, I return to the temptation of temporal messiahship, of millennarianism, to which some Christians might yield. There is a well-known image which shows the degree to which too great a success by Christianity could become the antithesis of Christianity, an asphyxiating society in which everything is foreseen except joy, freedom, independence, creativity. Fyodor Dostoyevsky presented this danger in his famous "Legend of the Grand Inquisitor." Beyond a critique of Roman Catholicism, upon which I will not dwell, he sketched a far more profound truth: a regime which has succeeded too well, one in which everything is foreseen except the presence of one essential figure, the person of Jesus Christ.

Has then Christianity contributed to world history some element that is unique? Perhaps the answer is the tension it fosters between the efforts which must be made to create a just society, and the need never to think that the loop has been closed. This is, perhaps, one of the keys to the ferment Christianity has and can continue to contribute to the history of humanity. According to the thinking of Jacques Maritain, with which I agree, together with Christianity, Judaism is also (and possibly more specifically) that invincible ferment in human society which constantly spurs people to seek new solutions to the eternal quest for justice, charity, peace, love, and communion.

At a conference in Kyoto in 1968, we discussed the essential experience of Buddhism and of Christianity, and the specific contribution of each to the world. The joint conclusion reached was that Buddhism should be more open to social responsibilities, and that Christianity had a great need to bear witness to the fundamental experience of God in his inaccessibility. This experience keeps me awake. It never ceases driving one back and forth between this world and the other, between the kingdom of God which is not *of* this world, but which must be more and more *in* this world.

Our expectation is this above all. It is in this that people will rediscover themselves in communion; the last word for me is the prayer of Christ, "that they all may be one; as you, Father, are in me, and I in you" (John 17:21).

17

Discussion: Toward a World "Community of Communities"

As this third session continued into the discussion period, achieving movement toward a worldwide "community of communities" became the main thrust. The new "we" of all humankind, thus formulated in Rabbi Lamm's phrase, received unanimous support, always provided that the smaller, particular "we's" retain their individual identities while each opens up sufficiently to form with others the wider, universal "we."

By the end of the discussion, nearly all the Colloquium participants had concluded that this unity in diversity, this plurality of community, should obtain in both the religious and secular fields. Faith communities must remain both closed and open, each setting itself apart from other faith groups while simultaneously opening to its conscious role in the world community of transcendental faiths. National, cultural, and ethnic groups should also retain their secular identities. Exaggerated nationalism, however, expressed through the "sovereign" nation-state, must be eroded in favor of structures tending toward world community, structures more adequate for coping with today's technological, economic, and political realities in their global dimension—and specifically for coping with the food/energy crisis.

The Colloquium also agreed that among the manifold roles of religion, in our context one stood out: While consciously becoming a world community of faith communities, religion must provide cohesiveness and openness for begetting a world community of *secular* communities—both of nation-states and of cultural and ethnic groupings.

But, agreed the participants, each faith community must guard against a double temptation in the push and pull of the next world and this world, in the dialectic between transcendence and ideology. On one hand, there is the religious temptation to flee the risky world of secular affairs, seeking too soon to embrace secure salvation in the completely transcendent absolute, in the *eschaton;* on the other hand, there is the temptation to degrade the transcendental by overesteem for the secular, to concretize and identify religion with ideology, with what Professor Askari called the "finite absolutes" of race, nation, money, land, ancestry, and sanctuary—and thus "to use" the transcendental for one-dimensional goals that are only of this world.

A long and complex discussion led the Colloquium participants to this unanimous thrust toward a worldwide "community of communities." In reporting it, however, I have shortened and simplified the exchanges, grouping them by major subjects and abstracting only the main arguments.

UNITY AND DIVERSITY OF RELIGIONS

The Colloquium accepted Professor Smith's basic affirmation that each faith community must be "both closed and open, in sharply varying proportions." So the participants, pulled by humankind's present need for a cohesive community open to all (such as the food/energy crisis requires), searched their traditions and highlighted the universal elements of each.

For example, Fr. Spae urged a "joint approach to a new spirit of asceticism, which could easily be shared by the non-Christian participants, very particularly by the Buddhists. Dr. Ananda has already referred to that faith's elements of detachment, which look very much like the *kenosis** movement within the Christian perception of religion. The extreme suffering of hunger calls not for a balance of power, but for a community of suffering." Fr. Spae also applauded Professor Smith's call for repentance on the part of faith communities—a repentance he agreed should be led by the Christians who have so often acted divisively in history.

However, the validity of each religious group's retention of distinctiveness and identity also received repeated support from

---

*Kenosis refers to Christ "emptying" himself of divine power to become the suffering servant foretold by Isaiah. See especially Paul's letter to the Philippians, 2:6–11.

participants. Even during the formal responses to Professor
Smith's paper, Dr. Sivaraman and Rabbi Lamm had launched
something of a counterattack to the vision of unity in their fear of
"state homogenization" and "religious homogenization or
ideological imperialism, whether conscious or unconscious," as
they put it respectively.

Monsignor Peter Rossano and Monsignor Moeller, both high
Vatican officials and respected theologians of the Roman Catholic
church (which until the Second Vatican Council had favored an
exclusivist position) also made significant statements backing the
virtue of plurality.

Monsignor Rossano, who is secretary of the Secretariat for
Non-Christian Religions, Vatican City, said: "I speak as a Roman
Catholic. . . . I am not ashamed to recognize the world of Voltaire
with its plurality of unique religions. . . . Religions are many and
they are different—typologically, historically, phenomenologi-
cally different. The very core of the Christian religion is different,
from a phenomenological point of view, from the core of Buddhism, and both are different from the Islamic faith.

"Multiplicity is not a curse; indeed, I think that multiplicity is a
blessing. I am certain from my Christian point of view that God is
creator of all and that this kind of understanding has a long
tradition. From scientific reason alone we can recognize that religions are different. We don't know why they are different, but I
appreciate them.

"What I do affirm is that every religion has the duty to develop
its intrinsic potentialities, to make a contribution to human problems, as Professor Askari said of the Muslim faith. Every religion
is concerned with liberation, salvation, and human welfare, not
only in the future world but also in this world. So every religion
must draw on and develop its intrinsic potentialities, must give its
contribution for the benefit of humankind from its proper resources. This includes resolution of the problems we are facing
today."

Monsignor Moeller asked for more profound study of the concept of "community of communities." "I agree with Monsignor
Rossano when he says that in some sense plurality of religion will
remain until the end of time, and that this is a blessing. I think
that in the Christian theological approach it is possible to integrate the fact of plurality; it is extremely important to see that."
But more than theological study is needed "to promote a world
consciousness—by which I mean a consciousness as universal as

possible. We need more outstanding prophets and heroes to be awakened to this world responsibility. Two examples of such men are Albert Schweitzer and Dom Helder Camara. Each was faithful to his own Christian religious tradition, but at the same time each gave a direction that provoked a kind of aspiration, a contagious admiration throughout the world, encouraging others to tackle the very special problems of injustice, food, and energy from a religious viewpoint."

Professor K. Satchidananda Murty also spoke to the value of diversity, as he corrected a common misunderstanding. "Usually westerners believe that Hindus hold the view that all religions are equal, that all lead to the same goal." This impression has been created by some Indian thinkers "who have traveled frequently in the West." They do want a synthesis of religion or "a universal religion to emerge, in the way in which people like Toynbee have hoped will happen. . . . But what they have said is not the opinion held by all Hindus. A good number of people in India hold the kind of view which has been expressed by Monsignor Rossano and Monsignor Moeller. They believe that diversity of religion exists and that there can be neither a universal religion nor a synthesis of religion, in the way some Indian thinkers want it."

Cardinal Arns returned the emphasis of the discussion to unity, recalling the historic founders of three of the great faith communities—Moses, Jesus, and Muhammad. "This morning Professors Smith and Askari said that if we studied the kernels of their three messages there would be profound convergences. But what about today? I ask, are not these personalities, in their messages, the bringers of a ferment which is of deep significance for the new times of the peoples who follow them? And I ask whether the Buddhists and Hindus could not add similar views from their own prophets and founders. Then I ask if the aspiration of the world's people today would not find in each of these traditions, these faiths, a content which could be brought to a meeting such as this today, a converging content about the sense of life and the responsibilities we hold in today's world for each other. And finally I ask whether the real voices of these faiths are to be heard from official spokesmen or rather in a more popularized source, in the speech and actions of the peoples who follow and believe these religions."

Professor Parmar countered that if "religions wish to play a helpful role, they may have to aggravate the divisiveness of religion." He specified that he did not mean "negative divisiveness which has historically entered all organized religion, even Hinduism, . . . not that separatism which means breaking up of community, building walls between people, sometimes even aligning with the forces of injustice. This negative divisiveness creates obstacles to the solution of the problems with which we deal today—the problems of poverty, of the use of the world's resources within a framework of justice—and, therefore, the first act of solution is to challenge this kind of divisiveness."

Professor Parmar urged attack upon such negative separatism, but he does see the need of "creative divisiveness. . . . The person of peace is sometimes a troublemaker. In fact, I would even go to the extreme of saying that the peacemaker is invariably a troublemaker. In my country we had the example of Mahatma Gandhi. He was essentially a religious man, a man of peace, but he was a great troublemaker within the Hindu faith, and between various sectors of organized religions. They were always uncomfortable with him because he was always a troublemaker. But he created divisiveness so that it could heal.

"The same was true of Martin Luther King. He was a man of religion engaged in a process of healing in his community. And I think his most spiritual document, his *Letter from Birmingham Jail* to the leaders of the Jewish and Christian faiths, is a document which shows the peacemaker as a troublemaker."

Rabbi Blank also asserted the value of divisiveness. "I think we have fallen into the trap of putting the equation in terms of opposing 'divisiveness' and 'unity,' of suggesting that divisiveness is without its redemptive aspect. We are also implying error on the part of those who insist on preserving a sense of individuality. But I would point out that every religious group had its genesis out of a situation of divisiveness. Therefore, to assume that divisiveness has no redemptive aspect to it is to imply that we are all in serious error in our ultimate commitments. I would suggest the possibility that 'unity,' as described by Professor Smith, is itself an error in perception because it becomes a self-imposed absolute. Therefore, to articulate an 'either/or' kind of situation is an error in perception."

But Rabbi Blank advanced a remedy to this word trap: "to 'divisiveness' and 'unity,' add another term, 'individuality.' What we want to do then is oscillate between all three of these points. We want to slip in and out of these relationships to the extent that particular situations require it."

The rabbi elaborated this last thought. Situations do change, he insisted, and with this tripartite conception we can change our focus to any of the three dimensions as needed. "There are times when we want to be very sharply divisive, when we want to articulate what we perceive as an error on the part of our fellow human beings. . . . There are times when we want to be highly individual, making no suggestion that those who do not follow us are in error, but simply accepting that they have a different kind of orientation in time and space than we do. And there are times, such as during the impending tragedy of this food crisis, that we want to be very much in unity."

But in seeking this unity, Rabbi Blank wants "to avoid the trap of self-imposed absolutes, which Professor Askari warned against. We may slip into this trap in our desire to overcome those barriers which at the moment are dividing us, so we hold back from really digging in on this problem of hunger and starvation, a problem which could conceivably lead to war."

While reading his prepared paper, Professor Askari had inquired in a spontaneous aside whether Jews and Christians are ready to recognize the prophecy of Muhammad. He now repeated this question and specifically asked Rabbi Lamm whether "there is any internal Jewish testimony to the 'community of communities.' "

In reply to the later query, Rabbi Lamm quoted from the prophet Malachi: "In the end of days each nation will go with the name of its God and we shall go in the name of the Lord our God." He also cited the Talmud, which does not expect non-Israelites to observe the "whole legal system," but rather "only seven Noahide commandments which are all fundamentally moral and ethical in nature, questions of justice and humanity." Additionally, "a great many Jewish philosophers (indeed, all of them with one exception) in their vision of the end of time, did not speak about the Judaization of the world at all, although they did hope someday for the Judaization of the Jews."

Then, said Rabbi Lamm, "getting down to the nitty-gritty of the problem, 'Are Jews and Christians ready to recognize the prophecy of Muhammad?' Well, I speak, of course, as a Jew. And to a Jew, anyone who observes the seven Noahide commandments (which means any human being who is moral and just, any human being who accepts as normative the principles of morality and justice) is considered a wise, good human being. And further, anyone who bases these principles of morality and justice on a belief in God and the Mosaic revelation is considered a pious human being.

"But in no way can I, as a believing Jew, affirm any element of Islam or Christianity or any other religion as an article of belief. Individual insight, of course. But totality of belief in the prophecy of Muhammad, no! For me to do so would not only be to slide into an easy kind of syncretism which would make all religions totally irrelevant for me; it would also implicate me in an unworthy activity, namely, the negotiating of affirmations of faith as if they were some merchandise on a counter."

Rabbi Lamm concluded by asking for "conceptual clarification of the nature of interreligious dialogue." He admitted, "I have always been in favor of interreligious colloquia which do not focus on religious problems. The moment that the focus of our dialogue becomes a theological problem, then we are going to get into such hot water that we will never get out of it."

Ambassador Sol Linowitz concurred with Rabbi Lamm, "that it is possible for us to work cooperatively without having agreed on everything, without having reached the point where we mean all humanity when we talk about 'we.'

" 'We' means different things for different purposes. You may remember, as I do, when Lindbergh first flew the Atlantic in his plane, *The Spirit of St. Louis*, he said upon landing in Paris, 'We have made it.' That 'we' meant Lindbergh and his machine, and that was the right combination for that purpose. There are other combinations right for other purposes—the family, the community, the country, and indeed our faith." But Ambassador Linowitz wanted the discussion to come down to the concrete role of religion for facing today's problems. He warned, "It is possible to express love for humankind and to walk over the beggar hungry in the street. I would hope that out of this group will come an understanding that the faith we possess should give us greater insight and a greater sense of how to relate to the hungry in the streets of this world. And that is how we can carry out the charge we have had, which is accepting the challenge to peace and the call to faith in order to deal intelligently with the food/energy crisis."

The time allotted for discussion on unity/diversity had run out, but Dr. Al-Nowaihi urgently asked to speak. "I do hope my coreligionist, Professor Askari, will forgive me if I say I believe he has overstepped himself. Indeed, I am entirely on the side of Rabbi Lamm. Islam does not require either Jews or Christians to recognize the prophecy of Muhammad, and it is unfair to expect them to do so. Islam only asks Jews and Christians not to wage war against the Islam community.

"I must say that I deeply admire the honesty and integrity of Rabbi Lamm. If we are seeking a real rapprochement among religions, it cannot be achieved by ignoring or minimizing the differences. That would be dishonest. Rapprochement can be achieved only by admitting our differences fully, trying not to cancel them but to transcend them. This is the way we must proceed."

Professor Askari responded, "Well, I am a little uneasy about this question and, therefore, I should confess to you what I feel. The problem of religious interdependence is somehow being stated in a form to which I cannot fully agree. The alternatives are not between syncretism and being together only to be concerned about nonreligious questions such as food and hunger. There are other approaches.

"I am more concerned, my friends, about seeing a religious meeting as a way of togetherness. What does it mean to be in a role like this, together with our special individualities? For me to be both interreligious and religiously interdependent is to seek from within and under my tradition a certain essential and religious critique of my own religious consciousness. Sometimes, in order to counter any process which would absolutize Islam within me, I look for the redeeming presence of Christianity in history. At other times I look to Jewish insistence on the individuality and specificity of the land and the people, as a corrective against my own superficial Islamic universalism. It is thus that my religiosity as Muslim evolves, and thereby I enter into new religious relationships with myself and with you.

"It was in this sense that I referred in my paper to the unity of God's revelation and the unexpected ways in which God does reveal. Therefore, I don't see a permanent, convenient gap to be retained in human history between nonreligious concerns and religious concerns. I don't see being together religiously only as an occasion to make a nonreligious involvement in history. I take this colloquium as a *religious* opportunity, with all the risks and opportunities therein."

NATIONALISM AND THE WORLD COMMUNITY

The position and durability of the nation-state in the world community and how religion deals with nationalism became the next hub of debate.

Fr. Hehir stated the first half of the question. In 1648 the Peace of Westphalia "settled a religious conflict by legitimating a series of self-contained nation-states. . . . And that is the way we have conceived the globe for the last four hundred years. But one sign of the times is that this system is under drastic stress today, that there is an erosion of the nation-state as the building block in the international system.

"I think the evidence is fairly clear from the military viewpoint. The two strongest nations on the globe clearly cannot defend themselves, in the traditional sense of defense. They deter one another, which means each needs the cooperation of the adversary or else they cannot carry it off.

"From the economic viewpoint, the implications of the present monetary system, of the role of the multinational corporations, indeed, of the economic system generally, tend to erode the capacity of the nation-state to control its own economic destiny. And from the ecological viewpoint, it is clear that unless your neighbor has clean habits, your own habits can be hygienic and you will still have dirty water and dirty air.

"Therefore," concluded Fr. Hehir, "there is no way that the nation-state can exist as a self-contained entity in the way we have conceived it during the recent centuries. Yet the problem is that, while there has been an erosion of the nation-state, I certainly see no empirical evidence on the horizon that says between now and the year 2000 there is going to be any quantum transformation of the international system toward 'global community,' by which I mean the disappearance of the nation-state. Indeed one could argue, as Reverend Mbiti has said, that there are functional values to the nation-state in terms of protecting certain concepts of independence and identity within the international system.

"So it seems to me that the structural gap we have to deal with, at least over the short term and the middle term, is that we are faced with a series of transnational problems, such as the multinational corporation, population, food and energy, and yet we make our decisions through national decision-makers."

Coming back to Professor Smith's paper, Fr. Hehir asked us to try to understand the role of religion in the global structural gap left by "that series of transnational problems and transnational actors who are only national decision-makers. As Secretary of State Henry Kissinger said at the World Food Conference in 1974, 'We are stranded between a conception of the globe as a series of states and a conception of the globe as a human community.' And that statement was from a man who believes in the nation-state system and is a master of the discipline."

Fr. Hehir argued for a threefold effort to transcend this structural gap, an effort in which religion must play its role:

"First, a conceptual effort: How should you think about the globe as nations and/or as human community? Second, a psychological effort: How should people become aware of their role in a nation *and* in the globe? And third, a political and economic effort: How can you build structures in terms of this gap?"

Fr. Hesburgh proposed double citizenship—in one's own nation and in the world community. Rabbi Lamm's concept of a religious "community of communities" appealed to him, "and it struck me that you could translate this into the secular order as well. We have to get a new way of looking at the world. . . . It has been said several times that the great enemy of interdependence, or even of thinking interdependently, is nationalism. But just as we should not give up our religious convictions, so in the secular order we cannot and should not divest ourselves of the race to which we belong, the color we happen to be, the nation in which we were born. . . . Indeed, I would disagree with Fr. Hehir and say nationalism is not about to fade out. In fact, it is growing stronger, I think, and that is understandable because in a post-colonial world people want to establish their own identity as a nation.

"But it would seem that, without fighting nationalism head on, we would make progress by creating this 'community of communities' not only in the religious sense, but also in a citizenship sense. We can do this if we all exercise the option of being citizens of the nation to which we happen to be born, but become citizens of the world as well. Such double citizenship and loyalty is necessary because in an interdependent world one cannot live in a corner. None of the problems we are facing, including the two we are talking about in the Colloquium, can be decided nationally."

Dr. Borlaug tackled the question of structure—and called us down to hard facts again—by re-entering the heart of the food crisis. He insisted that *producing* enough food for all humans is *the* major challenge faced by individual nations and by the world community. On this point he is in disagreement with Ambassador Martin, who laid stress on finding adequate means of distribution. Again disagreeing with the ambassador, Dr. Borlaug said he fears that insufficient food will cause political and social upheaval, and that even international war "is a good possibility, given the spreading of armaments."

Spurred perhaps by Dr. Al-Nowaihi, Dr. Borlaug also asked us to take seriously the astonishing annual increase in population numbers for whom more food must be produced each year, and the challenge this poses to the "we" of world community. The well-known figures he gave should enter our record. At the time of Christ, 250 million people are estimated to have inhabited the earth. It took 1650 years to double that population to 500 million. During that period living conditions had begun to improve; there was more adequate food, a little better empirical knowledge for control of diseases. So the next doubling—to one billion—took only 200 years, from 1650 to 1850. Then with the beginning of modern medicine and scientific agriculture, world population doubled in eighty years, to two billion by 1930. Next came antibiotics and much better control of infectious diseases. By this year (1975) the figure has doubled again, to 4 billion, after only forty-five years.

Dr. Borlaug called to our attention the fact, that, with the telescoping of time, we are doubling ever bigger numbers. When we again double from today's four billion to eight billion (which will happen by the year 2000 or thereabouts), that will represent a tremendous increase in the amount of food we have to produce in order to maintain current per capita consumption, which is already dangerously low.

Although he is loath to make long-range projections, Dr. Borlaug expressed serious doubt that we can produce that much. He pointed out that "in speaking of ways to cope with the food problem, many participants have said that we need revolutionary changes in structures. . . . I mentioned yesterday that this was done in the People's Republic of China, but I don't want to leave the impression that it was all good. They have made tremendous progress in producing more food and distributing it equitably, there is no doubt about that. But it is at a cost. A man has replaced God. By that I mean the word of the Party comes down to all levels—the Communist commune, the college of agriculture, the faculty of medicine. And that word is decisive. Now the word is coming down on family planning. The Party has said that the desirable number of children will be two in urban areas, three in the countryside. And it has ways of imposing this word, through shaming nonconformists as bad citizens.

"My question is: Is that the way we want to come to grips with adequate food production? Do we want our solution at the expense of personal freedom and the rights of the various religions?"

THE ROLE OF RELIGION

The discussion swung to the specific role of religion in today's complicated world of national structures and transnational problems.

Rabbi Siegman wanted to find ways to express our role as faith communities more concretely. "All our religious traditions clearly mandate feeding the hungry. We could all agree to that. So what is it that we are searching for?

"Here I found what Fr. Hehir said very helpful in terms of focusing the search. The dilemma we face is structural. In our age, the food problem, like so many other problems Fr. Hehir enumerated, is a transnational problem. And, as he stated so eloquently, we don't have instrumentalities to deal with such problems. What we have are national entities, which make decisions on the national level for transnational problems. . . .

"We all agree that the hungry of the whole world need to be fed, and we all want to feed them. So the questions we need to examine are: What is there about our national structures that prevents us from fulfilling that very humane objective? Are there certain values shared in our respective religious traditions that will enable us to bridge the gap Fr. Hehir identified for us? Are there values that will enable us to provide not only the motivation, but also insights, to support specific structures and to deal with very specific power issues, which have inhibited us in the past?"

It was at this point that Professor Parmar urged the role of "creative divisiveness" upon religion. He also made a second major point: "A change to new structures always comes from new values. Religion's role is to challenge the old values that support the old structures, and to advance new values in support of the needed transformation of structures. But, unfortunately, organized religion has not adequately challenged unjust structures; on the contrary it has often supported them. Do you not see the evils of distortions in the profit motive? In the way in which property is used? In the way in which so many economic forces operate in the world? Why does religion not speak about these evils? What stops religion from speaking about them? It can speak about good will. It can speak about brotherhood. Can it not speak about these very important and tangible determinants of whether or not brotherhood exists in society?"

In concluding, Professor Parmar demurred from Rabbi Lamm's hope for "enlightened self-interest as a basis for world community. I must confess that I do not believe in it anymore as a global approach. Perhaps the trick of survival should keep us together, but I do not think it will."

In a later statement Rabbi Lamm showed great sympathy for these doubts, recalling "a well-worn story going around in Israel. Two persons meet, and one says to the other, 'Are you an optimist or a pessimist?' He answered, 'I am an optimist.' 'Then,' asked the other, 'why do you look so sad?' He said 'You think it is so easy to be an optimist?' "

Bishop Rausch agreed with Fr. Hesburgh about the desirability of building a world community of national communities. But, he continued, the key question here is: "What can *religious* bodies do? What can we do that is unique, that is different from what anyone else could do?

"The answer is that we can develop a conscience among our people on the question of justice, because the food issue comes right smack down to an issue of justice. We can develop a conscience among our people regarding the issues of production, consumption, and distribution.

"Here I could not agree more with Professor Parmar. This brings us back to the question of power. As religious bodies, I think the best thing we can hope for is that we will be pressure groups in society. We are not really a power in society. It is true that in some places the church has power, but that has never been to the benefit of the church in my opinion. I know that we feel sometimes uncomfortable with the word 'pressure'; it appears to be a word that degrades. But that in fact is what we are or can be, and that is the context in which we have to operate."

Bishop Rausch also followed up Professor Parmar's point about religion's role of creative divisiveness. "What we do will not only be, in some sense, divisive among us; it will also probably be divisive within the broader communities in which we live. . . . In

Brazil Helder Camara is exposing the sore and is lancing the infection in the society in which he lives. He is not popular there; they are trying to make a nonperson of him. And yet it is his kind of prophetic voice, speaking from within the community, that ultimately develops a community of conscience. So let's get down to the business of discovering how do we do that."

Rabbi Lamm stressed the educational and inspirational role of religion, especially urging a campaign "re-emphasizing the dignity of farming." He recalled Dr. Borlaug's concern for "the lack of prestige adhering to the whole vocation of farming. . . . I believe that in many religions there are authentic resources that would allow teachers to emphasize the closeness of human beings to earth and the dignity of working it and of returning to the soil. Now this has been done in China, although by a method which we don't intend to emulate. It has been emphasized by western youth's counterculture, although that has been declining recently. In fact, historically it has emerged in romantic periods of many religious systems and traditions. For example, the kibbutz movement in Israel—which was a remarkable revolution for a people who had been city folk all their lives—drew for generations on biblical sources to a large extent, consciously or unconsciously."

Professor Murty agreed. "I am very much attracted by Rabbi Lamm's proposal—that people of diverse religions come together on fostering the dignity of manual labor. . . . Persons like Mahatma Gandhi and Simone Weil have thought that one of the ways in which we can reconstruct our civilization is to inculcate people with the dignity of manual labor. And this sort of thing can lead to an alliance of culture as well as civilization."

Chief Adebo expressed appreciation for Rabbi Lamm's concept of "community of communities," and for its application to both the national and the world levels, as well as to both the religious and the secular spheres. Within his own country, "we try to bring the influence of people of faith to bear upon Nigerian problems —which have not been reduced by the end of the Civil War or the presence of oil. In a sense they have even been compounded by the presence of oil." Among these problems are those of corruption and of choosing the right sort of technology. "We took the line that since the people of faith are going about preaching, then all people must come together, as much as possible, and talk like brothers. In order to promote a religious environment in which everything else might be able to flourish, then each within his own religious community should educate or re-educate the people into the belief in and creation of an environment which would promote development."

Chief Adebo believes this national experience could be projected "onto the international plane by means of the kind of Colloquium we have organized here. The world 'community of communities' concept seems to me to strike a balance between doing nothing at all to bring nations together, and bringing them so firmly together that they lose a certain sense of separate direction, or they break away again."

Bishop Moore also saw hope in interreligious, international meetings, such as this Colloquium. "I have found a tremendous sense of mutual support around this table in the last two or three days, and I have become much more motivated by it. It may well be that through conferences like this we could develop a network which would grow in size and depth over the years, so that we could have a multinational religious association to hold up as a factor among these eroding national states. It seems to me that my colleagues around America could use something like this. Through it we could escape our own isolationism and draw on the fantastic power which we sense together here as we join across the table, all relating to the Power which each one of us calls God."

CONCEPTUAL vs. PRACTICAL

During the hours of discussion, cries were heard from some participants that we must descend from the clouds and become more "practical." Bishop Rausch couldn't help thinking that "we have tended to go astray, we have tended to engage in some intellectual exercises that are beyond me." Rabbi Siegman was asking himself "rather incredulously whether we really need to engage in complicated theological discussion—if that is what we are doing—to find sanctions in our religious traditions for feeding the hungry." Even Rabbi Lamm, the professor of Jewish philosophy, warned against "ending up in pious resolutions, or even in excellent philosophical formulations."

Less surprisingly, Ambassador Linowitz pleaded for concrete proposals. Before making some of his own, he "epitomized" his worry over the abstract discussion "by the story of when the great Bertrand Russell came to Harvard to deliver a speech on the quantum theory. He was introduced by Professor Albert

Whitehead. When Russell had finished his learned discussion Professor Whitehead said, 'We are all grateful to Lord Russell, and I especially want to express my appreciation to him for having left the vast darkness of the subject unobscured.' I will be very disappointed if by the time we leave this meeting, we have left the vast darkness of the subject unobscured. And the subject with which we are dealing, as I read my program, is 'The Food/Energy Crisis: A Challenge to Peace, A Call to Faith.' My plea would be that we begin to put together the facts we heard yesterday and the theory we have heard today."

Dean Stendahl and Bishop Moore both urged that even theologizing must start from facts and action, not from abstract thought. The dean of Harvard's divinity school showed a smidgen of Ivy League tartness toward his former confrere: "Wilfred Smith is a master at warning us against false distinctions. But as I think about his paper there is one false distinction that I think pervades it, and hence our discussion today. That is the sharp distinction between theology and ethics, between thought and action. So I am wondering if what we are doing here is taking for granted that the right action will grow naturally out of the right thought.

"What we are faced with here today is an *ethical* problem of momentous dimensions. And I am very grateful to Norman Borlaug for having gotten a little shiver of reality into us after yesterday's clever soothing words, which somehow gave us the feeling that with a little American push and some cooperation called interdependence, we are about to solve the food problem of the world. In truth we are faced with a momentous ethical problem."

Dean Stendahl urged the group to focus "upon the hunger of people and then say, 'Let each of us see what we can do about it.' That sounds very naive, but it seems better than what we are tending to do—trying first to work out systems so that we can respond to the ethical problem before us."

Next the Harvard dean praised "the 'we' language, in the strong form Professor Smith gave it. It is a call for throwing out the old leaven (or having it thrown out for us) so that we are set free to the 'we' of interdependence, in order to respond to the issue at hand."

Still the dean was asking himself: "What is it that holds us back from moving in the way Ambassador Linowitz has pointed? One possibility is suggested by the history of religion. So often truth and faith have been born out of the problems at hand, not first put in reservoirs and then sluiced out into the world by clever theologians."

Bishop Moore, the busy pastor of New York City (he lives in Harlem), had relished the theologizing but recognized it was time to get back to harsh reality. "I was really enjoying myself much too much this morning. It was sort of nice to turn back to theology and matters of the mind, because yesterday's frank confronting of facts became more and more painful as we got closer and closer to reality. But after the lovely theoretical discussions today, I would agree with Ambassador Linowitz and Dean Stendahl that we should get back down to basics."

In trying to dig for root motives, the bishop went beyond and below Dean Stendahl's theory of the genesis of thought from action, into the irrational drives that move people to act. "As long as we have a good idea, people should be rational enough to move from the good thought to the good action. However, we know from our experience that this is not true. I don't think this conference is paying attention to the unconscious drives of humanity. Let me name a few. War is not a rational act; there are always all kinds of irrational drives that bring people to fight, besides the particular purpose they say they are fighting about. Nationalism—God knows—is not rational. Religion itself is not rational, it is unconscious. These things are obvious, but we have ignored this whole dimension in our conversation."

Bishop Moore then touched directly on a question germinal to the entire discussion: the relation of human ideology and transcendent faith. "If we are going to get into the nonrational, I would like to remind you of one thing from Monsignor Moeller's paper this morning: the difference between ideology and faith. In history, it seems to me, the tying of a person's unconscious loyalty, drives, and passions to an ideology, such as communism, has been a more dangerous release of those energies than the tying of a person's unconscious drives to a living God, as represented by the faiths around this table. I say this even though religion can also become demonic. But ultimately it is a healthier way to release our passions because they are more likely to be positive when they are related to a living God than when they are related to a fixed ideology."

Therefore, Bishop Moore ended, "I would like us to get down to business again with deeper awareness of humankind's unconscious drives and passions as barriers."

Before spading about the fertile ground of ideology/transcendence, I must record Professor Smith's responses to the conceptual/practical debate. In his wrap-up he confessed "bewilderment at the charge that, in effect, we have wandered a long way from reality and should come back to the concrete issue. Fr. Hehir has pointed out rightly that the world does not in fact have the political and economic structural mechanisms for dealing adequately with its new problems. I agree. I also feel, however—and apparently quite a few do not agree with me—that the world also does not have the *conceptual* structure with which to deal adequately with these problems.

"I have been wondering whether I could get out of my bewilderment by noting that, on the whole, it is the westerners who are saying that we should leave theory and religious conceptions aside, while, on the whole, it is the Asians who feel that there is, in fact, a close relation between feeding the hungry and religious or theological concepts. Perhaps this is an oversimplification, although I am still going to speculate whether there may be something in it."

(For the record, and to aid Professor Smith's ongoing speculation, the transcripts show that six westerners, all Americans, criticized the discussion as overly theoretical. No Asians did so, nor did participants of other continents and cultures; rather, they largely followed conceptual approaches. Pragmatism, the American philosophy, lives on.)

TRANSCENDENCE AND IDEOLOGY

In raising the subject of the relation (or difference) between ideology and transcendence, Bishop Moore had returned to a theme which had appeared in all the session's formal papers. It had been Professor Askari's seminal idea, packed with consequences if properly unfolded. Other writers had repeatedly interfaced transcendence and ideology—in confrontation, in dialectic, in cross-fertilization.

Yet, the theme barely surfaced in the ensuing hours of discussion. Probably the conceptual-vs.-practical debate pre-empted the time, and the strong statements by the actionists rang down the curtain on dialogue that would have been more theoretical still, in content as well as form. Perhaps, too, this theme suggested a subject for interreligious study in a more academic setting—but with a Dr. Borlaug or two about to inject that "little shiver of reality" so esteemed by Dean Stendahl.

Still a few participants did touch the subject obliquely in the course of the long debate. When the discussion period began, Professor Avineri launched into issues of ideology, although he did not use the word. "I very much agree with what Rabbi Lamm has said about the pre-eschatological object of our discussions here. We are not trying to secularize our eschatological leanings, if we have any; rather we are talking about something which is intermediate, not ultimate, in the sense of religious convictions." He asked "to be enlightened by our Buddhist and Hindu friends about what they consider to be the importance of a historical consciousness. What is their understanding of history within their own religious tradition, as distinct from their historical consciousness as individual human beings who live in the twentieth century? It may be that there are differences here, maybe there are developments and maybe there is one Buddhism that is more political than other Buddhisms."

Further on, Professor Avineri also alluded to the religious aspiration for transcending the subject/object polarity which has been imposed on modern society by science's "piecemeal" view of human affairs—a main point in Professor Smith's paper. The Israeli professor proposed that "we should strive to evolve an epistemology based on relation: that relation in which subjects have no meaning without being related to objects, and in which objects have no meaning if they are not recognized by subjects. This would be in the same way that individuals exist as individuals only if they relate to other individuals, and that collectivities and individuals are simply different modes of interpersonal relationship, and therefore no man is a monad, no man is an island."

Professor Avineri believes that "on this relational level, by trying to develop a philosophy . . . transcending both subject/object and individual/collective dichotomy, we may have a cognitive tool with which we can then approach the issues raised yesterday and today on a technical and scientific level."

Such a philosophic overture did not make for harmony in discussion, as we have seen. But, in my view, the Colloquium participants together should in due time and a more fitting setting sketch out blueprints for projecting Professor Smith's conceptual structure. Perhaps Professor Avineri's epistemology could provide ground for its foundation.

After Professor Avineri, Reverend Mbiti in the very next

statement—the shortest of the week—asked, "Exactly what kind of eschatology do we have in mind, from our different religious perspectives, as we discuss the question of peace?" On another occasion he expressed doubt that we could divest our faith commitments from our eschatologies, as Rabbi Lamm had urged.

Monsignor Moeller harked back to his own paper. In a manner mindful of Professor Avineri, he recalled that he had emphasized the "need to clarify some basic concepts: for example, faith and ideology." Now he wanted to "probe the distinction and relation between community and society, solidarity and communion, communication of consciousness. Also, what does 'the person' mean." On the last point, he contrasted "the Chinese view of person and the European one, which is obsessed by an individualistic preservation. . . . Another word and concept which must be clarified or defined is 'transcendent.' Transcendence can be trans-*ascend*ence or trans-*descend*ence. It can be transcendence about a personal absolute or about another subject, conveying different meanings." But for good or ill, none of these clarifications was attempted; of course, they could not be in our setting and time frame.

Only one more discussant returned to these philosophical-theological issues. Not surprisingly, Professor Askari, who had introduced most of them in his paper, raised two pertinent points concerning God in history and eschatology. With regret and awe in his voice, he said, "The discussions so far leave us indifferent to the question of God in history. When I hear the word 'God,' I tremble. Because it is not a concept, not an idea, but something more than that.

"And how can you disengage this 'community of communities' from any eschatological consideration? I can't presuppose God's unity in history without presupposing, however tentatively and earthly indeed, a certain unity of eschatology."

THE NEW "WE"

As the long discussion ended, our whole mood and momentum moved toward the vision of the new "we" of all humankind, of a world "community of communities."

Professor Smith, in his wrap-up of the session, spoke favorably of "a 'community of communities,' a notion which impressed me a great deal. But I do have some reservations. Maybe 'community of persons' would be the right vision that would have consequences for the number of people who will be hungry ten years from now. And I do worry about the consequences in terms of millions and millions of people."

Professor Smith remained convinced that we are "as close to the heart of the concrete, specific problem of suffering people in talking about theology, interreligious relationships, and the like, as when we are talking about any other matter. It seems to me this is very solid, very real. And the future is, in fact, bleak unless we can solve the conceptual and, if you like, theological and visionary issues that face us." He thinks "Professor Parmar is right; the inherited religious and secular positions presently at our disposal are part of the problem and not part of the solution."

As chairman, Professor Murty closed the session by evoking for us believers a parallel from the secular world, the effort at detente between the superpowers. "Just as the Soviet Union and the United States, in spite of ideological divergences, are now coming together and working together on a number of common goals, I believe it is possible for the Hindus, the Buddhists, the Muslims, the Jews, and the Christians also to agree on practical concerns and work together for some common goals—setting aside what they think about human destiny, the origins of the universe, and so on and so forth."

Sol Linowitz squeezed in just before the bell to ask. "What can we do to forge a closer community?" Then, ever prepared and practical, Ambassador Linowitz read two sentences already written up for our Colloquium's proposed statement:

First, out of our deep concern and religious convictions we call upon the nations of the world to support fully and promptly the efforts of the World Food Council to feed the hungry of the world.

Second, we call upon the religious communities of the world to accept responsibility for the just distribution of the world's food and energy, and to press their governments to give urgent and priority attention to the food and energy needs of all the world's people.

SESSION FOUR

STRATEGIES FOR MEETING
THE FOOD/ ENERGY CRISIS

Our three preceding sessions had dealt with facts of the crisis, its impact with the world political context, and theological reflection on religion's general role in society. Now we moved to more concrete strategies which faith communities are following, or ought to embrace, to help out in the food/energy crisis. All agreed that this dire human problem will be with us for a decade, probably through our generation, well into the next century, and that basic changes of economic and political structures are required to solve it. So a long-term view prevailed, while insisting that calls for emergency help in areas of sudden or chronic need must also be heeded.

Three presentations now provided elements from which faith communities might evolve their strategies, internal to each and among themselves. S. L. Parmar, professor of economics at Allahabad University, India, offered his major paper, prepared for this session, on "Political and Economic Structures Demanded by Our Interdependent World." A survey of "Programs Undertaken by Some Religious Bodies," written by Peter Henriot and Frank Harris, of the Center of Concern, Washington, D.C., was circulated. And Krister Stendahl, dean of the Harvard Divinity School, spoke on "New Styles of Life in Faith Communities."

Professor Parmar, a member of the Church of North India, has been teaching economics at Allahabad since 1970. Prior to that he was on the faculty of the Ecumenical Institute of the World Council of Churches, Geneva. From 1971 to 1975 he served as chairman of the World Council's Program on Church and Society. His paper was a wide-ranging compendium of his subject and represents, in my view, the prevailing positions of World Council leadership and staff—in the formation of which Professor Parmar has played a leading role. The paper is reproduced here in its entirety.

18

Political and Economic Structures Demanded by Our Interdependent World

by S. L. Parmar

For many developing countries it is inappropriate to speak of a "food crisis," because that gives the erroneous impression of a temporary deviation from an equilibrium between need and availability. Consequently, emphasis is likely to be placed upon palliatives through relief, rather than cure through development.

In the past, the crisis mentality encouraged "instant" remedies, such as food aid from countries with surpluses of it. But despite such assistance over the last two decades, hunger and misery remain; in fact, they increase. This has led to the *triage* philosophy, a "realism" which concludes that certain sections of the globe are beyond hope and should be left to their fate in order to concentrate in saving others with better prospects of survival. Strange fatalism of the rich on behalf of the deprived!

The food crisis is not an autonomous entity. It should be seen as a periodic outbreak of a deep-seated food problem, inextricably linked to underdevelopment. It is true that floods, droughts, wide-spread shortages, dwindling reserves, and high prices have suddenly exposed large populations to famine or near-famine conditions.[1]* But hunger, malnutrition, and misery are a persistent continuity for many societies; their influence is pervasive,

*Professor Parmar's scholarly references are reproduced immediately following the text of his paper.

though they do not always acquire as catastrophic proportions as they did in the Sahelian and Bangladesh tragedies. And in many developing countries, even when economic growth rates are fair to high and food production increases faster than population, the nonegalitarian pattern of distribution forces many people into subhuman existence.[2]

Our familiarity with this chronic misery has engendered a defensive indifference and pushed reality to the back of our corporate conscience. Occasionally, however, as at the present time, the problem forces itself into our consciousness, through the vision of unprecedented human agony, such as is occurring in the Sahel; it is then labeled a "crisis," as if it were new. But the crisis was immanent in the very nature of underdevelopment.

There is, thus, a fundamental, long-term food problem rather than a transient food crisis. Insufficient recognition of this essential fact is, in no small measure, responsible for the grim situation today. Many developing countries, in their zeal to emulate industrial societies, have failed to give top priority to agriculture, especially the food sector. Surplus producers, such as the United States, have been more anxious about the depressive impact of large food reserves on their economies and have pursued policies to limit agricultural production.[3]

But once the basic nature of the problem has been recognized, there may be good reasons for calling the present situation a crisis. First, such a designation can be effective in drawing attention of the world community to the magnitude and urgency of the problem. Second, it helps to indicate significant differences from earlier situations. A disquieting food gap is likely to continue over the next decade. Existing reserves and projected surpluses provide less cushioning than heretofore. Price trends in food and agricultural inputs impose disproportionately heavier burdens on countries with less resistance, especially on their low-income groups.

A solution to the food problem is possible only through overcoming structural underdevelopment. The experience of many countries over the last two-and-a-half decades has shown that resources, by themselves, cannot insure development unless undergirded by adequate structures. New relations of power and property, relations which promote social justice and self-reliant development, are necessary preconditions to maintaining satisfactory growth rates over time.

Food is the key to development. It is essential for survival and is, at the same time, the most important input for maintaining the population's productive efficiency. Food shortages and current inflationary trends sharpen the inequality of consumption in society and generate grave discontent. Quite often that leads to social dislocation on a wide scale, which disrupts development efforts. Much of the internal disturbance in India over the last year and a half can be attributed to high food prices, profiteering, iniquitous patterns of consumption, and a deep sense of deprivation among the disadvantaged sections. That kind of political climate can hardly be conducive to growth.

This view of the food crisis in developing countries suggests three significant areas of discussion for this paper: the interrelation between the food crisis and structures of society; the implications of interdependence today; and measures to deal with the crisis and their bearing on structural change and interdependence.

THE STRUCTURES OF SOCIETY AND THE FOOD CRISIS

Let us consider how structural factors aggravate the food crisis. Shortages represent an excess of demand over supply. In general, the demand for food is determined by population and patterns of consumption, while supply depends upon production, imports, distribution of stocks, and conservation (or wastage) of food.

Population Control and Struggle for Justice. Rates of population growth in developing countries are inordinately high and must be brought down.[4] This brooks no delay because a very large proportion of the present female population in most developing countries has not even reached child-bearing age and another large proportion will be capable of child-bearing for many years. Therefore measures initiated today to reduce birth rates will begin to change the aggregate situation only after ten or fifteen years. But in recent years, under the dominance of a neo-Malthusian approach, there has been undue emphasis on the technical or clinical measures of family planning. These have not met with much success, nor are they likely to in isolation.

It is now widely recognized that policies of social justice to the disadvantaged groups are essential for motivating them in favor of smaller families. Population planning will be effective only if it makes an impact on the rural sector, where the bulk of the population lives. Hence measures encouraging more socio-economic equality, better opportunities of employment, the provision of agricultural inputs (credit, seed, fertilizer, marketing facilities) to small holders through institutions that do not become tools in the hands of large-scale farmers and other privileged groups, land reform to give ownership to peasants and landless laborers, and so on, are absolutely necessary.

But the implementation of such policies involves a radical restructuring of society. Many institutions in developing countries now reflect an admixture of feudal, colonial, and capitalist values, and they obstruct more equitable use of productive resources and sharing of the output.

For instance, in India, community development programs, extension services, and cooperative societies have often served the interests of privileged rural groups with few, if any, benefits to the poor. In certain parts of the country the much lauded Green Revolution has aggravated rural inequalities and heightened social tension. Various other incentives have been beamed at the successful big farmer in efforts to accelerate output within the shortest time span. The result? The strong tend to become stronger. And all these efforts to stimulate production seem to have subverted, rather than promoted, social justice. Hence their support of population planning policies has been minimal, if not negative.

Structural change cannot be brought about by injecting more resources and giving incentives because these are appropriated by the controllers of socio-economic power. Therefore, political action becomes unavoidable. This fact needs to be recognized by the state, which is the repository of political power on behalf of the people. Not infrequently, however, the dispensers of political power are part of the country's vested economic interests and are hence disinclined to initiate changes in patterns of ownership and opportunity. Sometimes their selfish designs are camouflaged by verbal support to progressive, people-oriented policies. But nothing happens.

Some form of people's movement then becomes the only way to pressure the political authority into honoring its oft-affirmed promises. In this context, a struggle for justice becomes a vital component of structural change within and between nations.

The incursion of the struggle for justice into discussions of population and food problems may appear to be farfetched. If, however, measures to deal with these problems require structural change, reference to struggle cannot be avoided. In fact, it becomes even more important in an atmosphere of crisis. Those who control power insist that all social dislocation and struggle should be held in abeyance until the crisis is overcome. They announce order and stability as essential for increasing food production and assuring its availability to disaster areas. But such political sophistry conveniently ignores the fundamental nature of the crisis and the need to institute effective long-term remedial measures.

The success of any effective measures actually depends on more equitable sharing of power and on deployment of the political machinery to establish supportive institutions and norms. Order and stability are extremely important for development, but not as custodians of unjust structures which nullify developmental efforts. Structural change is the only effective guarantor of development-generating stability. Where the political system ignores this basic reality it invites instability.

The struggle for justice is, in essence, a form of creative instability. Therefore, one hopes that governments in developing countries, with their claim to serve the common person and their oft-reiterated determination to overcome poverty and injustice, will use the present crisis to establish new power and property relations that are conducive to such laudable ends. The food crisis has all the makings of human disaster in terms of suffering and misery. If its structural import is not fully grasped by decision makers, it could lead to political upheavals caused by the intransigence of power groups more intent on protecting their privileges than defending the interests of the people.

Changing Consumption Patterns. Patterns of food consumption in many areas are, at times, incompatible with nutritional considerations. This calls for a change in food habits, which, in turn, requires a substantial degree of cultural restructuring. It is not a simple matter of providing information but a question of changing social and cultural norms that have the sanctity of tradition and habit.

There is another disquieting aspect in this regard. Many of these societies have wasteful practices of social consumption for ceremonial and status purposes. These must be curbed. Perhaps the result may be of marginal significance purely in terms of the quantity of food saved, but a curb will create the sense of emergency so vital to mobilize public effort to fight the food crisis. Legalistic measures alone may not succeed unless a new social awareness, which decries wasteful consumption prompted by traditional obligations, develops a sense of social obligations commensurate with the needs of the hungry millions.

The implication of such an approach would lead to setting a maximum in food consumption as complementary to a minimum that can be assured to all. Obviously that would require curbing the influence of incomes and prices on the demand for food, as well as a rational simplification of nonessential consumption. Here again, the need for new institutions and social norms becomes unavoidable.

In terms of a global approach to population policies, a change in the pattern of consumption in affluent societies is now recognized as an important factor. Developed nations constitute 20 percent of the world's population but use 80 percent of its resources to stoke their ceaseless pursuit of affluence. In North America during the past generation consumption of cereals per head rose from 1,000 pounds a year to nearly 1,900 pounds. This formidable increase was due to the emergence of meat-eating as one of the symbols of affluence. The consequence is that over 60 percent of U.S. grain output—or something like 140 million tons a year—is consumed entirely by cattle, sheep, pigs, and poultry.[5]

The heart of the population problem is a disequilibrium between people and resources. This is caused as much by the overconsumption of the rich as by an increase in overall numbers. The high conversion ratio of food into feed is a normal economic effort if seen in isolation, but it represents misdirection of resources when judged on the basis of world need. Curbs on consumerism acquire significance as measures of population planning. Assuring a desirable minimum to the poor is the first step in the social justice that is expected to motivate them to reduce birth rates. It is becoming increasingly evident that its realization depends upon evolving some supportive global policy about maximum consumption.

Attempts to regulate consumption patterns in response to the food crisis will require structural changes in two directions: first, a rejection of self-propelling consumerism, and second, a mechanism to build up surpluses in rich countries and transfer them to poor countries, without a breakdown of the related economies. These are far-reaching changes and cannot be instituted under the present structures of national and international economies. But this may be precisely the point where the food crisis challenges us to search for new patterns of interdependence.

Changing the Supply: Distribution. On the supply side the most effective solution to the problem of chronic food shortage is increased production. However, in view of the urgency of human needs, distributional and conservationist approaches to the solution are no less important. These have the added advantage of being able to be implemented relatively promptly, given the political will necessary to insure social discipline. Increased production is a time-lag activity; it can meet the food deficit only after a minimum of one or two crop seasons—assuming that the requisite agricultural infrastructure exists. And if it does not exist, which is frequently the case, the time-lag will vary on a scale of several years, depending on the speed of providing essential ingredients, such as additional arable land, land reform measures, supplies of inputs, institutions to facilitate the flow of inputs to production and outputs to consumers, and so on.

Hence, of the options at hand, it seems more rational to begin immediately with a need-based distribution of what is available. This is not an easy venture because the establishment of an effective distribution machinery is a complex operation, and, more fundamentally, because significant structural change is involved. However, it is the logical primary response to the emergency. It is normal human experience that when a family faces shortages the first step is to make equitable use of what little it has. Within a family equity does not mean rigid equality. Usually, the needs of the weaker members—children, sick persons, the elderly—receive precedence; others make relatively greater sacrifices. Can this simple small-scale response be applied to a problem of national and international magnitude? One is reminded of Adam Smith's wise dictum: "What is sensible in the case of a family can scarce be folly in the conduct of a kingdom."

An egalitarian distribution policy will require fairly radical changes in the existing institutional framework. For instance, demand governed by price and income will have to be regulated. The deprived groups, the victims of hunger and malnutrition, do not possess adequate purchasing power to meet their survival needs. Left to the mercy of market forces they face starvation. Society has to provide them with a larger share of available supplies. That can be done only by separation of food from the vagaries of the market mechanism. (It is sometimes said that there is no food shortage, only an income shortage. As a bit of economic speciousness this may be admissible, but it cannot conceal the basic disability of a large section of the population.)

During periods of acute food scarcity in India the phrase "man-made famine" is often heard. It was first used during the 1943 Bengal famine, which is estimated to have claimed over a million victims. The phrase indicates deliberate aggravation of scarcity conditions by certain groups which exercise economic power. There are sound reasons for using this label today in Bangladesh and the Sahel, as well as in parts of India. *The World Economic Survey 1973*, citing the case of the Sahelian countries of Africa, observed "that food shortages in developing countries arise less because of the total supply of food than because of deficiencies in the system of distribution."[6] Practices such as hoarding, profiteering, adulteration, and so on have become rampant. Their brazen continuance would not be possible without some degree of political connivance from dominant economic power groups.

In a climate of "get rich quick" and "everything goes in business," the naked pursuit of private profit at the cost of human well-being has made cancerous inroads into the body politic. A new ideology of "profitism" is flourishing and gaining ground. Official statements from India indicate that adulteration of essentials, such as grains, fertilizers, edible oils, cement and seeds, has become well-organized business. Food adulteration has killed a number of people and permanently disabled even more.

In this corrupt atmosphere it is not unusual for materials earmarked for relief to be diverted into a burgeoning black market or smuggled into a more profitable market across the border. Recently a veteran of a relief program told me that only ten cents out of each dollar of relief aid reaches the poor. One could question the reliability of the percentage, but where human behavior is influenced more by personal greed than by social need, heavy leakages tend to occur.

Conventional economics emphasizes profit as a stimulus to efficiency, competitiveness, and the promotion of the consumer's interest. At one time, within certain limits, there was a rationale for that brand of profit motive. But what one often witnesses today is the negation of all these purposes. Producers and sellers, sometimes in collusion, work to strengthen their monopoly power—obviously at the cost of the consumer. When they take advantage of an inelastic demand for food, the only efficiency they show is a callous manipulation of the market to maximize their loot.

Yet it would be naive to regard all this behavior as merely that of selfish individuals or groups. It is spawned by the existing economic institutions and a concentration of power in unscrupulous hands. Such antisocial activities are embedded in economic and administrative structures and can be eradicated only by changing them.

Curtailment of Wastage, Imports. Curtailment of wastage is another factor in increasing the food supply. The use of consumption restraints for this end has already been mentioned. Equally important is the plugging of losses caused by inadequate storage, pests, rodents, stray cattle, and the like. For instance, according to a United Nations estimate, India is losing ten million tons of grain annually through such leakages, an amount equal to the anticipated worldwide requirement of annual food aid these days.

High priority, therefore, should be given to devising methods of protecting what has already been produced. Unfortunately, this is one of those oft-mentioned but neglected areas of endeavor.[7] Given the social will, it would not be difficult to evolve simple techniques to check the menace of pests without ecological backwash and to construct storage facilities by using indigenous labor, skills, and raw materials.

Imports can also help to meet the food gap. But most of the food deficit countries are short of foreign exchange; the rising prices of food grains, fertilizers, and petroleum products have put the balance of payments for many under a heavy strain. Over the next five years they are likely to face annual deficits of $3 billion.[8] Additionally, in recent months the prices of many primary commodities, the major exports of many developing countries, have been declining. (The bargaining power acquired by OPEC had raised hopes of obtaining better prices for other raw materials, but success seems doubtful at the moment.) It is, therefore, necessary to continue efforts for basic changes in the structures of international trade, which are now heavily weighted in favor of the strong.

Increasing Production. Undoubtedly the most important preventive measure against recurring food crises is increased production of food grains and other edibles. Some of the significant strands here are: shifting priority to agricultural development; giving primacy to the production of food crops, rather than cash crops; and using the improvements given by the Green Revolution for the benefit of those who need it. All of these involve reordering priorities and hence significant changes in economic structures.

Many developing countries have not given adequate importance to agricultural development. In line with the trickle-down theory, which assumes that aggregate increases in GNP will automatically percolate to the poorest sections and lead to distributive justice, rapid industrialization has been relied upon to promote agricultural development. It has been expected to generate greater demand for agricultural products and thus enable the price mechanism to become an incentive for increased agricultural production; to provide essential inputs for agriculture, such as implements, new technology, and fertilizers; to create employment and draw surplus labor from agriculture, thus improving the person/land ratio and enhancing the marginal productivity of farm labor.

Experience has belied these naive expectations. Developing countries are paying heavily for their propensity to imitate industrial economies and for their lack of adaptability and authenticity. Therefore, their first task must be to rectify this mistake by giving the highest priority to agriculture. In most developing countries, 70 percent or more of the population lives in the rural area and depends on agriculture. Since the focus of development is on the poor, this sector must determine economic priorities. It is ironical, almost scandalous, that predominantly agricultural economies have to be continuously dependent on industrial economies for their basic food needs.

This last point suggests another sort of reordering that is also needed in many developing countries. Monetization of the agricultural sector and its linkage with organized industry and exports have, at times, tilted production in favor of commercial or cash crops, relative to food crops. Without minimizing the importance of the former, it is obvious that the latter must be given primacy. Cash crops are inputs to keep industry and exports moving; food crops are inputs for human survival and sustained productivity. People must have precedence over industry and commerce.

Notice, however, that the need is for a new balance between these two kinds of agricultural production, as well as for a new balance between the industrial and the agricultural sectors, and not a jettisoning of industrial programs or cash crops as such.

Food production cannot, of course, be discussed without bringing in the Green Revolution. In a very short span of time, the use of the "miracle seeds" and attendant agricultural methods has undoubtedly succeeded in increasing food grain production and represents a major breakthrough. For instance, India's wheat production escalated from eleven million to twenty-six million tons between 1965 and 1972.[9] But the Green Revolution has not succeeded in establishing a firm base on which to maintain the tempo. On the contrary, certain negative influences, inimical to rural development, have come in its wake. These limitations can be attributed to a reliance on technico-economic measures without any concomitant radical change in social and economic structures.

The Green Revolution has depended mainly on large-scale farmers and landowners. Some of the latter do not cultivate the soil themselves but are absentee owners who provide inputs, use hired labor, and own and dispose of the output. Under the urgency of raising production, the interests of small holders and landless laborers have been bypassed. Before the Green Revolution, rural values and structures were already notoriously nonegalitarian. Now the prosperity it has bestowed on the relatively stronger sections has sharpened rural inequalities and, in many cases, pauperized the poorer groups. Growing social discontent threatens to jeopardize production.

Large scale farmers tend to find more capitalistic modes of production advantageous and are, therefore, increasing their use of mechanization and other labor-replacing techniques. This has serious drawbacks: It aggravates rural unemployment and underemployment, which are already high; it weakens self-reliant development by placing greater dependence on imported inputs and disregarding the indigenous manpower and skills available in abundance; it undermines the indigenous social justice by denying work and income to the needy and thus runs counter to the basic objective of development—overcoming poverty; it postpones land reform; and it violates the fundamental principle of optimal allocation of resources by implicitly denigrating simple technology, rural manpower, organic manure, and other readily available or potential inputs.

The dominance of capitalistic norms fosters production for profit, rather than for essential societal needs. In response to price variations the new technology encourages shifts from food crops to cash crops. (According to one estimate such diversion may be nearly 10 percent in the Green Revolution belt of the Punjab during the present sowing season.[10]) If food grain prices are kept high as an incentive, it intensifies the food crisis in the worst hit sections.

The profit motive also tends to encourage transfer of a large part of any increased production to the urban sector. This reduces demand for the products of rural cottage and small-scale industries. Additionally, under existing patterns and dominant interests, emphasis on increased agricultural production is often geared to urban requirements.

A related factor is the continuing hold of traditional vested interests (money lenders, middlemen, prestigious social groups) who have taken control of supposedly people-oriented service agencies, such as cooperatives, in the agricultural sector. Present economic ability, rather than potentiality, generally governs the direction and deployment of resources handled by these organizations. As such they are often only channels for bringing in resources, not for changing power and ownership patterns. On the contrary, they have added enormously to the strength and political capacity of the privileged classes and make the task of smooth social transformation immensely more difficult.

For these reasons, higher agricultural output does not necessarily imply agricultural development. The agricultural sector has always been exploited by the urban sector. The malady continues.

Positive Measures for Increased Production. The Green Revolution, as it has actually been applied in most cases, has not increased social justice and self-reliance in the food-deficit countries, any more than have the application of other capital-intensive modes of production or the dominance of the profit incentive. On the other hand, measures for the better distribution and conservation of food, as well as the reordering of priorities to and within the agricultural sector, do indeed support these goals.

The first step in self-reliance is to mobilize and use economically all the food resources a country possesses. If this is combined with schemes for constructive use of surplus manpower, it will promote capital formation. For instance, a creative way of using food aid is the "food for work" approach. If the "work" is used to build the infrastructure needed for conservation, it will convert labor into an important form of social capital and, thereby, turn relief into development assistance. The tendency to look to others to bail one out of difficulties not only leads to a neglect of existing possibilities, but also inculcates a spirit of dependence.

In a fundamental sense the spirit of self-help in a people is their most important social capital. It can become the fountainhead of new development resources. Capital is, after all, crystalized labor. With so much unused manpower going to waste, even seemingly simple measures of self-help can have a regenerative potential for a submerged group. Providing work opportunities to the underfed not only meets their hunger but draws them into the process of production. It is in that sense that policies of social justice and self-reliance stimulate and sustain economic growth.

Perhaps the most important part of self-reliant development is the achievement of self-sufficiency in food production, especially in predominantly agricultural economies, which obtain in most of the food-deficit countries. Existing structures have failed to bring this about, despite a commendable increase in aggregate food production and the reiteration of the objective of food self-sufficiency in economic plans, as in India. Therefore, structural change becomes the first step in the quest for self-reliant development.

The process of change can be started without delay by simple measures of self-reliance, such as using available material and human resources, employing appropriate technologies which are built from and make use of these resources, and emphasizing a concept of optimal allocation of resources in real terms of what the economy has, rather than what it can get from outside. Needless to say, structural change, beginning with economic structures, is central to programs of self-reliant development. And efforts for change will meet strong resistance from the entrenched economic values and production patterns, as well as from external economic influences which have come in through export patterns, mechanization, modern technology, and the like.

But the reordering of economic priorities in terms of available resource composition will confer important benefits on the rural sector. Rural poverty can be ameliorated by improved employment conditions. Per capita productivity is likely to rise as formerly unused labor is drawn into the production process. All this should enhance the potentiality to generate a larger surplus, which can be used to sustain both small-scale rural-based production and essential large-scale industries. Additionally, gainful employment for now-surplus labor and the use of indigenous resources and skills would establish the mechanism for a more equitable sharing of the social product. It would then provide the necessary base of social justice that I have already emphasized as a precondition for healthier demographic trends.

Self-reliance should not be misconstrued as economic isolation.

On the contrary, it is a positive way to strengthen an economy through effective mobilization of internal resources in order to participate in international exchange on a more equitable basis. It is the only way to break the domination-dependence relationship between developed and developing countries.

Two specific measures conducive to self-reliance are land reform and giving the small holder direct access to agricultural resources and services, such as seed, fertilizer, water, credit, expert advice and so on. And even at this starting point one can see the convergence and interdependence of self-reliance and social justice.

To sum up, an increased food production which provides a lasting solution to the food problem can be achieved only by a more equitable *sharing of power* in the rural sector and by mobilization of people and indigenous resources into production. It involves a stronger reliance on appropriate technology and the enthusiastic participation of the people. Achieving these goals calls for radical social transformation. Governments that claim to be committed to justice should act on behalf of the people and exercise their political power through constitutional means to usher in a new social order with minimal dislocation. If that does not happen, the people will be forced into extraconstitutional methods to insure that political power is harnessed for the eradication of poverty and injustice.

IMPLICATIONS OF GLOBAL INTERDEPENDENCE

Thus far I have focused mainly on internal action by countries which face the food crisis and I may appear to be ignoring international interdependence. The latter is indeed an important question, but before dealing with it I must emphasize that international action can only assist, it cannot resolve the problem. The national efforts and priorities of developing countries must, therefore, be central even to interdependence between nations.

Viewed in relation to the nature and dimensions of the food crisis the term interdependence may appear somewhat paradoxical. Countries already in the throes of actual famine, as well as others who are perilously close to such conditions, are going to be dependent on external assistance for some time. Most of them lack sufficient foreign exchange to pay for requisite food imports. This reflects an absence of complementarity in their relation of trade and payments with surplus countries. World prices for most developing countries' primary products (their chief exports) are falling or, at best, holding steady. In the meantime rising world prices for their essential imports is eroding the purchasing power of what foreign exchange reserves and earnings they do have. For instance, in 1972 India's purchases of crude oil, fertilizer, and food grain cost $500 million; in 1974 the price was over $1.2 billion, and it is expected to reach $2 billion in 1975.[11]

The interdependence advocated for the food crisis, therefore, has to be understood as meaning something like "a global approach," according to U.N. Secretary General Kurt Waldheim.[12] This usage must be carefully distinguished from the universalist concept of "interdependence" based upon specialization common in traditional theories of trade. That sort of interdependence, while claiming to be a mechanism for a just distribution of gains from trade and conducive to international equality, has in reality been strongly exploitative and served as an instrument of domination by the strong. This was clearly seen in the colonial pattern of specialization and trade, which still obtains in most of the world.

That mutuality of gain affirmed by conventional theory would have happened if the patterns of cash crop specialization in developing countries conformed to *their* needs and priorities and had risen out of *their* resource composition. But these have generally been projections of the dominant nations' economic interests. For instance, Latin America has the largest area of cultivable land of any continent. "And yet it imports most of its food and 60 percent of the arable land lies fallow, largely because the landowners find it more profitable to grow cash crops, such as sugar and coffee, for exports than subsistance crops to feed their own people."[13] Developing countries have been responding to impulses generated by industrial production in the developed countries.[14]

As a matter of fact, much of the specialization developed during the colonial days, and often still current, was contrary to the essential principle of comparative advantage; critical inputs were not locally available but came from the dominant nations, especially in the form of capital, technology, and managerial skills, to produce what they needed for their industrial society. This apparently neutral inflow of factors of production gave a dominant role to the industrialized country from the very outset of the specialization process. One need not refer only to economic history. The present scene, with the multinational corporations' awesome economic and political power, bears evidence to the current reality of this phenomenon. Specifically with reference to the food crisis, there is the example of the Sahelian region where "thousands of the best acres and a large share of the scarce water resources are assigned by multinational agribusiness corporations to the production not of foodstuffs for the native population, but of raw materials and other products for marketing in the developed world."[15]

Some benefits from this sort of relationship accrue to some groups in developing countries. But that can hardly denote true interdependence. The benefits flow mainly to the developing nations' internal structures of domination, which not only exploit the people but become willing tools for like-intentioned external forces. Obviously, a continuation of this pattern will undermine development and aggravate the food problem.

Rightly understood, interdependence of the global approach implies that specialization and trade be purged of their exploitative elements so that international economic relations will represent a mutuality of interest based upon the *human needs* of all members of all societies, rather than selfish national and regional interest and the quantum of politico-economic power controlled by one group or another. This would represent a new kind of interdependence, one which would change the domination-dependence relationship between developed and developing countries into one of just distribution and use of the world's resources.

But to shift from a power-based and profit-based allocation of resources to one based on need is not possible under existing national and international structures. Therefore, if the global approach is taken seriously, its first injunction is to change existing political and economic power relationships. Interdependence, thus construed, is a challenge to prevailing structures. As I have already said, such change always involves political action and some sort of struggle for justice; one wonders whether this controversial dimension has been comprehended by advocates of the global perspective.

Sharing Power and Resources. Since such a new understanding of interdependence emphasizes justice and solidarity between rich and poor nations, it questions the existing maldistribution of economic power achieved through nonequitable patterns of international economic relationships. The present arrangement of trade, investment, aid, and the transfer of technology, though representing some form of mutuality of gains, has, in fact, given control over a major portion of the world's resources to industrial societies.

As economic relations increase in range and intensity, the lopsidedness of this division of benefits also increases. If the resources of the world are to be used for the well-being of all humankind (i.e., on the basis of human solidarity), the first task is to convert the process of division into a more egalitarian one. Otherwise, under the guise of mutuality, traditional patterns will continue to dominate.

For instance, it is assumed that continued stability and growth in developed nations is an assurance of economic progress for the developing nations. According to this theory, a combination of inflation and recession, such as plagues the industrial world these days, reduces the real purchasing power and export incomes of the poor nations and causes serious setbacks to their developmental efforts. This does appear to be what is actually happening. The question is, does it indicate mutuality and interdependence or a state of dependency and helplessness? As a corollary to this theory, it is now being said that just as the survival of many developing countries depends upon food, the survival of the industrial world depends upon energy, and hence the food crisis and the energy crisis should be seen as qualitatively similar.

Nothing could be more misleading. The survival of the poor nations is at the margin of existence, that of the rich nations at steadily rising levels of material affluence. Any approach to interdependence that equates these two conditions actually implies a goal of helping the rich not only to become richer, but to appropriate a continuously larger share of total world resources for the benefit of a declining percentage of the world's population.

This kind of confused thinking was responsible for the false optimism of the 1960s, which claimed to see an inherent complementarity between the technological revolution of the industrial nations and the social revolution of the developing world. The former represented the ability to fulfill the aspirations reflected by the latter. Such thinking made it easy to assume that transfers of capital and technology, through the mechanism of international cooperation, would bring about a neat matching of ability and need, and in due time all nations could reach the economic millennium.

What was overlooked was that the very mechanism of international economic relations had been partly, if not wholly, responsible for the underdevelopment which was generating the social revolution; that capital and technology, the vehicles of mutuality, had acted as agents of exploitation and the prevailing international inequality; and that, therefore, all attempts to export the technological revolution would lead to greater subjugation of the weaker group, and thus subvert, rather than assist, their social revolution. Infatuation for a dubious mutuality led well-intentioned people of the industrialized world to overlook the most significant aspect of the social revolution—namely, that it was basically a quest for justice.

Human Need the Basic Criterion. More recently, an awareness of the limits to technology has led to a clearer realization of its exploitative character over nature and society and its inherently acquisitive attributes on behalf of the strong and affluent. More and more individuals are coming to understand that if human need is to condition interdependence, it is necessary to use radically different criteria for the allocation of global resources. Priority should be given to the provision of a desirable minimum to all humankind. Eradication of poverty and injustice would then become the first charge on world resources, with international specialization and trade the means for attaining this objective.

But even changing the patterns of international trade will not suffice to reach true global justice. Because the world presently has insufficient resources to combine that goal with an ever-rising affluence for the already prosperous, justice obviously also implies that the "haves" voluntarily accept some kind of a maximum on the use of resources—food, energy, raw materials, and the other bounties of nature. That would, in effect, mean halting the triumphal march of consumerism in both rich and poor nations; reconstructing production patterns accordingly, and establishing new mechanisms to transfer the resources thus released into the development process of the nonindustrialized nations.

In other words the optimal allocation of scarce resources must be determined by global rather than national needs. And some individuals and groups are beginning to put forward certain significant proposals regarding changes in the food habits of the rich, reallocation of supplies of agricultural inputs (such as fertilizers) to developing nations in preference to their use by industrial societies, and so forth.

It is very encouraging that renowned experts and organizations of international importance now begin to see "malnutrition in the form of overnutrition in the industrial countries"[16] and to question the propriety of nonessential use of fertilizer in the United States because it is nearly equal to the amount used on farms in India.[17] They now express dissatisfaction with "the structure of the international fertilizer market" (this from no less an establishment than the World Bank),[18] deplore the fact that Americans have recently added 350 pounds per head to the annual diet, largely in the form of beef and poultry—an amount very nearly equivalent to an Indian's entire diet for a whole year,[19] and are disturbed by the fact that it takes eight pounds of corn to produce one pound of beef.[20]

Such statements represent an emerging world conscience, so vital to a responsible use of resources. Such concerns reflect a desire for justice and solidarity, and could help to begin a process for changing national and international structures so they would subscribe to true interdependence.

INTERDEPENDENCE DEMANDS STRUCTURAL CHANGE

The Global Level. The concept of an interdependence that is expressive of a global approach to the earth's resources may appear unrealistic, even utopian, in a world where short-term national self-interests determine international economic relationships. Therefore, its advocacy imposes an important educational task: First, to build a public opinion to the view that human survival and well-being depend upon a just use of the world's resources; second, to promote studies that would clarify its substance and policy implications; third, to prepare a sound case for its economic and political feasibility.

For instance, under present structures the curbing of consumerism and overuse of resources in developed countries will cause a serious economic crisis there, through unemployment and other recessionary problems. The exports of developing countries would also be adversely affected, jeopardizing their efforts for development and even survival. Indeed, in recent months the fear of recession has prompted a number of industrial countries to stimulate consumption through fiscal and monetary measures. And many developing countries are seeking new ways for export promotion.

These tendencies run counter to the direction indicated by the global perspective. But unless there is a workable alternative model which allows radical structural changes to be made without a collapse of the world economy, any proposal for a new kind of interdependence will be brushed aside as mere sentimentalism.

Similarly, it is not enough to advocate a just sharing of resources unless there is also provision for a new and effective mechanism that will actually do so under equitable international economic relations. Assume that developed nations were to agree to adjust their consumption and production patterns so that surpluses would be available to be transferred into the development process of the countries of Asia, Africa, and Latin America. How is that to be accomplished without reducing the recipients to permanent dependency? It is, therefore, vital to work out, in operational terms, the economics of sharing. This is a difficult, but not an impossible task. (There is a parallel in some studies on the economics of disarmament, which deals basically with the same question of optimal allocation of released resources.)

The National Level. But the primary arena for action toward interdependence is in structural change at the national level, in both developing and developed countries.

For example, in the context of the food crisis, the struggle for land reform, for new institutions to which the small holder has easy access, for employment-oriented policies and technology, for more equitable sharing of foodstuffs irrespective of income differentials, and so on, has to be part of a comprehensive internal process of social transformation. Involvement in such efforts would give these countries the credentials, moral authority, and political will to strive for international justice. Even more important is the fact that such efforts would help establish an internal structural framework in which an inflow of resources from outside could assist development programs instead of perpetuating inequality and domination by the strong, as it tends to do under existing conditions.

A parallel and complementary struggle is necessary in developed countries, exemplified by efforts to discipline consumption, to shift resources from animal feed to human food, to regulate the might of the multinational corporations, to refrain from use of food aid as a political weapon, to curtail the wastage of important inputs (such as fertilizers) by diverting them from nonessential uses to farms in developing countries, and so on.

International economic structures are a projection of domestic structures and the priorities of the traditionally dominant nations. Therefore, without slackening efforts through the United Nations, its agencies, and other international forums, the effective evolution of a new world economic order requires changes at national levels.

Technical vs. Structural Remedies. For example, the implementation of the proposals that emerged from the 1974 World Food Conference can be helpful in relieving the food crisis. But, by and large, these tended to be technical and programmatic rather than structural.

It is true that international organizations lack the political machinery and power to initiate structural change in national economies and, therefore, in the global one. However, the failure to highlight the importance and primacy of a radical change in economic, institutional, and socio-political conditions, which have been the main constraints on agricultural development, reduces the proposals to innocuous palliatives. Increased food aid, loans on relatively soft terms, provision of fertilizers, and so on, are familiar solutions which have generally increased the dependency of the weak and strengthened the forces of domination, within these nations as well as for their international accomplices. The director general of the Food and Agricultural Organization has stressed the importance of getting "rid of antiquated and often oppressive agricultural structures,"[21] but there is not much evidence of such measures in the final recommendations. Even short-term remedies must be an essential part of the long-term structural solution.

If the global approach is to be actualized in dealing with the food crisis, it is necessary to move beyond the recommendations of the World Conference.

Such observations may seem naive in view of the present politico-economic climate in some industrial nations, particularly the United States. Their problems of inflation and unemployment have acquired serious dimensions; consequently, instead of a globally oriented shift in economic policies, there is a movement into insularity. Consumption is being stimulated to maintain levels of production and employment. Restraints have been placed on exports of certain commodities, such as soya beans, corn, and fertilizers, under pressure from domestic producers hit by inflation.

Certain political setbacks, such as in Southeast Asia, have heightened an isolationist mood in the United States, the most important controller of food surpluses. Preoccupation with its economic and political problems seems to have pushed the world food crisis into the background. There is a feeling, perhaps not quite justified, that the developed nations' "sudden interest" in a global approach to the distribution of world resources was prompted by the energy crisis, and that the food and population problems were marginal in their considerations.

Certainly, at the moment, it appears doubtful whether even some of the World Food Conference's recommendations will be implemented. Since initiatives here lie with nations with ability rather than nations with need, this does not look promising for a resolution of the food crisis. Against this backdrop, in the developed world perhaps it would be more sensible to talk about food aid and immediate relief operations, rather than about fundamental changes in economic structures and power relationships.

I feel, however, that the discouraging international climate makes the need for structural changes within developing countries even more urgent. They cannot continue to rely on external help. Their real remedy is self-reliant development through a total mobilization of national resources and energies. As such structures and mechanisms are established, whatever assistance comes from the world community could be more effectively used than it presently is, without imposing the priorities and patterns of donor nations in the process. Thus, in a fundamental way the challenge of interdependence is a challenge to strengthen self-reliant development, paradoxical though that may seem.

The ramifications of the call for global interdependence and prerequisite structural change are endless. The space here permits suggesting only two areas that are sometimes overlooked —certain aspects of population planning and the question of disarmament.

Population Planning. Two aspects of the population problem have an important bearing on interdependence. The first is the cooperation of all nations in facing it. It is now generally accepted that the success of population planning depends as much on reduction of birth rates in developing countries as a reduction of consumption levels in the developed. This represents a mutuality of responsibility and conforms to a global approach to the question.

A similar interdependence must be recognized between different parts of the developing world. Latin America and Africa do not have an unfavorable people/land ratio. Quite often their spokespeople say that they do not have a population problem. That cannot be accepted. The inability to assure a desirable minimum represents a serious population problem, irrespective of unharnessed potentialities. More important, however, is that countries in Latin America and Africa, even if they do not think that high birth rates are a long-run burden, must agree to their reduction as a solution of the global disequilibrium between resources and numbers. This is only just if rich nations are being asked to reduce per capita use of world resources as a part of world population policy. After all, there is no national economic compulsion for affluent nations to curtail their consumption. And yet, we from developing countries insist upon it in the light of total human needs, of solidarity and justice. So it becomes incumbent upon developing countries to adopt the same perspective in shaping their economic behavior.

A second interface between the population crisis and interdependence has to do with the choice between policies which promote rapid economic growth and those which promote justice, national and international. For some years a popular demographic notion assumed that a per capita income of $200 represents the level at which the material standard of living starts to curb the birth rate. Consequently, great stress has been laid on rapid economic growth in order to reach this self-regulating level of population. But it will take some developing countries, especially those most in need of population planning, two or more generations to reach even this modest income level (which rises if adjusted to recent inflation). And their problems demand immediate attention.

Happily, policies of social justice are now being recognized as an essential prerequisite for success in family planning. Because of this and because of the desperate need for action that can show some rapid effects, international cooperation to correct the population/resource disbalance must rely more on the promotion of justice within and between nations than on the promotion of growth in isolation. There is ample evidence that growth without justice is counterdevelopment and, therefore, detrimental in the long run to the success of food and population policies.

Peace and Disarmament. One much neglected area of development discussion is the question of world peace and disarmament.

It is not inappropriate to draw attention to this in the context of the food crisis, especially because there are frequent condemnations of India's nuclear experiments precisely in relation to its food problem. A country beleagured by hunger and malnutrition is deemed to be wrong in diverting scarce resources into a nuclear program. Purely in a polemical spirit one could refute many of these criticisms. But polemics serve no constructive purpose, certainly not when we are concerned with interdependence. Therefore, one should go beyond partisan stances and consider the basic human issue.

The whole process of armament, in all countries, represents a gross misuse of the world's resources. True interdependence is impeded by any armaments race, whether between the superpowers or between less powerful nations, such as India and Pakistan. Resources are not being used in response to societal needs, but according to the dictates of power and realpolitik. Spending money and using resources for armaments leaves that much less for the war against poverty and injustices. The accumulated overkill capacity in the world, especially that at the disposal of the superpowers, has crossed the limits of absurdity, and yet this inhuman competition continues.

Additionally, in many situations, militarism has become the strongest opponent of structural change. Developing countries are allocating the largest proportion of their budgets to armaments. Industrial countries encourage such trends because it is good for their business and also increases their hold in areas of influence. Many aspects of the domination-dependence relationship, which is now recognized as one of the major causes of underdevelopment, can be directly linked to military relationships and defense-oriented production and trade. The technological direction taken by the armaments industry imposes highly advanced, capital-using technology on the organized sector of the economy and is likely to stifle the development of appropriate technology, which is so important to eventual self-reliance.

Obviously, a global perspective on the use of the earth's resources calls for a strong movement toward disarmament and peace.

From the Economics of Greed to the Economics of Community. In conclusion, the global approach brings a basic challenge to prevailing structures, which means, in effect, to the values and social norms underlying economic systems and socio-political organizations. Justice and solidarity require a responsible use of society's resources in the corporate interest, in other words, a movement toward a communitarian economic order.

That calls for fundamental changes—from private ownership to community ownership, from production for profit to production to satisfy global needs, from a narrow concept of incentives which favor the more dominant groups to those that promote people's participation, from a blind pursuit of material prosperity to a quest for quality of life, and so on. These norms can scarcely be fitted into existing economic patterns and the exclusivism that tends to mark political sovereignty and nationalism. But are such expectations too idealistic for the workaday realities of our world?

The great Indian revolutionary, Mahatma Gandhi, who was nothing if not a hard-headed realist, proposed an attitude of trusteeship toward resources. He said that "everything belonged to God and was from God. Therefore, it was for His people as a whole, not for a particular individual. When an individual had more than his proportional portion he became a trustee of the portion for God's people."[22] He saw property as not a personal possession to be used for satisfying the owner's unbridled wants. His emphasis was not on ownership but on stewardship.

One could enlarge this idea to suggest that the wealth of each nation exists for the well-being of the whole human community. The basic criterion for apportioning resources then becomes distributive justice on a world scale. As Gandhi said: "There is enough for everyone's need, but not for everyone's greed."[23]

Some perceptive analysts of Gandhian ideas have said that Gandhi lived ahead of his time, that he was essentially a man of the future. Our preoccupation with international interdependence, sparked off no doubt by experiencing the scarcity of essential resources, is really a concern about the future survival of humankind. If Gandhian ideas have relevance for the future, it might be well for the world—certainly for India—to take a more serious look at them. In the shadow of the food crisis we need values and structures that can change the economics of greed into the economics of community, of the "people as a whole."

NOTES

1. In 1974, "even while the world had added nearly 70 million people since the last harvest, world grain production dropped by 5 percent from 1973." This was only the second time since 1962 that such a fall occurred. The fall in production in North America and the Soviet Union was mainly due to unfavorable weather, but in Asia, in addition to climatic factors, the insufficient availability of fertilizers and energy contributed to the decline. According to an estimate by the U.S. Department of Agriculture, the Indian wheat crop fell by one million tons "solely as a result of lack of fuel for operating irrigation pumps." Food reserves were "the lowest since the year immediately following World War II," barely enough for a month (Quotes are from Lester R. Brown and Erik P. Eckholm, "Beyond the World Food Conference," *The U.S. and World Development: Agenda for Action, 1975,* James W. Howe and the staff of the Overseas Development Council [New York: Praeger Publishers, May 1975]).

Elsewhere Lester Brown also gives these figures: In 1972 rice cost $9.40 per 100 lbs., while in mid-1973 the same amount cost $19. Similarly, in 1972 wheat cost $1.75 a bushel and jumped to $3.80 a bushel by mid-1973. Soyabeans cost $3.38 a bushel in 1972, as compared with $6.20 by mid-summer 1973 (*In the Human Interest* [New York, W.W. Norton & Co., 1974]).

2. Robert McNamara describes poverty in Asia, Africa, and Latin America this way: "One-third to one-half of the two billion human beings in these countries suffer from hunger and malnutrition. About 20 percent of their children die before their fifth birthdays, and millions of those who do not die lead impeded lives because their brains have been damaged, their bodies stunted, and their vitality sapped by nutritional deficiencies. The life expectancy of the average person is twenty years less than in the affluent world. They are denied 30 percent of the lives those in developed nations enjoy" (Address to the Board of Governors, World Bank Annual Meeting, in Nairobi, September 1973).

3. "By the 1950s the dominant agricultural problem for the U.S., Canada, Australia, and some European countries had become a problem of 'surplus food disposal.'. . . The U.S. Government paid subsidies to farmers to withhold land from production, gave away, or transferred on concessional terms, very large quantities of foodstuffs and feedstocks, and still paid as much as a million dollars a day to store grains and other food products. . . . If the nightmare of some is famine, then the nightmare of others is glut" (Thomas W. Wilson, Jr., *World Food, the Political Dimension* [Washington, D.C.: Aspen Institute for Humanistic Studies, 1974] pp. 15, 20).

4. "When the nineteenth century opened, only 4 million were being added to the world's population each year. A century later that figure was still only 10 million. By 1950, it had risen to 22 million; today it is about 75 million" (Lincoln Gordon, "Population Trends and Prospects," in *World Population and a Global Emergency,* by Thomas W. Wilson Jr. [Washington, D.C.: Aspen Institute for Humanistic Studies], Appendix A, p. 33). "Approximately half of the total population of the developing world today is under 16 years of age" (ibid., p. 17).

5. Geoffrey Barraclough, "The Great World Crisis I," *The New York Review,* January 23, 1975, p. 25.

6. *World Economic Survey 1973,* press release ECOSOC/646, p. 3.

7. "Despite declaratory intent, neither governments nor international agencies appear to have made serious efforts to conserve supplies by systematically minimizing losses. And research on requirements and techniques for food conservation has received until now only low priority" (Wilson, *World Food,* p. 34).

8. Estimate referred to at the World Food Conference, 1974.

9. Brown and Eckholm, "Beyond the World Food Conference."

10. *The Overseas Hindustan Times,* April 24, 1975, p. 11.

11. Norman Borlaug, in an address to the World Food and Population Commit-

tee, as quoted by Dougal N. Ross, *Food and Population* (Ottawa: The Conference Board, 1975), p. 16.

12. In a statement to the 57th Session of the U.N. Economic and Social Council, Geneva, July 3, 1974. Press Release SG/SM/255/ECOSOC/647.

13. Barraclough, "The Great World Crisis I," p. 26.

14. W. Arthur Lewis, *Aspects of Tropical Trade* (Stockholm: Almquist & Wiksell, 1969), p. 7.

15. Barraclough, "The Great World Crisis I," p. 24. Barraclough also quotes the World Bank on Mali: "Production of food for domestic consumption . . . has declined steadily . . . from 60,000 tons handled by official marketing channels in 1967 to a current 15,000 tons, but export crops—notably peanuts—have increased during the same period despite the ravages of the recent drought."

Another description of the same phenomenon: "The tragedy of the Sahel does not result merely from drought . . . (but) overexploitation and destruction of the soil by too many animals and men using inappropriate technologies and crops. Both technologies and crops were imposed on them by governments and by national and international trading firms concerned with their own growth and profit" (Pascal de Pury, as reported in *CCPD Network Letter* 1, June 1974, World Council of Churches, Geneva).

16. Quoted in Barraclough, "The Great World Crisis I," as a statement of the Norwegian delegation.

17. Brown and Eckholm, "Beyond the World Food Conference."

18. Quoted in Barraclough, "The Great World Crisis I."

19. Barbara Ward, "The Fat Years and the Lean Years," *The Economist*, November 2, 1974.

20. Ross, *Food and Population*.

21. "The World Food and Energy Crisis," an address by Addeke Boerma, Rome, Food and Agricultural Organization, p. 8.

22. J. S. Mathur and A. S. Mathur, *Economic Thought of Mahatma Gandhi.*

23. Ibid.

19

Programs Undertaken by
Some Religious Bodies

*extracts from a survey by Peter Henriot
and Frank Harris*

Professor Parmar had ended his presentation with a call for "values and structures that can change the economics of greed into the economics of community." I repeat that his paper drew heavily from positions held by the leadership and staff of the World Council of Churches, and that he himself had played a major role in the formation of these positions during the past decade. Catholic social teaching on global justice and the development of peoples closely parallels, and is often identical with, that of the World Council. So a large majority of the Christian churches—Orthodox, Protestant, Catholic—have reached basic consensus on changes needed in economic and political structures, national and worldwide.

Professor Parmar, it must be noted, appealed directly to "the great Indian revolutionary, Mahatma Gandhi," as a moral authority. For Gandhi, "Everything belonged to God and was from God." The so-called owner is a trustee; the stress is on stewardship, not selfish property holding. "As Gandhi said: 'There is enough for everyone's need, but not for everyone's greed.'"

But are religious bodies promoting this trusteeship and change of structures which Professor Parmar proclaimed? Do they show concrete concern for human needs, in current emergencies and for the long term? Are faith communities trying to "convert" adherents from mere profit hunting to a ministry of caring and serving? From the economics of greed to the economics of community—to embrace even the new worldwide "we" of all human communities?

In planning our Bellagio meeting, we saw the need of a survey of religious responses to the food crisis. At our request this was prepared by Peter Henriot and Frank Harris, staff members of the Center of Concern, Washington, D.C. This new research center wants to become more ecumenical and interreligious. At this stage, however, its network of related bodies is dominantly Christian. Consequently, this survey drew almost exclusively from programs related to Christian churches, with some data from Jewish initiatives, and contained very little from the other three world faith communities.

Comparable reviews of Hindu, Buddhist, and Muslim programs are much needed, particularly since most of these have begun reaching out beyond local areas only in recent years, their development having been held back by western domination, among other factors. Further, almost all Christian and Jewish organizations form stable associations at national and global levels; Hindu, Buddhist, and Muslim bodies have but recently begun comparable federation and fellowships. Consequently, the first two bodies are more poised, geared up for action, than are the three last named. (Wilfred Cantwell Smith made this point several times during our Bellagio meeting. Below I will report that in later exchanges he continues to stress this difference between the more "westernized" bodies, Jewish and Christian, as compared with Hindu, Buddhist, and Muslim bodies, which are dominant in Asia and in much of Africa.)

The survey of existing religious response by Henriot and Harris was circulated among the participants. It was eighty-nine pages in length; I can reproduce only brief extracts, slightly edited; the numerous examples, almost wholly Christian and Jewish, and lengthy statistics of the original have had to be left out. What I have emphasized are three more general parts of the original paper: factors that motivate religious response, types of programs, and evaluation.

FACTORS THAT MOTIVATE RELIGIOUS RESPONSE

The character and extent of response to the challenge of world hunger by leaders, organizations, and members of faith communities seem determined, in general, by at least four factors: theological worldview, organization, geography, and history.

Theological Worldview. The particular theological stance toward human development appears to be the single most critical factor influencing the response of faith communities. No set of religious teaching is totally unrelated to the material status —economic, social, political, cultural—of men and women in this world. Nor is any group of religiously motivated persons totally callous or unconcerned about the sufferings of their brothers and sisters. Yet the nature of the response will vary considerably from group to group depending upon views of each on the nature of human persons, the demands of human solidarity, the relationship of this life (world) to other lives (worlds), the meaning of suffering and/or happiness, the relationship between religion and politics, and so forth.

Organization. Religious bodies differ considerably in terms of their patterns of organization. Some are elaborately structured, with centralized and definite leadership extending to national and transnational levels. Others are more loosely structured and more locally controlled; with these groups it is difficult to point to any organizational "center" beyond the local or provincial area. Still others are religious "bodies" only in a very extended sense, since that which links them together is their common theological worldview and not an organizational network. Accordingly, response to social issues, such as the food crisis, will be more organized the more structured the religious body is, and more occasional and personal the less organized that body is.

Geography. The factor of geography influences response in two ways. First, a religious body that has a strong presence in a particular region—indigenously or because of missionary activity—is influenced by the character of the food problem within that region. Second, religious bodies that are active in the industrialized developed nations with significant food reserves and technical capability are more drawn to respond in terms of promotion, of sharing, and the like.

History. This factor is related to the previous three; it simply designates the influence exerted at the present time by longstanding historical commitments by religious bodies. Some groups have been actively involved in relief and development work for many years; others are only recently responding. The previous historical response influences present response in both positive and negative ways.

TYPES OF PROGRAMS

For an overview of activities by religious bodies, it is possible to distinguish four types of response. These are not, of course, completely discrete categories, but interrelated emphases. The four program areas are: humanitarian relief, agricultural development, political action, and education about the problem.

Humanitarian Relief. In many circles today—religious as well as secular—it is unfashionable to speak of *relief* assistance. Charges of "too paternalistic," "too temporary," "too subject to abuse," are made to question, discredit, or at least down play the role of humanitarian gifts to those in great need. Yet the fact remains that relief assistance continues to account for a highly significant portion of the response being made to the food crisis by religious bodies around the world. And at a time when millions of people are in dire need of immediate food in order to survive, programs of relief assistance are a necessary and fitting response.

Two categories of relief assistance can be distinguished: emergency disaster aid, and prolonged aid. Within the first category would fall special programs mounted after natural or manmade disaster—earthquakes, hurricanes, wars, civil strife, and the like. Religious bodies tend to respond to these disasters with generous contributions for humanitarian assistance. Special appeals for funds are made so that foodstuffs may be purchased and shipped to the afflicted areas. The ordinary channels of presence in the afflicted areas (regular institutional operations, established "missions," or specialized teams) are used for dispensing the assistance. Such aid is frequently linked, in a variety of ways, to official governmental responses, at least in the case of western religious bodies, especially those from North America.

Within the category of prolonged aid fall the numerous relief programs operated by religious bodies on a continuing basis in chronically destitute areas. One easily identified example is the "soup kitchen" some groups run in poor sections of large cities (in both developed and less developed countries). Rather than being a response to some "emergency" situation, such programs of prolonged aid go on continuously because the need is continuous. Marginal people—unemployed masses in urban areas, poor farmers following crop failure, many small children and elderly persons—are always in need of assistance. Many faith communities, both indigenous and missionary, have run relief programs for these people for years.

Recent global food conditions have prompted greater voluntary response by many religious groups in providing relief assistance. But some significant difficulties also have arisen: for example, the rising price of foodstuffs has often meant that increased expenditure (calling for increased fund-raising efforts) has not purchased more food. Other difficulties arise when relief programs become entwined with or dependent upon governmental policies, either those of governments assisting in providing aid or those of governments exercising control in areas where relief takes place.

It is noteworthy that, despite the economic difficulties in the industrialized world, appeals for money to help bring relief to the less developed countries continue to be heard. Members of these groups in the developed nations have not yet made a notable cutback in their generosity. It is not yet clear how long this might continue, given the economic problems in these countries and the repeated calls for contributions. It must be noted, however, that the great bulk of food aid to other countries is financed by governments of industrialized nations; voluntary contributions, for religious and humanitarian motives, account for only a small fraction of the total in recent years.

Agricultural Development. "Give a man a fish and you will feed him; teach him how to fish and he will feed himself." This old adage underlies the increasing emphasis many religious bodies are giving to projects for agricultural development. Such groups recognize the built-in limits of humanitarian relief. Assistance can, at best, bring only temporary alleviation of human misery, not long-term solutions, because such programs treat symptoms, not causes. Moreover, they can establish undesirable patterns of dependence by recipients upon donors. The promotion of self-reliance through true development becomes, therefore, a critical priority for religious bodies concerned with alleviating world hunger.

In the less developed countries about 60 percent of the population live in rural communities and spend the major portion of their time tilling the soil. Yet recent development models have tended to bypass the agricultural sector, concentrating on the industrial sector. Professor Parmar's paper went into this at length. This emphasis has had increasingly serious consequences for feeding people. Hence, the 1974 World Food Conference in its "Declaration on the Eradication of Hunger," urged that prime importance be given to "effective measures of socio-economic transformation by agrarian, tax, credit and investment policy reform and by the reorganization of rural structures . . . such as the reform of the conditions of ownership (land reform), the mobilization of the full potential of human resources, both male and female." If implemented, this part of the Declaration means significant attention should be paid to programs that promote rural development in terms of land reform, credit unions, technical training, services for health and adult literacy, and provision of adequate fertilizer, seed, and water.

Therefore, many faith communities are giving greater importance to the agricultural sector. For several decades some western missionaries have been involved with a variety of development programs: training in farming techniques and leadership skills, formation of cooperatives and credit unions; assistance for meeting fertilizer, water, and seed needs; organization of peasant leagues, etc.

But interesting problems face religious bodies which become involved in promoting agricultural development. The first relates to the political implications of development. Advocating land reform, building up institutions and social infrastructures, encouraging peasant farmer movements, and similar activities are not politically neutral. In some areas, religious groups have found themselves in conflict with official government policies.

A second question arises from the kind of modernization represented by the techniques of the Green Revolution. Although its supporters contend that the Green Revolution's high-yield grains, intensive fertilization, and sophisticated machinery are not per se out of reach for small holders, this technology has, in fact, been most effective on a scale requiring large areas of land and heavy capital investment. Many religious groups, particularly those oriented toward peasant farmers, have protested development based on such intensive technology, which consumes, of course, much energy. A third problem is avoidance of domination by nonindigenous religious leadership. Religious agencies that promote credit unions, for example, face the challenge of rapid preparation of local leadership.

Political Action. Faith communities, no matter how well motivated or organized to respond to the food crisis, cannot become the principal actors in the fields of humanitarian relief and agricultural development. Government response remains the most influential element in terms of authority, programs, finances, and organization. For this reason, religious bodies in many areas have increasingly been involved in political action, by urging governments to respond with more relief and development assistance. Many religious groups are devoting personnel and money to such advocacy and lobbying; several organizations have been established explicitly for this task.

But there is another, more profound dimension to the political pressure exercised upon governments by some faith communities. Many people now recognize the food crisis as symptomatic of a more substantial crisis in the international order. The Third World has issued a fundamental challenge to the structure of relationships between the developed and the less developed countries in its call for a New International Economic Order, which addresses basic issues as trade patterns, commodity prices, investments, and control over resources and decision-making processes. It calls, in short, for fundamental changes in the planetary system of economic power which was established during the period of western colonialism. (This period, dating from about A.D. 1500, corresponds with the outsurge of Christian missionaries from the West.)

Situating the food crisis within this wider context of economic and political relations between rich countries and poor countries, many religious groups have broadened their lobbying efforts beyond food aid or development assistance. Leaders of faith communities are appealing to governments to deal with trade issues, the price of commodities other than food, and domestic agricultural and economic policies. And although such groups generally support increased bilateral and multinational foreign aid expenditures, many are also criticizing these operations—their standards, procedures, and control by a few rich nations.

The 1974 World Food Conference, sponsored by the U.N. Food and Agriculture Organization, served as a focal point for many religious bodies in bringing political pressures upon governments. Prior to the Conference, faith communities in several developed countries urged their nations' representatives to take generous and cooperative stands in endorsing both short-term and long-term programs to meet the food crisis. During the Conference itself, many religious groups were represented among the nongovernmental organizations which took part in the proceedings. Within the FAO, moreover, several religious bodies enjoy permanent consultative status; almost all, however, are Christian.

One paramount problem is associated with the increasing political character of religious response to the food crisis. While there may be little controversy connected with direct humanitarian assistance (although even here some controversy does arise), political activity almost always stirs up controversy. Some members of faith communities object that their religious leaders or organizations have no business trying to tell the government what to do; others do not object to some political emphasis as long as it stays very general and abstract; still others insist that political pressure must become very specific, even to the point of evaluating particular political candidates on the basis of their stance toward the food crisis. Since it is not possible to please everyone, controversy seems inevitable once political action of some sort is undertaken.

During the 1974 Food Conference, two world leaders of the Christian churches, Pope Paul VI and the Reverend Philip Potter, general secretary of the World Council of Churches, spoke to the delegates. The major thrust of both was that response to the food crisis had to move toward structural reform at national and international levels. Speaking as religious leaders, they took seriously the political dimensions of the food crisis and the need to address the issue in a political fashion. Pope Paul questioned the operation of the free market system in allocating food in a hungry world, and Reverend Potter endorsed the call for a New International Economic Order.

In the United States there have been widespread efforts by Protestant, Roman Catholic, and Jewish groups to urge appropriate government response to the global hunger problem. In November 1974, an ecumenical coalition of religious leaders, headed by Fr. Theodore Hesburgh, president of the University of Notre Dame and chairman of the Overseas Development Council, called for the United States to commit reserved grain to famine-stricken areas. In the spring of 1975, the Interreligious Task Force on U.S. Food Policy was set up in Washington to help faith communities bear witness to the issue of responsible government food policy. A specific "Christian lobby" for hunger and poverty issues, Bread for the World, began in 1974 under the leadership of the Reverend Eugene Carson Blake, former general secretary of the World Council of Churches. It has grown to over 15,000 members whose local groups pressure the government for programs to meet both domestic and global food concerns.

The World Conference on Religion and Peace is composed of leaders from all the major faith communities; in August 1974, during its second international meeting in Louvain, Belgium, it issued a strong statement on the food crisis and endorsed the New International Economic Order. It has also linked the food crisis to the call for disarmament.

Education. During the past decade there has been a very significant shift in the language used to arouse awareness of and response to the food crisis among religious bodies. The reason is twofold: growing recognition that hunger is neither an accident nor due only to natural causes—it results rather from the structures of society; and acceptance that today there exists a "right to eat," in the words of Pope Paul VI to the 1974 Food Conference. In its "Declaration on the Eradication of Hunger and Malnutrition," this Conference stated: "Every man, woman and child has the inalienable right to freedom from hunger and malnutrition in order to develop fully and maintain their physical and mental faculties." These two factors, of structure and right, have given rise to the use of "justice" language when speaking of religious obligations to respond to hunger, in addition to traditional "charity" language.

This shift in language has important implications for educational efforts by faith communities. For example, traditional publicity programs and campaigns for relief funds underlined the suffering of the victims of famine. Pictures of hungry children, ribs exposed and bellies distended, were used to motivate generosity. The themes of solidarity with brothers and sisters, the universal family of God, stewardship of the earth's goods, were also emphasized. The appeal was to charity, to love of neighbor, and was intended to impel the committed religious person to respond by sharing with the needy, giving alms, alleviating hardship.

More recently, however, education programs of many religious groups have emphasized not only the crisis but also the economic, political, and social structures underlying it. Contrasts are made, for example, between the amount of grain consumed directly by persons in poor countries and that consumed indirectly through heavy meat diets by persons in rich countries. In addition, analysis is made of the positions taken by governments on emergency grain reserves, agricultural development programs, and the like. The appeal to action—either through short-term relief assistance or through long-term economic changes—is made in terms of justice. Injustice is described, often quite specifically, in terms of carryover from colonial practices, unfair bargaining positions of multinational business, and different consumption and waste patterns.

New educational methods have been developed to encourage a "justice" response from members of faith communities. Printed matter and films, entire issues of magazines and newspaper, radio and TV presentations, curriculum content, sermon guidelines are used. One popular educational tool—which also has significant political usage—is a formal "statement" from prominent religious leaders, organizations, or conferences. Seminars, workshops, and lectures have also aimed to inform and motivate local groups, who then approach their local media and political leaders.

Such educational efforts have become so widespread that religious bodies begin to wonder how to continue to educate their membership without alienating them through oversaturation. As with any topic that receives widespread publicity, the world food crisis may be in danger of becoming passé in many developed countries because there have been so many vivid descriptions and heart-rending appeals. Efforts which seem to have been particularly effective in surmounting this overdose have been those which make very explicit religious ties to the topic (for example, encouraging the traditional practice of fasting), offer concrete opportunities for response (for example, proposing specific projects for financial support), and link global food problems to domestic issues (for example, rising food prices).

A major effort at "development education" has been undertaken by the World Council of Churches through its Commission on the Churches' Participation in Development. According to its rationale of development education, it is not enough to ask what people in the less developed countries can do to take a role in their own development; one must also ask what people in the developed countries can do to bring about structural changes more in keeping with global justice. The Pontifical Commission Justice and Peace, Vatican City, carries out a comparable program within the Catholic church, through dioceses and religious orders. Orthodox, Protestant, and Catholic churches cooperate in many nations, and globally through the SODEPAX Committee set up for this purpose in Geneva and the Vatican.

Religious communities in the United States have issued major statements on the food crisis as instruments of education as well as political pressure. The Synagogue Council of America, in January 1975, called upon the Jewish community to re-emphasize its religious, legal, and historical traditions in order to mobilize support for public policy decisions on food problems. Particular reference was made to simplifying religious celebrations and promoting less consumption and waste. Similar calls were made by the National Council of Churches in the "Graymoor Covenant" of December 1974, and by the National Conference of Catholic Bishops in a "Pastoral Plan of Action" issued in November 1974. These statements helped educate the faith communities to the need for sharing immediately with the hungry, for effecting long-range changes for more justice, and for adopting simpler life styles.

The Protestant and Catholic churches of Canada together promote an annual educational effort entitled "Ten Days for World Development." The Christian Conference of Asia, in May 1975, adopted as one of its three major priorities a "Programme to Combat Hunger," aimed at educating its member churches to the structural aspects of hunger; this includes cooperation with the older faith communities of Asia.

EVALUATION

In planning future responses to the world food crisis, religious bodies should take two sets of factors into consideration: long-term trends that appear to be developing at this time, and the evaluation of past responses and programs in terms of future trends.

Five trends are now discernible. The first is that world hunger promises to get worse before it gets better. Population increases, inflated prices for fuel and fertilizer, erratic climate conditions, the failure of the developed nations' political will to respond, and the lack of purchasing power among the unemployed poor in developing countries are some reasons for this pessimistic forecast. Accompanying this grim picture is a second trend: indications that the intense interest the food crisis has generated in the developed countries may already have begun to "peak." The "fad" character of response is probably already declining and what will remain of solid commitment for long-term action and sacrifice remains to be seen.

A third trend is that the moral principles for determining food allocation in times of scarcity are being questioned. Debates over "triage" and "lifeboat ethics" will be more intense. (These proposals take for granted that the planet cannot carry its mounting quantity of humans; many must die, willy-nilly; by the selective process of "triage" only those nations and groups should be helped which give promise of providing for their own needs within reasonable time; let the others slip off this life raft Earth into the hungry sea of death.) Religious response to this profound moral issue will be demanded as the crisis mounts. A fourth trend is that the food crisis is becoming increasingly political. Humanitarian relief can become a political weapon, and agricultural development—because of its tie to overall development questions— affects the character of international economic relationships. Food policy enters into debates over the New International Economic Order.

Finally, a fifth trend is that, with increasing interdependence between rich and poor countries, the developed countries' patterns of affluence, consumption, and waste are being more and more challenged. Lifestyle questions will, therefore, have to be addressed by religious bodies.

Evaluation of the past and present response of religious bodies to the food crisis should include serious consideration of the following questions:

1. *How systematic* is the response? This question is designed primarily to get at the relationships which do or do not exist between the relief, development, political, and educational aspects of the response. The coordination of these various aspects of response is important since it is central to the effectiveness of programs. For example, an education effort that emphasizes the "disaster" character of the food crisis may promote relief assistance but do nothing to inform members of the faith community about the development side of meeting the crisis. Political pressure for government aid may or may not be linked to pressure for more effective bargaining positions for the less developed countries.

Another area a systematic approach must examine is cooperation both within and between religious bodies, especially cooperation with those groups indigenous to the area affected. (For instance, many would say that Christian missionaries from Europe and North America have made little or no systematic effort at cooperation with the Hindu, Buddhist, and Muslim communities of Asia and Africa. And what of these three faiths; what is their attitude now that they have freed themselves from western domination?)

2. *How effective* is the response? A prior question should probably be, "How does one measure the effectiveness of programs?" One approach would be to figure the number of persons actually fed by the relief programs being examined and to calculate the amount of food actually produced as a result of agricultural development assistance. A cost-benefit analysis might then be done in terms of the amount of effort and money put in by the religious body or bodies responsible.

Another, more profound approach would seek to measure how the quality of life of the people aided has been improved—not just in areas of hunger and malnutrition but in other areas of socio-economic development as well. For example, have any relationships of dependency developed that could have long-term harmful consequences? The effectiveness of political emphasis is particularly difficult to measure because the role of pressure groups is always ambiguous in the final outcome of decisions. The impact of education programs can be measured not only in terms of response to funding appeals, but also in terms of the memberships' ability to move from the facts about hunger to an analysis of why hunger exists, i.e., to a structural approach to the problem.

3. *How politically sensitive* is the response? Feeding the hungry is not a politically neutral act, so questions need to be asked in order to get at a series of politically significant issues involved in responding to the food crisis. First, what consequences are there to the fact that religious bodies in the United States, for example, distribute food under the auspices of the government's food program? Is dependence on government aid creating or paving the way for restrictions by the government on the religious agency?

Second, what are the implications of any support the religious body is giving socio-economic movements in the less developed countries, especially movements involving structural change, such as organizing peasant farmers, advocating land reform, promoting cooperatives and credit unions, and the like? These have political aspects and consequences which may be heightened if the supporting religious body is from outside the country.

Third, how radical a restructuring of society—national and international—is the faith community willing to support if this appears necessary to meet the food crisis in a lasting fashion?

4. *How religious* is the response? This question is more profound than might immediately appear since it requires evaluation of the

degree of interior commitment that motivates response. If the concern of any particular faith community for a social cause —even a cause as serious as the present world food crisis—is only peripheral to what it considers true religious spirit, then commitment can always be conditional. If, on the other hand, social concern is integral to the regular program of the faith community, more demands can be placed upon its members.

Another way of putting the question is to ask whether response to the food problem is seen as a matter of charity or a matter of justice. If the latter, what place does justice play in the character of religious response for the community? More and more this becomes the key question—and debate—within most faith communities.

20

New Styles of Life in Faith Communities

presented by Krister Stendahl

(Strategies to be pursued by religious bodies in view of the food/energy crisis was the subject of this session. Professor Parmar had concluded that political and economic structures must undergo basic changes, at national and world levels, because all the planet's peoples have become dependent upon each other. This interdependence requires a new international order. With passion and compassion, this important expert on world justice for the Christian churches had pleaded for religious commitment and moral values "that can change the economics of greed into the economics of community," because, "as Gandhi said: 'There is enough for everyone's need, but not for everyone's greed.'"

(Even the brief extracts given above from the survey by Henriot and Harris show that responses by religious bodies are indeed focusing on the changes of social structures which Professor Parmar urged. Religious groups are modifying their own educational programs and their own forms of ministry so as to promote changes in secular society, because all have "the right to eat" and the duty to help.

(The next presentation to the Colloquium spoke of change and truth still more central to the religious message. Dean Stendahl meditated about self-control and self-diminution as believing persons and as powerful societies, of simpler lifestyles that make visible our faith in the holy, especially the holiness of bread through which God continues to share life with us.

(Besides being dean of the Harvard Divinity School, a post which confers international prestige among theologians and academics just about everywhere, Krister Stendahl is also active in many church organizations. Most fitting for the interreligious character of our Bellagio meeting, he is chairman of the Program on Dialogue with People of Living Faiths and Ideologies, of the World Council of Churches, Geneva.

(Dean Stendahl spoke from scanty notes with no attempt at a well-outlined, cohesive pattern. Rather, he shared glimpses into himself, a series of vignettes strung together on the thread of his lifestyle theme. His presentation was so effective that I have reproduced it in its entirety from the taped transcript, editing only to add subject subheads and to allow for transfer from the spoken to the printed word. His first person singular is retained.)

*   *   *

My topic is responding to the challenge we are confronted with. I'm not quite sure how to define that challenge—perhaps it is the challenge of interdependence, perhaps the challenge of new styles of life in communities of faith. And perhaps it does not matter because more and more I think that is two ways of saying the same thing.

EXEMPLAR OF RELIGIOUS INTERDEPENDENCE

As Professor Parmar has already invoked the name of Mahatma Gandhi, I would like to tie that person in with our discussion of yesterday by pointing out that here was a real manifestation of religious interdependence. One of the fascinating things about Gandhi is that no religious tradition can claim him totally. He is unthinkable without his Hindu, Indian roots and Buddhist influences. He is unthinkable without the prophets of the Old Testament, as we Christians call the Jewish Scriptures. He is unthinkable without the Jesus of the Sermon on the Mount.

Here is interdependence in a beautiful way. None of us can claim him but God, yet all of us listen as if somehow he spoke out of and into our own faith.

FEAR AND GLOBAL INTERDEPENDENCE

The interdependence of our world is not a lofty idea, it is a fact. It is a fact we may not be willing to accept, but it is a fact.

If it be true that the starvation is not only a crisis phenomenon but a lasting one; if it be true that life and brain damaging malnutrition is an even vaster reality; if it be true that the arable land on earth cannot be much expanded; if it be true that the four billion inhabitants on this little speck of the universe will be eight billion in the early part of the next century and, I guess, sixteen billion not too long after that; if it be true that many, if not most, of the measures taken so far to alleviate these situations have an almost built-in tendency to make the rich richer and the poor poorer on the village, national, and international levels; if all this be true, then there is much to be afraid of.

A certain amount of fear, as Rabbi Lamm told us yesterday, can galvanize people to joint, speedy, even imaginative action. But much fear, overwhelming fear, has a paralyzing effect. Christian theology has long discussed whether people are good or bad by nature; I have never been able to resolve that argument personally, but my observation brings me to believe that human beings can be very nice and they can be very ugly. And, by and large, nothing makes them more ugly than fear, overwhelming fear.

Is the fear that is upon us of that nature? Interdependence means, as far as I can see, in our present situation, a problem of sharing and distribution in order to break the vicious circle by which the rich become richer and the poor become poorer. That vicious circle is to me the most scary of all, because in the long run, it can only lead to catastrophe. In the long, long run it leads to catastrophe for the rich after enormous catastrophe to the poor.

THE WEST MUST DECREASE

In the West we are beginning to feel the danger inherent in continuing the vicious circle. The sensation may be fleeting, sometimes ignored, but we do begin to feel it. That sense of danger presents a problem to the West—a problem that is spiritual.

Interdependence means different agendas for different peoples, because we are now so different in situation and the amount of power we hold. For example, the much delayed national liberation of Vietnam is a defeat for the United States in historical terms. What is victory for one is another's defeat.

Because I am a westerner, I look at interdependence's agenda for the West, and I speak as a westerner. The spiritual problem for the West that emerges from the demands of interdependence is the fear of giving up power. Over the next years and decades we will have to cope with this fear and learn how to handle it.

Make no mistake; this is a real problem. It is unusual for a people with huge privileges to decide by free will to shrink, to diminish their power. I am not sure it has ever happened in history. But what interdependence is clearly demanding of the West is what I call "the John the Baptist principle." In the Christian Scriptures, when John the Baptist saw the Jesus movement coming forth, he summed up his situation: "This is as it should be, that I decrease and he increase."

John the Baptist's response is a model that requires much grace in all theological and secular meanings of the word. We have become used to much power, to many comfortable things in life. Now the challenge is upon us: Resources are scarce on the global level; redistribution is necessary for the simple reason that no nation, no church, no person can ask any other group or individual to tighten their belts as long as the asker has a belt looser or better filled. Can the West find the grace to adapt John the Baptist's response to this situation?

THE ESCHATOLOGICAL ITCH TO EXPERIMENT

The challenge has started, in a playful funny way, to lead to experimentation with new lifestyles in the West. That is, in itself, an affluent phenomenon. On the level of subsistence one does not discuss lifestyles; one does not have a choice.

These new lifestyles are experiments, perhaps protests. In my western, Judeo-Christian tradition they are an expression of what I like to call the eschatological itch—that itch for the kingdom whereby somehow believers find themselves to be guinea pigs for the kingdom or feel themselves called to such ventures.

Lifestyles have much to do with reaching for, with achieving a new climate in which to cope with the situation at hand. So let us first examine some of the meteorological data behind some of these attempts to change the climate, to find more appropriate lifestyles for the West.

BREAD IS HOLY

The first idea in this context is that bread is holy. Albert Schweitzer spoke about the reverence for life; in our setting it is important to break down the bigness of that language into the little crumbs of life, thereby lifting up reverence for bread.

Speaking out of my own heritage—and for the Jewish heritage, too, if I may—attention to bread is central to our religious tradition. Fasting and feasting are the two basic religious acts circling around the bread; things as small and worn out by sheer habit as prayer at meals signal its holiness. Such a signal is capable of true renaissance, even outside properly religious circles.

Rabbi Blank has reminded us that many of our religious traditions have an awkward attitude toward material things, and toward bread. Jesus once said, "Man does not live by bread alone" (Matt. 4:14). I almost wish he had never said that or, more precisely, had never quoted the verse of Old Testament he took it from. When that line is used today it is often forgotten that it was first spoken to a well-fed, prosperous, affluent Israel that had forgotten the holiness of bread (Deut. 8:3), and that although Jesus spoke in such fashion to the devil and to himself, when he found hungry people he fed them. So both Jews and Christians should be careful about using the line out of context or as a whole truth; there is much in both traditions that teaches bread is very important and very holy.

BREAD AND LAND NEVER OWNED ABSOLUTELY

Behind the holiness of bread lies another idea which, I think, is at the heart of our matter: that bread can never be owned.

In my native Swedish, everyday things like bread are sometimes jokingly termed "the loan from God." That sort of language has become slightly worn out, slightly funny. But isn't it true to say that bread can never be a commodity? That there is a difference, a uniqueness in the *air* we breathe, in the *water* we use —both of which we have in a certain sense managed to turn into commodities—and that next comes *bread*? Bread could, should never be owned.

In the Judeo-Christian tradition, there are two chapters from the Jewish Scripture that don't get much attention today: Leviticus 25 and Deuteronomy 15. These give the legislation about the years of release, the Sabbath years, and the year of Jubilee. All of it is grounded in the sentence, "The land shall not be sold in perpetuity for it is mine." Land cannot be owned.

This Jewish legislation contained both very general and very specific attention to the periodic cancellation of all debts and the release from loans after seven years. This was one way of breaking the vicious circle of the poor getting poorer and the rich getting richer.

So the bread and the land are holy. And the farmer is, too. And that's a point where I think Norman Borlaug could help us out a great deal. As a child of the city, whenever I start to speak about the farmer, I find myself falling into all kinds of Rousseau-like romanticisms. Nothing is easier than to glorify the farmer. My religious tradition has done so very well, partly for the simple reason that almost all the beautiful parables of Jesus are agricultural.

But what does it mean to say that if bread is holy, then farmers are priests, that they really tend the temple. What does it mean in terms of legislation, in terms of remuneration? What does it mean in terms of education, dignity, and the scale of prestige? We modern people need to ponder these questions about the holiness of bread and the priesthood of the farmer.

RAPING NATURE NICELY?

Another factor in the western search for new lifestyles is the growing realization of the interdependence of nature. I'll not speak much about this, partly because it's so complicated and my time is limited. But it strikes me that the crisis of resources pulls us between the anthropocentric stance and the cosmic stance. And I'm torn between them, with their grave ramifications for lifestyles.

There are those who always argue that if we do not behave ecologically, we will have no air to breathe, no clean water, and so on. They take for granted that this is the only thing to say, that the only perspective is the human one, as if the whole world, the whole cosmos were there for us to rape—but nicely. And that's very difficult to do, I'm told.

Therefore, one might question whether their self-evident anthropocentricity, with everything centered around humans, is not one of the sources of misjudgement, one of the causes of the problem rather than a solution to it.

CONSCIOUSNESS-RAISING

It is true that in the Judeo-Christian tradition's story of the beginning of the world, human beings were told to name the .

animals, be master of all creation. But that over which they were set was God's creation, not just a big supermarket with full shelves for their use. From this perspective what are the functions of religious leaders in choosing or changing lifestyles? I would like to think that they are part of consciousness-raising.

In an earlier discussion we were told that changing the affluent's wasteful habits of eating and air-conditioning and energy use would be a negligible factor in solving the crisis of resources. I have a note here which I think we should clear up. Dr. Hannah told us that all these wonderful beef cattle the West enjoys eating are raised by just grazing the land which could not otherwise be used for grain production. But in Professor Parmar's paper we were told that 60 percent of the United States' annual harvest, 140 million tons of grain, goes to domestic animal feed.

The discrepancy in information here is stunning. And I would like to know which one is right.

The value of changes in lifestyles, however, is not limited to the question of reducing wasteful consumption.

Lifestyle choice is, in a certain sense, a protest and a symbol; it falls, therefore, in the area of education. And as education it can be seen as consciousness-raising, perhaps more precisely as setting the climate in which one can stand the reality which one has become aware of. The feeling that the wasteful habits of the West are obscene (a word often used) may strike many people as an overreaction. But it is a very basic experience, and it is an experience which is hard to live with.

I'm not going to speak here in detail about eating habits, cutting down, changing from meat, and the like. The point I am making is that in the West the way to get people thinking about these matters is to begin with those areas where the religious community has a say. Therefore, I think that the line taken by the Jewish statement at the Aspen Conference about an educational process against the lavish use of meat, lavish and wasteful overeating, in the name of religious celebrations, makes a very good point.*

CONSUMERISM OF CONFERENCES.

Another lifestyle point we should think about has to do with conferences. I'm not just speaking about what we are all aware

Editor's note: The reference is to a conference on the food crisis held by the Overseas Development Council at the Aspen Institute for Humanistic Studies, Aspen, Colo., June 1974.

of—how well we have eaten here—but a much more basic question.

The conference has become a phenomenon of our lifestyle —an unquestioned one. It took a group of our black students at Harvard to start me thinking on this. They wanted to achieve something, and I had to go over their budget for what they were going to do. And when I said, "You have no travel budget in this thing," they answered, "We have found conferences to be a very wasteful way of working. We have our contacts and we plan to do this by mail, etc. . . ." And that struck me as rather interesting.

I'm not going to deny that conferences have accomplished a lot of good. But the students are right; conferences use a lot of resources, which are always limited. And I think it is fair to say that one of the most intellectually and spiritually stimulating means of exchange the world has ever known has almost disappeared out of our experience—the old fashioned exchange called correspondence. We might think that there is something very new in our coming together physically. But history tells that careful correspondence over sustained periods of time, between persons like us present here, was part of the intellectual and spiritual and religious life for ages. And it was cheaper, both in terms of time and money, and it might even have been more productive.

There is another point to be made about the style of conferences and the lifestyle of the church. Since 1954, when I came to the United States, we have gone from the old-fashioned gathering where you met in a church and were housed with various families, to meeting on a campus (which had the advantage of enabling the exchange of deep theological thoughts while shaving in the common bathrooms), to meeting in hotels, and on to super hotels. It has all escalated, almost unnoticed, in a very short time.

The complete opposite of this is possible. Take the Taizé Community in France, where they hold meetings for up to 25,000 people and house them in tents. The brothers have refused to build buildings because they don't know how long the Lord might be with them, and they don't want to be stranded with real estate.

This is typical of the new lifestyle. It is not just a petty detail or quirk; it is a decision coming out of a consciousness and thereby continuing a consciousness. I could go through a list of all the specifics such a conscious lifestyle involves, but to save time I'd rather refer you to the report of the Aspen Conference I just mentioned. For the United States, at least, this lists ways for resisting the force of consumerism, built-in obsolescence, fertilizing of lawns, and so forth. Here I would rather summarize by saying: Set your consciousness and let your imagination work out the means in each case.

ADVERTISING

One very real problem is how does one accomplish a change of lifestyle and consciousness within a consumer economy, especially under the pressure of advertising. There is no question that advertisement, which has been a problem in the United States for some time, is now spreading far beyond our borders.

As an American, I can only express the hope that the United States, which was sold such a miserable president by high-powered advertising, would soon wake up to the absolute impossibility of continuing the advertisement-consumer economy mode and mood we are living in, and that our bad example will become a warning to other cultures.

POPULATION CONTROL

Professor Parmar's argument that global interdependence means that wherever an increase in population occurs it adds to the planetary total, and therefore population control must be worldwide, seems reasonable at first. But I am also impressed with the argument that such reasoning is too one-dimensional. Who is to decide that the proportions of cultures and nations and races should be frozen at the present level? Might it be that different parts of the world are on different timetables? Large parts of Africa are certainly not overpopulated.

We in the West must understand that our favoring of global birth control has in it certain selfish elements; we are concerned lest we be even more outnumbered than we are now. Additionally, experience tells us that, in this area as in most, new lifestyles come about not by command from outside, but as a finding of new freedom and new choice.

PRAYING—AND PUTTING THE PIECES TOGETHER

Let me just finish by saying this. I have always been fascinated by the historical fact that the early church used to pray: Let this dirty earth go to pieces. And let your kingdom come.

When the earth as they knew it did go to pieces, with the collapse of the Roman Empire, the only people who were not paralyzed, the only people who could start to put the pieces together, were the ones who had prayed that prayer. To me that strange fact says volumes about the role of a faith in the affairs of women and men.

21

Discussion: The Powerless vs. the Powerful: Faceup for Faith

The discussion period for this session centered on confrontation between the powerless and the powerful in an interdependent world: What, if any, is the role of religion in redressing this inhuman faceup? By what process can change be effected—through violence, countervailing force, peaceful means? Toward which models of human community should we be working? What spiritual and material hungers and motives will animate us?

(Eddies of words whirled around these thematic eyes—each eye prismed through the ego-I in diverse plurals, the particular "we's" of human communities; each "we" seeking to preserve its own identity of self and its power for self-realization, for human fulfillment in and through community.

(In this broad, muddy Mississippi of crisscrossing currents, the whirlpools of "we's" are carried by the river's majestic flow into the future, pulled by the gravity of interdependence and the heavy consequences of going it alone. Perhaps downstream can be found that greater "we" of a world "community of communities," laid out by Rabbi Lamm and lauded by so many yesterday.

(The structures of power, the rising wrath of the weak, and the winds of change confront us of the world faith communities with such force that our millennial "we's," the elder communities of humankind, must rouse ourselves to respond. And, if we could and would, that response might be made together, because Yahweh, our Creator God, Allah, the Great Reality is/are perhaps pulling us together *by means of* the mundane reality of human interdependence, through our awakening to human need.

(And why not? Don't we people of the Book—Jews, Muslims, Christians—believe that our one personal Creator God keeps all reality afloat in being and on the move, energizing all electrons and galaxies, attentive to every inner thought and outer act of every human? Buddhist and Hindu friends, is that not *the* Great Reality (which I as Christian call creating-God-and-created-nature), somehow bound together into the Greater One? For you, monist oneness is already and always here and everywhere; for me, there is movement through time toward the final blossoming of God's full embrace of all-there-is, all creation gladly becoming God's kingdom, already begun and still to reach fulfillment.

(I am then a monist, too, but only so as seedling thus far and never of myself alone. Perhaps my transcendent Creator God is the greatest Monist of us all, and I become monist like unto him to the degree that I embrace and become one with all creation, particularly with all humans and our many community "we's." How does it feel, dear Hindu and Buddhist friends of Bellagio, to be already and everywhere at one with All Reality?)

Back down to the themes of earth that revolved round our discussion table.

THE STRUCTURES OF DOMINANCE

The fact of domination went unquestioned. Professor Parmar's analysis of unjust systems at national and world levels was accepted as fundamentally sound. So how to change the structures of dominance became the first focus of debate.

As usual Professor Avineri led off. "May I first say how impressed I was by what Professor Parmar was telling us." The Israeli social scientist continued, "One of the major problems of the developing nations after 1945 was that when they gained independence, they modeled their political and economic arrangements on the western pattern." The new countries of Asia and Africa drew from "the political, social, and economic philosophies of the western countries from which they became liberated. . . . It didn't work.

"That may not be a great tragedy. Even if it had worked, it

would have produced a duplication of the western social economic model with its concepts of a highly atomized individualism, which is, after all, at the root of some of the problems we are dealing with."

Professor Avineri then urged attention to other development models: the Maoist, the kibbutz, the Amish, and the ideas of Libya's Colonel Qaddafi, "who is trying to evolve an authentic Islamic form of communitarian life.... As an Israeli I have a great many differences with Colonel Qaddafi and I cannot agree with all his actions. On the other hand, when I listen to him describe some of the ideas which he is trying to follow, I cannot but be impressed by his quest to create something that is not modeled on either western capitalism or Russian communism."

Fr. Hehir began to probe how the food crisis in general, and the World Food Program in particular, might lead to U.S. support for "structural change in the international system. One of the best means I have found for educating the public to the need for change is to start with the food problem; I go through the food problem to the larger problem. The food problem is a prism that people can grasp. And when they understand its reality, I think they can be brought to understand some of the larger structural problems."

Fr. Hehir echoed Professor Parmar's concern that more food aid increases dependency and that the World Food Conference proposals "tend to be technical and programmatic rather than structural." He cited the Indian economist's insistence that even short-term remedies must be an essential part of the long-term structural solution, and then went on to ask him, "Do you see the Food Conference proposals as inimicable to the long-term structural change that you advocate? Or do you see them as short-term measures that are good but not enough, and therefore should be supported as long as we also prepare to go beyond them?"

(Professor Parmar had no chance to respond immediately to Fr. Hehir's query; however it became clear that he concurred with the latter's second formulation: as short-term crisis measures the Food Conference proposals are acceptable, but they do not change structures and are therefore inadequate for solving the problem.)

Nor did the father of the technology-based Green Revolution, Dr. Borlaug, question the harsh reality of "the structures that chain and prevent change that could increase food production and distribution." But he did worry about the poorly planned but drastic land reform which can result from violence, fearing repetition of cases "where the structural change came from bloody revolution, which really broke the power of the landed aristocracy and also of the church."

And he wondered whether the results in such cases compensate the suffering. He asked about Professor Parmar's reference " 'to really destroying structures.' I am sure he means in a peaceful way because I know he is a peaceful man."

Even after drastic land reform, Dr. Borlaug sees another injustice mounting against farmers from "the industrialized sectors with their strong unions which have already battled to get better incomes for urban laborers. But much greater injustices remain at the farm roots. After these open, sometimes bloody conflicts bring about change, how can we be sure that these revolutions will then become social evolutions? How can we assure better benefits for the rural sector where we hope to see them go."

Finally, said Dr. Borlaug, "we all wring our hands about the drift from the countryside to the cities, yet we do nothing about it. In most developing nations the vast majority of the population is on the land, even at this date, but the pattern of migration to the cities clearly continues. I think this can mean that we haven't done an equitable job in distributing the benefits from the production of bread that Dean Stendahl spoke about. We talk, but we don't take action or even seem to discuss possible action. Of course, I know how it is done in the Soviet Union and the People's Republic of China—it is just not permitted; if you are born on the farm you stay there. But perhaps there are alternatives between that course and letting people drift away. On the kibbutzes, for example, how are people kept from migrating?"

Dr. Hussein Fawzi, former dean of the science faculty, University of Alexandria, and former deputy minister of education under President Nasser, moved the discussion of unjust power systems from the domestic to the international stage, starting with problems these cause for his own country. "I want to remind you that Egypt has been a victim of foul politics almost since the end of pharaonic times. . . . As soon as the Suez Canal was dug all nations had to try to possess Egypt. Even today that game is still played, not by all nations but by two superpowers. I do not intend to distribute blame. There is no doubt that both of them honestly seek peace, no doubt about that." But the game causes many problems for a country caught in the middle.

For example, Dr. Fawzi stressed the obstacles to development posed by the arms race. He compared the plight of poorer peoples to the situation of the "great nations, superpowers. These are arming, yet they can manage to retain high living standards. But for the poor countries in the Near East, what do you imagine it's like to be loaded with heavy payments for armaments? . . .

"Egypt—as a nation and as the present regime—tries against all odds to realize peace. But the hindrances on the road to peace are against all that Professor Parmar proposes [for disarmament]. We cannot stop spending for war materials before we realize peace and security for all the nations of the Near East. That is what we are really for: security and the recognition of all nations in the Near East."

On a different tack, Dr. Fawzi concurred with Professor Parmar that transnational interdependence makes population a world-wide issue. "Of course, the explosion of population is one of the hills blocking development in the poorer countries. But consumption levels in the developed countries must be reduced as well. My point is how can you do that?" He also regretted that population reduction may be impeded for "religious reasons."

Another Egyptian, Dr. Al-Nowaihi, turned to the need of religious leadership in promoting the rights of the weak against the powerful. "Professor Parmar said that we must have a change of social structure. He believes that the regenerative power for this change must come from the people. Agreed. But the people will never start the needed process. They must be stirred up, even agitated, by their religious thinkers. Why is that? Because to effect the needed structural change, we must change the people's conviction that the present scheme of things is the right one, the morally correct one, the divinely sanctioned one.

"If I may judge by my experience in Egypt and other Arab countries, it is this conviction, not the repressive power of government, that is the chief obstacle to change. And this conviction has been instilled into the people by the religious establishments in their alliance with privilege, of which I talked yesterday. That is why religious leaders must now effect the conceptual change.

"This agitation has already started in both Christianity and Islam. The agitators have been dubbed rebels, heretics, and worse. But look at what happened at the last Synod in the Vatican—the Vatican which has been the principal butt of the enemies and detractors of religion. The Catholic bishops ended up issuing emphatic documents on justice and human rights.

"A similar process has been occurring in the Arab world since the early 1950s. Religious leaders have begun to reassert the original Islamic aim of redressing economic imbalance and giving justice unto the poor. . . . But I won't use this opportunity to make propaganda on how Islam tries to effect needed justice.

"If you ask me what the prime aim of this Colloquium should be, I'd say to foster this agitation. We must do this first by convincing more religious leaders of the changes in the concept of and the role of religion. We must not forget that many religious leaders, if not most, are still unconvinced about this role.

"The other thing we must do," Dr. Al-Nowaihi concluded, "is to spread our new interpretation of religion's role among the people of our several countries. And toward this end, I think Dean Stendahl's suggestions have been a pretty good beginning. It is leaders like him who may save religion from its enemies by cutting the ground from under their feet. And by saving religion they may save humanity from the imminent threat of doom."

(As I prepare this record from a transcript of our taped discussion, I recall that Dr. Al-Nowaihi was not reading from a prepared text; I don't think he even had scribbled notes. He should not be held to the details of my rendition, only to its larger meaning. His heart, his very soul, was speaking as much as head and tongue, hand and eye. He reminded me of a great biblical prophet, yes, a Hebrew prophet.)

Professor Murty questioned some of the proposals advanced by his compatriot, Professor Parmar, because they were based on Gandhi's thought and he doubts that this still exercises "clout" in today's India. He agreed that political parties there do proclaim the ideals of the simple life, self-reliance, and the promotion of justice. Many religious leaders also propose this kind of thing and teach "trusteeship"—that the rich are the trustees of the poor, and therefore they must share with others what they have. "But this kind of thing, it seems to me, is too impractical. . . . Gandhi is almost never referred to now in any serious political debate. He is invoked, of course, with the same respect as the Buddha commands. But he is not followed by anybody."

The basic fact, Professor Murty continued, is that "India, to use the phrase of Gunnar Myrdal, is a 'soft state' and not a 'hard state.' " A number of people, he reported, now believe that the use of force is the only solution left for the Indian nation. "I do not necessarily concur, but I put this forward to show that now in India many people don't swear by Gandhi anymore." True, some frustrated politicians still talk of him; some communist leaders who follow the Chinese line do also, trying to show that there is no difference between their ideals and those of Gandhi. "The difference," for Professor Murty, "is how they achieve these ideals, and that is the crux of the problem."

(A few weeks after these points about India being "a soft state," and the belief of some "that the use of force is the only solution left for the Indian nation," Prime Minister Indira Gandhi drastically curtailed political freedom and civil rights in her country. Two years later free elections were held and Mrs. Gandhi was voted out of office.)

ATTITUDES TOWARD FOOD

The Reverend Mbiti asked the Hindus, Buddhists, and Muslims present to add their own "theological understanding toward food" to that voiced by Dean Stendahl and others of the Jewish and Christian traditions. Perhaps this could be done during the afternoon work groups, the African Christian added, together with some discussion on the avoidance of certain foods for religio-cultural motives.

Professor Askari wanted "to confess my own Muslim testimony to what Dean Stendahl said. It was a remarkable convergence of theology and political economy. . . . I felt like crying when he referred to John the Baptist's principle, the response of a contemporary of Jesus; John said, 'Let him increase and me decrease.' "

Following up Professor Parmar's concern for "the given structures of economy within each government, particularly in the developing societies," Professor Askari urged that there be set up a national food council within each country, parallel to the World Food Council. "Thereby the party leaders and generalists and religious leaders can join together, not as a governmental body but as a voluntary national organization, to fill in this gap."

Rabbi Siegman combined the questions of structure and of the holiness of food: "We all seem to share the notion of the holiness of food—that food is qualitatively and spiritually on a somewhat different level from other commodities. I found Dean Stendahl's comparison of food to air particularly provocative. If we take this reminder that air is not something we sell as a commodity and extend his comparison, would it not be possible—without necessarily altering radically all our existing structures—to lift this one aspect, food, out of our existing structures and treat it differently, just as in some countries the health services have been nationalized without necessarily altering radically all other interrelated economic structures?

"Is there not some way," the rabbi insisted, "by which we can lift up food as qualitatively different and deal with it structurally in different ways than we do today?"

Dr. Ananda brought us more good news about social teaching and practice in Buddhist societies. "Now, according to the Buddha, problem number one facing humankind is the food problem.... To him hunger was the greatest disease. The Buddha, of course, never wanted people to waste food. Therefore, he asked his followers, his disciples, his monks to take food only to the extent it would help them to maintain life. . . .

"Then coming to Professor Parmar's paper, I think it would interest him as an economist to find in Buddhist teaching certain key ideas, such as social justice, self-reliance, equal distribution of food, structural change.... And these did not remain as mere theories in Buddhism; they have been put into practice in Buddhist societies.

"On the issue of structural change, the Buddha really went down to grassroot levels. He wanted structural change to start with the family, then ascend to local society, and finally to the national level."

(I can only repeat my hope that Dr. Ananda, perhaps with other Buddhist leaders and pastorally oriented monks, will write a systematic, book-length exposition of Buddhist social teaching and its practice in today's "ministry" at the national and transnational levels.)

CONCLUSION

In his final remarks, Professor Parmar did not add to his statement on structures, which he had already masterfully covered in his paper. Rather, he addressed some of the viewpoints and questions that had emerged during the discussion period.

For the method of changing structures he stated that he preferred a "people's movement—a militant, nonviolent movement; to be effective the emphasis must be not on a kind of namby-pamby nonviolence, . . . but on the word 'militant.'

"But that is a matter of personal conviction. Many would say that this method doesn't work, and I am not going to tell them this is the only way. Obviously, the world doesn't have many examples of the real success of such movements."

Turning to Dr. Fawzi's question: "The global picture on the population issue is a lack of equilibrium between numbers of people and resources. Numbers should be decreased to reduce the strain on resources. But overuse of resources should also be decreased. An example is the United States where 6 percent of the world's people consume 40 percent of the world's resources —that's overconsumption of resources.

"So the global shortage of resources is also generated by the excessive rate at which resources are being consumed in affluent societies. But the less affluent countries are also imitating this pattern of increasing the use of resources. The whole economic process in the entire world seems to be demanding and over-demanding resources." Therefore, although the reduction of population through the reduction of the birth rate is important, "reduced per-capita consumption of resources is also an important factor in balancing this issue."

Taking finally Dr. Fawzi's other questions on peace and disarmament, Professor Parmar admitted he might seem "self-righteous in charging others, especially when my own society of India has so many things wrong with it, but still I must say this. The problem is that since the big powers, the superpowers, have so much to lose, they are not prepared to confront each other directly. They will avoid that to the very end. They confront each other by proxy, and unfortunately we of the developing nations offer ourselves as willing pawns in that game. So whether the breaking of peace is in the Middle East or in the Indian subcontinent or in Vietnam, it's quite often a clash of the big powers by proxy.

"And I don't know when some awareness of this process will develop within the developing world, when we will be able to see that what is really weakening us . . . is our allowing the big powers to export their own tensions and the possibility of direct confrontation."

Dean Stendahl's windup remarks also concentrated on power, but he first asked for additional insights from the Hindu, Buddhist, and Muslim traditions on the holiness of food. He had purposely derived his own statement from the Christian and Jewish heritage, anticipating that input from other faiths would be added.

The Harvard dean then concentrated on the question of power. "When the history of western theology during the 1960s is written, I think it is reasonable to guess that the new dimension which will show up is awareness of the power factor. During the past decade this has been thrown into theological thinking and theological sentiment in Christianity. And one of the striking facts is the previous absence thereof.

"This is an interesting absence because the Jewish and Christian Scriptures are all documents written out of powerlessness, documents about a God who identifies with the weak to the point of saying, 'I am on your side to equal the power balance.' These religious documents go so far that one could say that grace, in biblical terms, means God's built-in bias in favor of the weak. This is why, for example, in the black theology of the United States, it seems that the Scripture fits perfectly and doesn't need any complicated reinterpretation. It is back home.

"But what happens with such a Scripture of powerlessness when it falls into the hands of the powerful?" For Dean Stendahl, "This is the trauma of western Christianity today.

"Now how does one with power live in this situation. The answer always is: know who speaks to whom and listen to what they are really saying. When the hungry steal a piece of bread, the 'haves' quote God's law: 'Thou shalt not steal.' But it is awfully hard for the hungry to hear the unpolluted will of God because it is too tainted by the self-interest of the 'haves.'

"Secondly, in terms of power, *my* guilt helps nobody. Perhaps it makes for good rhetoric and some spiritual purification, but guilt cannot be eaten. I am therefore inclined to think that the answer to our guilt is the empowerment of the weak and the divesting of power from those who now hold it."

(The dean did not specifically cite his John-the-Baptist principle again, but he obviously appealed to it here. The repeated applause this decrease-increase dialectic received from spokespersons of all five faiths must be remembered and handed down as a promising seed within our embryo movement.)

Dean Stendahl wound up with doubts that we should rely upon the trusteeship principle because the trustee is, by definition, powerful. "Theoretically it should work, but I am a Lutheran and I believe in sin. As a parallel, in the United States we have learned that the slogan 'separate but equal' is intellectually a very good idea for race relations and might work among angels in God's

kingdom, but doesn't work very well on earth. So it is that trusteeship without conflict and pressure from the needy doesn't work.

"I used to think, as one having a little power, that I made my
best decisions when I had slept well, prayed a little, and had not
yet been interrupted by all the pressures that came my way. I
think I have now learned that this is not so.

"I don't want to romanticize the student revolution of the 1960s.
But during some of its worst days, when I spoke with some of the
youngsters over a glass of beer, they said: 'Do you understand now
why we make you scared? No? Well, you see, unless *you* are scared,
we aren't equal.'

"And this has much to do with the question of power. It is one of
the striking new data in the theological computation."

SESSION FIVE

THE WORK GROUPS AND A
HAPPENING OF THE HEART

22

The Work Groups and Their Reports

Three work groups chewed over food facts, societal structures, and the role of religion for about five hours. The quick ingestion of the rich fare resulted in bouts of mental indigestion. These showed up in oral discussion and in the written reports, but assimilation proved quite satisfactory. Dean Stendahl was asked to draft a statement embodying our consensus, which, with the approval of an editing group, was published and distributed as a folder a month after we met, the only official document of our Colloquium. It is reproduced in the opening pages of this book.

The work group reports were presented for discussion by the entire gathering. General approval, however, was not sought; no votes were taken because the Colloquium did not conceive itself to be a formal body which makes resolutions and takes positions to be advocated in the public forum. (The Colloquium's function and program, as a continuing organization-movement, received much attention during the two years since Bellagio, as we shall see further on.) The three reports do record the agreed views of each small group; all follow a logic of notable similarity and by their convergence record the flow and thrust of the Colloquium as a whole. Each report is given in its entirety; the chairpersons and rapporteurs responsible for each final version are indicated.

REPORT OF WORK GROUP ONE

Chairman: Hussein Fawzi; rapporteur: Hasan Askari

At the outset of its deliberations the group agreed upon the unity of the political, the economic, and the religious. It was, however, seen that such a unity could be approached both from within a given religious situation and also from an interreligious perspective.

This unity—of the political, the economic, and the religious—is expressed in the organic interrelationship between the different themes which the Colloquium has been identifying and discussing with varying degrees of emphasis. Even autonomous responses presuppose communication between: (1) how we react to the commitment and program of the World Food Council; (2) how we explore, within each other's spiritual traditions, the potentiality to enforce what the World Food Council is doing; and (3) how our spiritual tradition could offer a critique to structures blocking the equitable distribution of food and energy.

It was not forgotten that the very spiritual traditions on which we so hopefully rely for regeneration of a spirit of justice and peace were interlocked with great political and ideological strategies which both argue and act against justice and peace.

The group, while addressing itself to the question of food reserves, was conscious of its limited competence to deal with areas such as food production and distribution and technology, trade, and the world monetary system, in which the world food problems are structured. It was also admitted that it was difficult to disengage the food question from politics. The food problem, it was stressed, however, should not be permanently subordinated to political and economic reasoning; it is not unrealistic to hope, from within our spiritual commitments, for food to become available to all men and women in the world irrespective of political, ideological, and economic blocs and barriers. This hope and commitment should be a complement to the working and the success of the World Food Council.

Regarding the institution of nongovernmental national food councils, the group, under the advice of Dr. Borlaug, felt that these should not be only voluntary agencies operating in the area of food aid and relief. Dr. Borlaug argued that national food councils be instituted in such countries where there is inadequate voluntary commitment to the questions of the food crisis. Such national councils may go a long way toward stimulating interreligious, interparty, and interregional consciousness in the developing countries on the global perspectives of the food problem.

As the group went about the question of the spiritual and religious commitment, it was led by the Judeo-Christian symbols of the holiness of bread to explore similar symbolic constructs in other religious traditions so that approximation of the symbolism of religious commitment could be identified in the world community.

The point was also raised that the symbol of the holiness of bread may not speak meaningfully to cultures where such symbolic association does not obtain. Parallel and convergent symbolism of reverence toward food (in the Sino-Japanese culture) and of sanctification of food (in the name of Allah, in the Islamic instance) were identified. A diversity in the symbolism of food, it was felt, extends rather than qualifies the Judeo-Christian sacrament of food.

It was pointed out also that the symbolism of the holy presupposes a polarity of the secular and the sacred, and that where there is no such polarity the symbolism of holiness might not work. It was also brought out that the religious symbolisms of food are a reference to a vast problematic of people's relations to their world, pointing, of course, to the rediscovery of the sanctity of nature.

The discussion on holiness of bread was also an occasion for exploring the idea of food being lifted out of the present techno-economic structures. Food is, indeed, a commodity among other commodities, but one with a difference. This difference may be recognized by the analogous relationship of food with water and air.

This marvelous analogy, it was admitted, can be seen only by the eye of faith. The facts are that water and air are abundant and food is scarce. It is the latter fact that makes food an instrument by which people enslave themselves to economic and moral exploitation. The discussion on the analogy of food with water and air was, however, profoundly significant as it led the group to stress clearly two things: the human right to food, and the body of religious symbolism of food as a commentary, from the religious end, on the autonomy of the techno-economic and political determinism of the food situation.

The religious reply, both in terms of the holiness of bread (and the analogy of food with water and air) and in its projection of the right to food, should not in any way be taken as a judgment on any ideology that tends to look at the food problem in purely materialistic terms. Nor is the religious reply to be understood as leading to a dichotomy between the religious symbolism of food and the massive technical and economic efforts being made toward solving the food problems.

As the group took up the problem of the energy crisis, it was admitted that the Colloquium had not discussed the energy crisis sufficiently, and hence any commitment by the Colloquium to one or another way of resolving the energy crisis would not be desirable. There was, however, a difference of opinion in the group regarding two questions: whether the food crisis and energy crisis are equally important, and whether the West was justified in resenting the energy situation as it obtains today.

It was also noted that, more than food, energy is intertwined with the power politics of the world. Two problems were identified in the energy crisis: the discovery that the supply of energy is more limited than what was thought, and the swift rise in prices. It is the latter which links the energy crisis with the food crisis.

The group, while it took into account several intricacies regarding the problem of energy crisis, decided to report its point of view in the energy crisis on the following terms: Food and energy are closely interrelated; the food crisis is aggravated by the energy crisis; energy policy, one way or the other, should go a long way to help or hamper the resolution of the food crisis.

It was also felt that possession of food or energy resources by one or another group in the world should not be an occasion to assume postures of ideological *triumphalism.* Humankind looks forward to a world of equality and justice, not to a world wherein the basic needs of food and energy are subordinated to political ideologies and goals.

REPORT OF WORK GROUP TWO

Chairman: John Mbiti; rapporteur: Shlomo Avineri

We welcome the establishment of the World Food Council and look foward to its work with great expectation, although we believe that the world food crisis cannot be adequately confronted without structural changes in many spheres of human life.

Nevertheless, the World Food Council is the first overall effort supported by the international community to help resolve this problem. Attention to and recognition of its activities and programs should be given, and we see one of our major tasks within our respective communities as disseminating information about it and helping its activities so that people all over the world will become aware of the scope of the problem involved. We also recommend establishment of local voluntary bodies to advise on procedures and means of distributing the food that will be channeled through the World Food Council.

We recognize that historically one of the roles of religion has been to serve as critic of existing institutions. Measuring institutions against the moral norms inherent in the various religious traditions, we find that religion has a mission beyond the role of merely helping the weak within the framework of existing conditions.

Investment in instruments of war deflects enormous resources that could be used to solve the problem of hunger. On the crucial issues of war and peace, religion must be a force on the side of peace. We, therefore, condemn the use of religious beliefs for warlike aims and urge religious leaders in areas of conflict to bring their influence to bear upon their political leaders to work toward peace and reconciliation. We believe it is particularly important that religious leaders and institutions support the drive toward disarmament, thus freeing resources for the fight against want and poverty.

Iniquitous trade terms should be revised, and the transfer of technology should aim at mutual help rather than considerations of gain and power politics. Bread should not be treated as a commodity, nor should food be used as a political weapon. Wealth should not be viewed as power, but as a trust in which resides an inherent obligation toward society. Given the social and economic disparities prevalent in our world, we urge business corporations to plough back part of their profits into the areas from which they derive their incomes.

We consider labor as the source of all wealth. Hence physical labor—especially agricultural labor, which creates food—should be regarded as ennobling and not demeaning. We should seek to bring out those elements of our religious traditions that enhance these values and attempt to integrate them into the educational system of our respective societies.

Innovative lifestyles that are responsive to a sense of responsibility to fellow human beings and transcend mere egoistic individualism should be encouraged. Religious institutions should become a nucleus for new modes of production and distribution. Lifestyles that do not involve useless wastage of scarce resources should be encouraged, and the conspicuous consumption that is sometimes associated with religious festivities, be they public or private, should be condemned and discouraged.

The areas most drastically affected by the energy crisis have been precisely those countries suffering most cruelly from the food shortage. We must seek ways in which countries of the Fourth World can be relieved of the excessive price of oil.

The moral and political influence of our religious groups should be used in our respective countries and on a global level to lobby for programs that will help solve food and energy problems. While our deliberations may not produce ultimate solutions to these problems, we do possess enough social influence and power to make a significant contribution toward the restructuring of institutions and the redistribution of resources that will be necessary if these problems are to be adequately solved on a global level.

REPORT OF WORK GROUP THREE

Chairman: James Rausch; rapporteur: Marga Klompe.

(As with other work groups, this one's report was prepared by its chairman and rapporteur; however, Professor Mohammed Al-Nowaihi proposed adding an annex of his own, which was accepted.)

The group considered the question of why religious bodies should be concerned with the issue of world hunger, international peace, or, for that matter, any social, economic, or political issue. These points of agreement emerged.

First, the human being is not only spirit, but spirit and flesh, or, as Buddhist thought puts it, form and mind. If religious bodies have at times given too much attention to the human being as a disengaged soul, now is the time to realize that people are also flesh and blood, and that religion must minister to them as total persons.

Second, all religions agree that each human being has inestimable worth. This results in responsibilities, both spiritual and material, toward one another. Justice, therefore, demands that we feed the hungry and work at the development of institutions and structures that will enable all people to achieve their full human potential, both spiritually and materially.

Religious bodies and individuals have a threefold function: prophetic, educational, and operational.

The credibility of our prophetic visions and our actions rests upon the example we set by our own lifestyles, as religious bodies and individuals. The group agreed that in many religions bread is a very special gift of God. In Islam bread is considered a remembrance of God and his goodness and the sign of gratefulness to God.

In Christianity bread is ever sanctified in its central sacrament. In Buddhism food assumes significance as a prime human requisite. The Upanishads state that food is *Brahman* (holy, priestly).

The right to food becomes then a most fundamental human right. The group therefore agreed that the food problem should be given special treatment, apart from *other* economic and political problems.

In education and preaching each faith community has to clarify to its people that at the root of the food and energy crisis there lie economic, racial, and political structures in its own society which have to be changed. Only when individuals and groups are willing to work on a restructuring within their own countries will it be possible to change world structures. In this respect the following suggestions are made.

In the *developed* countries:

1. Surplus stocks should not be misused to influence world market prices nor to exercise political influence.
2. Developing countries should be given an equal share in the decision-making in world economic and monetary matters.
3. Fair prices should be paid for raw materials coming from developing countries.
4. In contracts of governments or transnational corporations with developing countries, no conditions should be set which would impede the development of such countries.
5. Restructuring of industrial and agricultural production systems should be pursued in order to facilitate a new lifestyle and to create a more equitable global distribution of labor and food. The status and the dignity of the farmer should be especially improved.
6. There should be general self-scrutiny on how the developed countries exercise political, economic, and cultural imperialism.

In the *developing* countries:

1. Stress must be laid on a policy of self-reliance.
2. Agricultural development should be promoted with the tools and the energy present in or appropriate to the particular country, initially on a small scale.
3. The imposition of foreign cultural patterns should be resisted.

4. The gap between rich and poor must be narrowed.
5. A system of social security and economic assistance should be promoted.
6. The dignity of those who work on the soil should be more appreciated, socially and materially.

The operational role of religious bodies in promoting more just structures and a more just society means being prepared to get involved in social action. Many of the suggestions mentioned above can be implemented only through measures and legislation taken by governmental and intergovernmental bodies. But governments will not so act if their people are not willing to accept the consequent sacrifices. Therefore, the spread of information and education on these issues by religious bodies and leaders is imperative. Suggestions for changing structures should be brought to the competent bodies and advocated with great sincerity and skill.

In addition, the following issues should be given attention by religious bodies:

1. Promotion of universal disarmament, and removal of the scandal of trade in arms.
2. Early and effective activation of the World Food Council and the International Fund for Agricultural Development, avoiding excessive bureaucracy.
3. Expansion of agricultural areas by irrigation, drainage, and desalinization.
4. Programs by which energy saved in the oil-producing and industrialized countries would be put at the disposal of developing countries, especially for the production of nitrogen fertilizers and irrigation systems.
5. Establishment of an information clearing house to spread knowledge of food facts in the whole world.

Faith communities should promote lifestyles that are more fitting to our new human situation. Religious bodies and individuals, in their teaching and preaching and way of living, should lay stress on values that are truly religious and human. Individuals are too often judged by their income and social status. But the value of people lies in what they are, not in what they have. We must combat the attitudes of consumerism which go counter to the dignity of the human being. A new lifestyle should not be limited to certain groups or individuals; a campaign should be promoted within the whole society, without becoming compartmentalized. Such an effort should include these elements:

1. No waste of food and energy.
2. Reduction of food consumption by the rich.
3. Careful scrutiny of one's own budget. (How much is really needed?)
4. A mind and heart more open to one's neighbor and to the deprived, inside one's own country.
5. A respectful use of nature, avoiding and combating pollution.
6. Refusal to buy nonessential commodities.
.7. Greater restraint in using leisure time in ways that require consumption of material goods.

All these elements are pertinent for the rich; some are also applicable to the deprived.

The group stressed the urgency of studies on consequences of new lifestyles for the social and economic life of a society: How can existing production systems be restructured? How can the burdens of unemployment and other consequences be shared by all, instead of being put on the shoulders of particular groups in society?

In conclusion, the work group realized that many of its suggestions will meet strong opposition in many circles and that some of the measures required will take a generation to be fully implemented. This, however, is no reason not to work and press for getting them under way. This initiative belongs to the prophetic role of religious bodies and individuals.

The group saw signs of hope. Contrary to the false optimism of the 1960s, humankind now realizes that it is confronted with huge problems and it is more aware of the unacceptable catastrophes which will result if we do not act both individually and collectively. In their endeavors to develop a new lifestyle the Canadian churches have adopted this theme: "To Care, to Spare, and to Share." These are the imperatives that will cure the world's ills.

ANNEX, BY MOHAMMED AL-NOWAIHI

(The annex from Dr. Al-Nowaihi amplified the view that religion has a role to play in meeting human material and social needs on this earth.)

There can be little doubt that the fundamental aim of religion is the ennoblement and refinement of human beings, giving ascendency to their spiritual side over their animal side. However, in the past this has led religious bodies to concentrate almost exclusively on what they considered to be the proper way toward the salvation of the soul.

In this they too readily forgot that people have certain basic material needs that must be satisfied. Thus they became rather lukewarm in their attitude toward the endeavor to ameliorate wretched physical conditions, hunger and disease, as well as toward the injustices that were often perpetrated on people by those who had power over them. People's yearning for justice and equity and for the improvement of their lot on this earth was thus ignored or belittled.

We believe that justice, equity, and the lessening of physical suffering are religious imperatives that must concern both religion and individual religious men and women. We believe that full human dignity cannot be assured unless these imperatives are implemented. Without them religion's fundamental aim will not be achieved, and religious bodies and individuals will have failed their supreme duty.

The implementation of these imperatives will inevitably call for a certain amount of change in the existing social structure. Furthermore, it will entail many technical operations. We do not wish to set ourselves up as political agitators; neither do we claim, as a group, to have technical expertise. In both arenas, however, the needed change cannot be achieved by the politicians alone, nor by the technicians alone. People's religious and moral attitudes and values must be taken into account, with the fullest sympathy and the utmost sensitivity.

That is how we understand our role as an interreligious colloquium. It is a dual role: on the one hand, alerting the people of power and the technical experts of the need for the religious approach; and, on the other hand, persuading the people of the appropriateness and imperativeness of change.

23

Discussion and Finale:
Shalom and Salam

The wrap-up discussion had three aims: to clarify the meaning of the work group reports so that all would understand their content; to provide guidance to Dean Stendahl and his editing group in drawing up a statement setting forth our common mind; to give the "we" of our colloquium community a final chance to express our fresh feeling of solidarity.

Then, at the last second a sign of this new-found community unexpectedly appeared, a happening of the heart beyond the measure of mere ideas.

But first the ideas, four of which did receive new emphasis and fresh twists—despite the late hour and myself as martinet chairman allowing forty-six speakers but three minutes each.

REVERENCE FOR FOOD

Reverence for food, to some the "holiness of bread," is a religious insight, feeling, or symbol of deep and universal power. All our faith communities share this in various ways. We must cultivate and enhance this shared heritage as a high value, of which we have become deeply conscious at Bellagio. This reverence for food provides nourishment for the world "community of communities," another symbol which grew among us.

But the Buddhists were anxious not be be misunderstood. Dr. Ananda made clear that he could not accept "the theory that food was a gift of God. As you know, the major difference between

Buddhism and other major religions of the world is that we don't believe in a God as you do believe in God. . . . We do not consider food as a gift from any divine person to us; it is a natural thing of the earth. And we, as Buddhists, take everything as things are, in their present condition. . . . So as a Buddhist, I would like to restructure that particular phrase, as Monsignor Gremillion suggested: 'Some religions believe food to be a gift of God, but others consider it a natural gift.' "

Another Buddhist on the other hand, Professor Palihawadana, insisted that food is "the prime need . . . that should be consumed for living. It is the prime need for existence. I certainly do not see any objection to the word 'reverence' being used in this formulation."

And so it was done, in crescendo from Dr. Fawzi's telling touch of nostalgia: "As a Muslim boy, if I would find a piece of bread on my way, I would take it and sometimes kiss it. . . . I cannot tread on a piece of bread."

Dr. Smith saw that two significant symbols were coming out of our Bellagio week: "the world community of communities," introduced first by Rabbi Lamm; and "reverence for food" on which we now agreed. But he didn't want to reduce our particular views to a lowest common denominator; we must not omit the specificities of our different faith communities. "My point is that the 'holiness of bread,' which is a phrase that actually moved me greatly, is specifically Christian. . . . It is not inconceivable that moving the Christian world to act in this realm might turn primarily on building on precisely this symbolism of bread, on two thousand years of Christian history. The power of that symbol to move affluent westerners to act so that something really significant is done is not negligible. Part of our trouble is precisely that those symbols that move some of us, leave others of us cold or even offended.

"We mustn't skirt this issue just as Rabbi Lamm did not avoid his point about community and ended by enriching us all with his image of 'community of communities.' "

Dr. Ananda at this point graciously urged that the phrase "holiness of bread" be kept in the statement. "I would like it to be there, because that is the Christian traditional viewpoint and it should be there. If everyone would agree, let me work it out with Madame."

(Marga Klompe, rapporteur for Dr. Ananda's work group, was the "Madame" referred to, the only Miss, Mrs., or Ms. among our thirty-odd participants—doubly odd during International Women's Year, but quite normal among leaders of the world religions and of transnational business and government, from the time of Moses, Buddha, Confucius, Christ, Muhammad, from the era of Hammurabi through that of Adam Smith to the present. Perhaps we need a five-faith colloquium on the "holiness of all humans," or at least "reverence" for women, for their dignity and rights.*)

FOOD AS A COMMODITY

Food is not just another commercial commodity among commodities and cannot be so treated by society or by the world's economic and political institutions. This is the societal consequence of reverence for food, the prime need of life and/or a gift of God, a sacred symbol to our several faith communities. It is also a consequence of our new planetary interdependence—new in fact because of technology, and new in the consciousness of persons and nations.

Bishop Moore said, "I was fascinated by even the possibility that food would be lifted out of the normal interchange of economics and politics. I don't know whether this is a dream, whether it's a practical thing even to think about. But the idea of putting food in a separate category internationally is fascinating to me. I'd like to hear it explored by those who know more about it than I."

Professor Parmar answered that members of "the Overseas Development Council, Lester Brown and others, in speaking to their own countrymen and leaders in the United States, have emphasized being careful that food does not become a political instrument, because it is obvious that, at the moment, the U.S. controls the major portion of world food surpluses and will continue to do so for some time. It is this line of thinking which seems to put food in a *qualitatively* different category from other commodities."

For Professor Parmar this is a moral question that also relates to the energy problem. The rich and the poor peoples are affected by the energy shortage in basically different ways. In developed

---

*A year after I wrote this, such a conference was held, on "Women, Development, and Religion," sponsored by the Center of Concern, Washington, D.C.

countries "the energy crisis affects luxury levels of consumption. Any cut-down of consumption arising out of the energy crisis starts primarily with overconsumption. On the other hand, in many less developed countries, even the energy crisis hits at the level of necessities, because it is linked with food." It is so linked because energy is required to provide fertilizers, pesticides, irrigation, and other inputs for producing food. "So if food is politicized by those who control the surpluses, then a combination of the energy crisis and the food crisis really hits certain developing countries very hard.

"For this reason, even the narrow socio-economic standpoint is giving food a qualitatively different status. Additionally, more and more social scientists are getting concerned with moral aspects. In our discussions here we have lifted the question even higher. This pleases me as a social scientist; I am helped by it."

Fr. Theodore Hesburgh, besides being president of Notre Dame University and prominent in several civic bodies, is also chairman of the Overseas Development Council. He wanted to reinforce Professor Parmar's moral position. "Sometimes facts nail down moral situations better than just talking about 'justice' in the abstract. The reason the food and energy crisis got locked together is that both began raising costs of the people who could least afford them, but needed them most.

"We wanted energy to drive massive autos that were unnecessary; the poor peasants in India needed energy to get water out onto their fields. If we had no oil, we couldn't drive our cars so much. If they lacked energy, water didn't irrigate their fields, their crops didn't grow, and they may have died of starvation; or they lacked fertilizer, and therefore, their crop dropped to one-tenth of what it might have been. Now let me give you the facts that link these two together:

"In 1974, the Third World had to pay $10 billion more for energy than it had the previous year and $5 billion more for food, because the prices of both these commodities went up. Those two items practically wiped out all the aid to the Third World, which had totalled about $16 billion annually. The Overseas Development Council has been insisting on the deep moral responsibility of those who produce food and oil, that they ought to take special concern for the poor of the world, especially for the Fourth World countries that simply can't afford to pay current prices for food and oil.

"Peoples of the Fourth World simply cannot continue to exist if they have to pay these prices. So what we proposed was that a prime obligation of those controlling oil and food production would be to take a concessional approach toward the poorest countries of the world.

"This may look like redistribution of wealth," Fr. Hesburgh concluded, "and it should be. It recognizes the interdependence of the world and recognizes the fact that some people cannot deliberately wipe out other people on earth and look upon them as brothers and sisters while doing it."

Professor Avineri raised no objection to the views of Professor Parmar and Fr. Hesburgh on planetary social justice. But he objected to the complete equation of food with air and water, "which are natural givens, whereas food is mediated through human labor. Part of my anthropology is that the human being is a food-producing animal; making that analogy between air and water and food is to lose this specific aspect of the human being as a laboring human being." And from that aspect of human nature flow a number of consequences, such as the sources of wealth, what capital is, and so forth. Still, he agreed very strongly "that food and energy, specifically in reference to the developing countries, should not be treated as commodities."

CRISIS PSYCHOLOGY

What will result from the psychology of crisis that now encircles the globe? Some thought that collective fear generates isolationism and the goal of national self-sufficiency. Public opinion in the United States and the attitudes of that country's Presidents Nixon and Ford were cited. Others saw a positive possibility, a mood of hope.

Professor Parmar objected, "Personally I am very much against crisis psychology. It could push us back into our pre-1960 ghettos on a planetary scale, the kind of ghettos with which we are more familiar each in our own societies."

Chief Adebo responded, "But fear can also lead to cooperation, the fear of common disaster."

To Fr. Hesburgh it seemed "that we're always caught in the dichotomy between optimism and pessimism. . . . We are always somewhere in between; for example, we speak of love of God and fear of God." He hoped that "our report will have a different tone and mood to it than that from the World Food Conference. Somehow they never got around to giving the reasons why one thinks peace is better than war, or why feeding people is better than letting them die of starvation."

Fr. Hesburgh added, "Our conference here is a kind of reflection on the relationship between religion and science. That relationship is best understood when a religious person can accept science as another one of those givens which is developed through human talent, yet has to be used. It must not be used capriciously and wildly, as we have, for destroying people, but toward elevating, ennobling, helping people to have a better life, and somehow to promote the kingdom."

All these elements of crisis and fear disturbed Dr. Askari. "They make me feel afraid that our lives are being determined historically, that we are interlocked in a given mundane situation. Does this leave room open for a religious breakthrough, not conditioned this way or that, by the directives of crisis and hope within history. I would very much like Dr. Smith to comment on this."

Professor Smith thought the hunger problem might get "frighteningly serious before it is solved." That's why he is seeking a very deep, firm, solid religious fundamental "which in some fashion transcends both optimism and pessimism, which is able to act in the face of disaster, or even in hope."

But this dean of interreligious scholarship was more concerned with the concrete, with the critique of existing structures and the upbuilding of new ones. "I may see some light out of this uncertainty. The World Food Council is a new structure, and perhaps we haven't given it the applause it deserves. At last, faced with a major new world challenge, the world community of nations has come up with a new structure calculated specifically to deal with it. And it's one in which the rich countries and the OPEC countries have collaborated, really for the benefit of the Third and Fourth Worlds. So here is a political structure that is new and appropriate and to be admired."

Professor Smith then objected to "the idea of taking food out of politics. We have come to disparage the political, in a way that only Dr. Klompe is here to remind us not to do. The food problem challenges us to move toward a better conception of politics, a better actuality of politics, than we have had. But we mustn't maneuver ourselves into a position of saying, 'We are righteous and those politicians are dreadful people,' because in some senses the ultimate future of humankind is in the hands of political leaders, virtually by definition.

"A politician is the person to whom we give the mechanism for deciding our future. Humanity's progress will depend much less on its ability to criticize existing structures than on its ability to modify or to construct new ones that will serve humane and just purposes."

THE PURPOSE OF THE INTERFAITH COLLOQUIUM

Mr. Cyrus Vance, active for decades at the highest levels of U.S. public life, recalled, "I was privileged to serve as a participant in the discussions leading to this Colloquium.... We concluded that indeed there was a need to try to draw on the strength of the religious bodies around the world to attack some of the problems that are besetting the world and seem so difficult of solution. We came to the conclusion that there was perhaps one issue, namely the issue of food, which could be lifted out of all the others and which included within it the problem of justice and so many other global issues."

Mr. Vance then turned to the role of religion. "The question before us is what religious groups can do that politicians cannot. It seems to me that religious groups can bring their moral strength to these particular problems. And this is terribly important, because politics is affected by the moral strength that is brought to bear by the constituents of all of us who have been involved in politics across the world. I think it is most appropriate then that we have decided to attack this particular subject, to bring it to the special attention of the various religious communities around the world.

"I am very pleased to see what we have been able to accomplish here and to observe the fact that it is possible today to come out with a statement of principles after discussion. These I think can be helpful in mobilizing thought around the world, and for action in coping more effectively with this problem, which transcends most others.

"I hope then this meeting can serve as a base for future gatherings which will address similar problems that need resolution and mobilize the strength of the various religious communities around the world to attack them."

Professor Smith, however, objected that all religious bodies are not structured to carry out such a role in today's society. "The Roman Catholic church is certainly the most beautifully organized for action, and many of the Roman Catholics among us are people of real importance in this organized action of their

church. The whole Christian church, even the Protestants, are
somewhat organized. But in the case of Islam and Buddhism and
Hinduism, these communities—if that's what they are—are not
organized for action. I think the representatives among us from
these groups feel as powerless as I do individually. The whole
ambience in which they move is simply not structured toward
operational movement."

This difference of religions in structure and disposition for action, Professor Smith concluded, had wide implications for the
Colloquium's plans. Six months later Professor Smith, responding
to a prospectus on the follow-up to Bellagio, again raised this and
other problems for collaboration among religious communities.

Professor Murty saw the problem raised by Professor Smith.
However, in his view, "Although some faiths represented here,
such as Buddhism and Hinduism, probably don't have institutions
or formal organizations for operating within their societies, it is
possible for individuals from these faiths to speak effectively on
the problems raised here. Religious leaders and the professional
religious people have a particular duty in this connection; that I
have long felt, especially from my experience in India. It behooves
all truly religious people, when they want to speak authoritatively
on the food problem, to do what people like St. Francis of Assisi
and Mahatma Gandhi did—adopt holy poverty, sincerity, and
simplicity of lifestyle. If religious leaders share what they have,
not getting more than what people in their own nations and communities generally have, then they can tell their own communities and the world, 'Do this, do that.' "

Lastly, Professor Murty raised the possibility of having a similar meeting in the East. "It would be interesting to see if an
eastern setting would change the conclusions or ideas we now
have."

A HAPPENING OF THE HEART

Then, at the last second, something occurred which I must call a
"happening of the heart"; two humans reached out across the
Sinai Desert of Yahweh-Allah to embrace each other. Even this
hard-boiled church bureaucrat became speechless, as did my confreres.

The discussion was just about over. As chairman, I was just
clearing my throat and shuffling notes, ready to give the final
wrap-up, when Professor Avineri asked for ten seconds and got my

nod. "For me as an Israeli," he said, "this was a particularly significant and moving occasion. I had the good fortune to meet two people from Egypt, and I know that both, Dr. Fawzi and Dr. Al-Nowaihi, have become and will always remain great friends to me.

"I was very much encouraged by our very ability to sit around the table discussing things. If people had not known our countries of origin, I don't think they would have guessed that there an Egyptian was speaking and here an Israeli was speaking. We have been talking as human beings sharing our concerns. And perhaps for some of us, beyond the universal concerns we shared here, there were also particular concerns.

"My hope is that one day it will be possible for the follow-up to this Peace Colloquium to meet in a City of Peace which is dear to three of our traditions, where I think we would be able, all of us, to meet.

"Certainly I, for one, would be very happy to meet our Egyptian friends in Jerusalem. Thank you. Shalom and Salam."

Dr. Fawzi, seated two places away, stood and reached out his hand to the Sabra dean. Stumbling across the legs of neighbors they drew closer and embraced.

Silence. Moist eyes. We clapped hands and each others' backs. Quiet again.

Shoving notes aside, I could only say, "Further words are not only unnecessary but unspeakable after this." A few more seconds of silence, then I asked Dr. Smith to close with the final prayer.

Oh God, thou who are so great a mystery that we hardly know whether to call thee Lord,

Whose splendor and majesty are so great that we hardly dare enter thy presence,

Whose nearness is so utter that thou art within us as well as around us and before us, working within us to do thy will, sustaining us, strenghthening us, guiding us,

We tremble before thee and before the awesome specter of the hunger of the world, the inscrutable terror that so many suffer while we are well fed.

Give us the humility to recognize how little we know, how weak we are, how much we must do.

Give us the grace to open ourselves to thy willingness to work through us.

Let us be ever astonished at it, but let us respond.

Give us the imagination to realize our unity with each other through love, the compassion to realize our unity with the poor through service, the reward of realizing through that love and service our unity with thee. Amen.*

---

*Dr. Smith's was the last of the five-minute prayer services which opened and closed each day's work. They were led by adherents of the different faiths, each of whom prayed as he would within his own community—Hindu, Buddhist, Jewish, Muslim, Christian. Regrettably only this closing one was recorded.

THE TWO YEARS
SINCE BELLAGIO

24

A Call for Follow-Up

Our last evening together, Fr. Theodore Hesburgh and Rabbi Henry Siegman led an informal discussion on "Where do we go from here?"

Rabbi Siegman reviewed the steps that had brought us together. These he knew best; two years before, my friend Henry had visited me in the Vatican to share his vision. He had also approached some ten other friends who formed the temporary steering committe to plan Bellagio. (These are listed in the appendix.)

Fr. Hesburgh then ticked off the many problems besides food and energy which face the human family: war, disarmament, and peace; trade, aid, the monetary system, and related issues, which have been brought together by UNCTAD and the goal of a New International Economic Order; terrorism; human rights; public health; academic and popular communications through travel, print, and the electronic media; safeguarding the environment; the nuclear hazard; the use of space and of the seas; multinational corporations.

He invoked Barbara Ward's image of Spaceship Earth carrying five passengers. One of the five consumes 80 percent of the capsule's limited resources, leaving 20 percent to be divided among the four others. Four have but 5 percent apiece of the air, water, food, and energy, while the affluent one enjoys 80 percent of these necessities. "And that favored one, representing only one-fifth of the human family, is probably white, probably Jewish or Christian, probably western unless he is Japanese.

This gap between the North and South, Fr. Hesburgh con-

cluded, cannot continue. That's the message of so many recent
U.N. meetings—at Santiago on trade and development, at Stockholm on the environment, at Bucharest and Rome on population
and food, at Caracas on use of the seas. These are finding focus in
the series of sessions on the New International Economic Order.
They all witness to our growing awareness of global interdependence, to the fact "that you can't have a national answer to a world
problem. These problems are global, and the solutions must be
global. Our new vision must be the vision of global justice.

"And interdependence is ultimately deeply religious. In the
book of Genesis the first question a man asked God was, 'Am I my
brother's keeper?' Blessed with the enormous gift we call humanity and with God's grace and wisdom, if we want to we can together
forge a new vision of the earth. We can learn how to live in harmony with the nature that surrounds us, and how to make justice
a reality in our times."

Professor Askari said he wanted our Colloquium to continue in
some form, because he agreed with Fr. Hesburgh that the Spirit
had been working among us, helping us to see the problems of
global interdependence. He made a concrete suggestion on organizing a follow-up: ask the existing steering committee to appoint a small caretaker group to assess what we had done, to
project another session in perhaps two years, and to consider
enlarging the steering committee with members from other faiths
and regions of the world.

Cardinal Arns supported Dr. Askari. "The group which created
this Colloquium out of nothing is certainly strong; consequently
they should continue the responsibility for a certain time, until
other persons come to the fore who can carry on. As an additional
thought, the next Colloquium should have a similar theme, in
some way related to food and famine. I think, for instance, of
justice."

A dozen others expressed general agreement. For example, Dr.
Ananda said, "We have hope in the future. Rome was not built in a
day. This is a first step, and I think it is a first step in the right
direction. Therefore, we should continue. But I also endorse Dr.
Askari's view that it would be very good if a Buddhist, a Hindu,
and a Muslim were on the steering committee."

Another Buddhist, Professor Palihawadana, was not so sure. "I
feel a great sense of trepidation in saying 'no,' this is not the best
or the most effective way. Only I have been asking myself a lot of
questions. . . . In no way can I say that I speak for all Buddhists or

for the Asians or anything of that kind. But personally I have been reflecting upon this conference with mixed feelings. I feel optimism as far as the immediate issue of the food and energy crisis is concerned, but pessimism as to the deeper question of interreligious communication. . . . Maybe this is all too western for me. Or perhaps I am not the right kind of person for this type of meeting."

Professor Murty followed, ending the discussion on a strong upbeat. He believed "participation has been of great value to almost everybody here. I, therefore, would endorse this suggestion made by the Cardinal and Professor Askari, that there should be a continuing group to work for interreligious dialogue. . . . As I said yesterday, the Soviet Union and United States, despite their different ideologies, can agree on common action, at least in some causes. If they can do so, I don't see why Hindus, Buddhists, Jews, Muslims, and Christians can't agree on certain things and undertake to do them together."

Professor Murty also asked that the continuing Colloquium include the Jain religion, "which is now being accepted in India as a major religion in its own right and has contributed a good deal to the civilization of humankind." Finally, he seconded the "proposal which has been made by the Cardinal that the next Colloquium be devoted to justice—the way it has been realized so far, and the way it might be realized in different social systems and political systems."

Fr. Hesburgh summed it up: "Dear Lord, give bread to those who have hunger, and to those who have bread, give a hunger for justice."

25

The Interreligious
Peace Colloquium

Two years after Bellagio, the Interreligious Peace Colloquium
(IRPC) is taking form as an organization-movement. The original
sponsors accepted the participants' advice: Cyrus Vance, Henry
Siegman, and I were named to a "continuation committee"; we
asked Matthew Rosenhaus to join us. The very idea of the Colloquium had come from this philanthrophic and business leader, as
was explained in the Foreword of this book. (He had been pre-
vented from attending Bellagio because his wife gave birth to a
daughter that very week.)

Our group of four met ten times during the fifteen months after
Bellagio. Through correspondence, visits, telephone calls, and do-
zens of small sessions, we received ideas and critique from most of
our Bellagio "alumni." Our interest group was enlarged, especially among Muslim leaders.

After much discussion it was decided that we should first form a
group based in North America. Participants would be mostly
Christian and Jewish, in keeping with the religious composition
and culture of Canada and the United States. At the same time,
leaders in other regions would be encouraged to form their own
groups—in, for instance, West Europe, the Mideast, East Europe,
South and East Asia, Black Africa, Latin America. These would
reflect the religious presence and culture of their respective
areas. As these take shape, they could come together as equal
partners in a world federation.

Accordingly, the North American unit of the Interreligious Peace Colloquium (IRPC) was formally incorporated, in the state of New York, in August 1976. The founding directors and officers were Matthew Rosenhaus, president; Cyrus Vance, vice-president; Henry Siegman, treasurer; myself, secretary and executive officer, with the title of coordinator. The board of directors of fifteen to twenty members is being elected. (See Appendix.)

As noted earlier, Cyrus Vance resigned in January 1977 when he became secretary of state of the United States. I must record that his participation was decisive in the formative months of IRPC; he attended nine of our ten planning sessions and gave significant leadership within as well as outside our small committee.

During these fifteen months after Bellagio, the four of us so charged drew up a Prospectus which sets forth our vision of what we are and whom we might become, insofar as we understand ourselves. By August 1976, the sixth version also projected four program areas we would pursue. The major parts of this Prospectus are reproduced below.

NATURE AND PURPOSE

1. A first Interreligious Peace Colloquium was held at Bellagio, Italy, May 1975, on the food/energy crisis and the challenge this crisis presents to the five world faiths—Hindu, Buddhist, Jewish, Muslim, Christian. Participants in and sponsors of this interfaith experiment have decided to form an organization composed of leaders who are adherents of these faiths, or of their religious cultures. The motives and insights leading to this decision grew out of the Bellagio experience and discussions since. Principal among these are the following:

A. All five faiths, and the cultures they help generate, teach views of creation, man, and society, together with values and ethical principles consequent to these views, which are applicable to current issues of human rights, justice, development, and peace, at national and world levels. As these are jointly explored, significant common ground is found, as well as factors causing conflict. Bases for commonality and roots of division should be pursued together. They are made more specific by focusing on concrete issues of which the food/energy crisis is a first example.

B. Common ground exists particularly among Jews, Muslims,

and Christians; however, conflicts between these communities have darkened our history for centuries.

1) Jews, Muslims, and Christians share similar faith sources: revelation inspired by teachers, lawgivers, and prophets, handed down in holy writings, to the "People of the Book." These three religions also share belief content: the one personal God, creator of the universe, just and compassionate judge of all the human family; commandments and counsels addressing the whole nation and society, as well as each person privately, with appeals to inner conscience and to the common good; the possession by all humans of innate dignity and freedom, from which derive basic human needs, duties, and rights.

2) Adherents of the three religio-cultures are concerned with pressing issues which still cause dangerous confrontation and harsh conflict within and among several nations in which Jews, Muslims, and Christians are numerous and influential; also between three regions in which these faiths and ethical systems play significant roles, by historical inheritance and at present: the Middle East, Europe, and North America.

That the Holocaust happened in their midst still haunts Christians of the West. Constantly it alerts them to ambivalent effects of religious conviction—for and/or against other faith communities, and the freedom and rights of all. A large portion of the Jewish people live in the Soviet Union where they share with many Christians and Muslims serious disabilities in public life.

Today tensions between Muslims and Christians deeply affect nations and regions. Current cases are Lebanon, Cyprus, areas of Black Africa, and the Indonesia-Philippines-Malaysia triangle. This interacts with issues involving the Jewish people. These problems sometimes attain such dimensions that they endanger the rights and well-being of hundreds of millions, and even world peace.

Religious adherence has played a key part within Zionism and Israel, among the Arab nations and Palestinians, and in the turbulent events of the Middle East for three decades.

2. Bellagio participants also became more conscious of the changes, or challenges to change, being experienced within their five faiths. They are influenced by the impact of technology and

modernization and by the expansion of the traditional concerns of each faith beyond nation and region to embrace the new planetary dimension of today's secular institutions—economic, political, social, and cultural.

Sometimes the societal impacts are evolutionary and peaceful; most religious groups become open to them. However, the faith communities are often caught up in revolutionary transformations which include violence. These radicalized situations pose fresh dilemmas to the faith groups; their commonality is confronted by civil conflict, heated up by the fuel of religious divisiveness.

3. Motivation for organizing the Interreligious Peace Colloquium (IRPC) derives also from consciousness among secular and religious leaders of striking changes underway in the power relations among nations, blocs, and regions. Since 1973, a chain of events—involving food, energy, inflation, and Third World demands—has accelerated these transformations and deepened this awareness.

A. Many interpret these changes as a process of historical dimension. Nonwestern regions and blocs increasingly demand and assume decisive roles: The Chinese, Japanese, Arab, and Islamic peoples now acquire positions alongside North America, West Europe, and the Soviet Union in the world power equation.

Others, and the Third World as a whole, begin to forge new linkages which enhance their voice and participation in decisions affecting the well-being, rights, and peace of half the human family. They even urge "a New International Economic Order" based upon interdependence. The Third World now enjoys a strong majority in support of this and other positions in the United Nations, particularly in solidarity with Islamic countries, as seen in the Israel-Arab debates.

B. Without passing judgment on motives and rhetoric, many now recognize that in today's polypolar world new levels of interdependence among nations and regions do indeed arise. Some leaders of the regions formerly dominant begin to acknowledge that this factual interdependence requires fresh approaches to transnational relations and exploration of new structures in the global power framework.

Peoples and cultures which have taken mutual conflict for granted now are reconsidering, with measured progress and expected setbacks, the continuance of their historic struggles. A prime example is the conflict, hot or cold, which has endured for 1200 years between Muslim Arabs-Turks versus Europeans-Americans of Judeo-Christian heritage.

C. While demand for power-sharing and economic equity among nations rises to the fore, the advance of human rights and civil freedom falters *within* many nations. Together with its promised but still inadequate satisfaction of food, health, educational, and other needs, modernization too often brings as well new motives and technologies for thought control, denial of religious freedom, political suppression, and terrorism. This "negative development" weaves a different and dangerous web of interdependence. It should come as no surprise that vaunted technological change, being ethically neutral, can be used for people's good or to their detriment.

4. Religious officials and secular leaders concerned with religio-cultural values are becoming *jointly* attentive to the new reality of interdependence and the enduring reality of conflict, as seen at Bellagio, because:

A. Tragically, religion has too often contributed to divisiveness and conflict between peoples and cultures. To cite our western and Middle East experience, the contribution of "holy war" and "crusades" to the Islamic/Christian conflict over the centuries is clear. Today the religio-cultural tradition of the Jewish people comes into conflict with the cohesive unity of Islam. Economic, political, and national motives obtain added strength and staying-power from religious convictions. Religious and ethical values frequently compete and fuel conflict. At the same time, the need for moral discrimination and political judgment on true human good is as great today as ever.

B. Within the nation a faith community can contribute positively to national identity and internal cohesion, as seen among most European peoples for over a thousand years, and more recently in Japan, Israel, and other Asian and African nations. This unifying action among adherents of one religious culture can also help draw together citizens of several nations, and/or the "sovereign" nations themselves, toward identity and unity, in regional or other formulas. Current examples are the European community, the Zionist movement, and the Islamic world.

C. However, exclusivist or dominant claims by one faith community within the nation have frequently injured the economic, political, and human rights of other groups. Conflicting factions use such religious motives to buttress their positions, even to justify violence, imprisonment, and torture.

D. Some believers charge religion with another fault: One member of our sponsoring group criticizes its failure to inspire "men like us who are in business and political affairs" to meet the challenges of hunger and poverty, oppression and violence—challenges flung worldwide at human consciences. He asks whether and how could religion help vitalize day-to-day life and work for building up society and history, for fulfilling the true human potential. For him "this is the religious heart of the matter."

E. Through all this there is reason for hope. Helped by recent interreligious exchanges the realization begins to emerge that essential elements of each faith partake of a certain universality which make them common to all faiths. Interreligious openness, pluralism, community become possible.

Bellagio particularly demonstrated by lived experience what scholars already knew: that Jews, Muslims, Christians share broad areas of commonality in their faith sources and content, which offer bases for cooperative relations as fellow humans and nations. In today's changing world, shared ground among the three faiths could bring constructive elements toward solving economic, political, and related problems within three regions in particular—the Middle East, West Europe, North America, and among the five world faiths, for bettering the international economic order to provide for the basic needs of all humans and a material foundation for the exercise of their full rights.

5. Realizing that current economic, political, and military answers fail to meet many of today's challenges, secular leaders might welcome appropriate religio-cultural elements within the customary *realpolitik*. Indeed, because the absolutes of religions are at a higher level, they should help to harmonize competing political and economic values without sanctifying these middle principles into absolutes. The sponsors of the Interreligious Peace Colloquium propose its formation therefore for these basic purposes:

A. To identify and reduce divisive factors which religions historically have brought into our national and regional cultures and aspirations; and to strengthen factors favoring cohesion, nationally and regionally.

B. To grasp and to espouse the cause of the weak and oppressed in conflicts between the powerful and the powerless, between haves and have-nots within nations and among regions or blocs.

C. To promote human dignity and freedom, as values which the faiths at their best are able to nourish, for assuring human rights and self-fulfillment among all groups and classes.

D. To make manifest and to reinforce within each faith, by conscious experience of interdependence, the universal and essential elements we share in common.

E. To cooperate as believers from the several regions and blocs for generating a sense of conscious interdependence among the whole human family, "a world community of communities."

6. This community of believers must also help beget that human understanding and appreciation, mutual trust and friendship which gives cohesiveness and true life to society, at local and global levels. Bellagio participants did experience this animating sense of community; they wish to continue, deepen, and expand this experience with others.

7. Whatever the formula, structure will be kept minimal. IRPC is to be a loose gathering of leaders in world affairs—especially from government, business, research, communications, education who come to know and to respect one another. It is hoped that they will become a "community of friends" who appreciate and interlink the religious values of each, to reduce conflict and to enhance solidarity between their respective cultural regions. Participation will be on a personal basis, not as delegates of religious or other bodies.

8. IRPC intends to carry out the following activities among faith adherents and their organized bodies:

A. Continue communication with Bellagio participants, strengthening and enlarging our embryonic "community of friends"; urging all to regional and national initiatives; broadening our circles through comparable programs.

B. Encourage interreligious concern for social issues within faith or "ecclesiastical" communities and through exchange among them. Bodies which may be included are Synagogue Councils and rabbinical associations; Catholic, Orthodox, and Protestant churches, with the confessional "families" and world networks, such as the World Council of Churches; comparable Buddhist, Hindu, and Muslim bodies, constituted by monasteries, ashrams, and mosques and their abbots, nuns, monks, ulemas, imams, and other religious leaders (e.g., World Buddhist Sangha Council, World Muslim Congress, Ramakrishna Mission, etc.); missionary societies, religious orders, sisterhoods, brotherhoods, etc.

C. Most world religions are reviewing their doctrinal statements and ethical systems in terms of current changes in national and global society. Several are seeking to restate their teaching on society, human rights, justice, development, and peace in terms more adequate to the daily needs and fresh vision of their people. IRPC will offer help to the world religions for articulating their social teaching in forms more responsive to current reality, always seeking to identify elements which contribute to conflict or to solidarity within and among nations.

D. Seek relations with religio-cultural bodies, as distinct from official faith communities just cited. Examples are the new Buddhist, Hindu, and Islamic associations (of laity, of universities and students, of economists, sociologists, etc.); World Jewish Congress; YMCA, YWCA, Conference of International Catholic Organizations; also with social agencies of religious inspiration, such as Church World Service, Catholic Relief, and Red Crescent.

E. Seek cooperation especially with bodies which focus on religious and ethical dimension of world issues (e.g., Council on Religion and International Affairs; World Conference on Religion and Peace; Center of Concern; Gandhi Peace Foundation; Justice and Service Unit of the World Council of Churches, Geneva; Justice and Peace, Vatican City; and SODEPAX, Geneva and Rome [Committe on Society, Development, and Peace, constituted by the two Christian bodies last mentioned]).

F. Foster dialogue between faith communities and adherents of philosophies that are expressly antireligious, such as Marxists; and between faith communities and followers of belief systems that are agnostic or nonreligious, e.g., humanist or Confucianist.

9. The Bellagio meeting brought together three categories of participants: scholars, secular leaders, and religious officials. Wilfred Cantwell Smith, the pioneer of comparative religious studies, presented the key paper on "Divisiveness and Unity: The Role of Religion in Politics and Society."

IRPC will seek out other thinkers and researchers who, as individuals or as groups, can deepen perception of the issues in their manifold dimension. It will encourage studies in this interdisciplinary field and pursuit of these subjects in educational systems, religious and secular, for youth and adults. The cooperation of the private foreign policy community will be sought in all IRPC programs.

10. IRPC proposes transregional programs on four interlocking subjects:

> Program One...The Changing World Economic Order: Challenge to the Five World Faiths
>
> Program Two...The Future of the Middle East: Can Its Three Faiths Work for Healing after Centuries of Conflict?
>
> Program Three...Religion's Role in Current Struggles for Human Rights
>
> Program Four...Religion as a Divisive and/or Cohesive Force in Today's Interdependent World

Each of these programs will provide a more concrete *focus* within the larger purpose of IRPC. Each will follow its own track of studies, work groups, meetings, publications, etc., to pursue that focus. However, all four programs will be constantly linked and will nourish one another. Program One, on the changing economic order, is more advanced in the IRPC process because it builds upon Bellagio, which focused on the food/energy crisis. Already at Bellagio, the three other themes—the Middle East, human rights, conflict/solidarity—repeatedly came forth from the exchanges. The four subjects are like fingers of the hand, each confronting the thumb of religion. So the four will be pursued separately, but with strong awareness of their constant linkage.

11. To be remembered in all programs is the larger purpose of IRPC: To animate a movement of leaders in transnational affairs—from economic, political, communications, academic, science, and related circles—who, inspired by their religio-cultural heritage, become a "community of friends" who are committed to justice, development, human rights, and peace among the whole human family.

Its further purpose, with and through these lay leaders, is to stimulate officials of religious bodies, theologians and scholars, toward engagement of their faith communities to advance social justice and development, human rights and peace—offering a ministry of conflict resolution and reconciliation, instead of fueling division and hate as has occurred too frequently in the past.

A SYMPOSIUM ON THE CHANGING WORLD ORDER

In November 1977, at Lisbon, Portugal, the Interreligious Peace Colloquium sponsored a symposium: "The Changing World Economic Order: Challenge to the Five World Faiths." This was a logical outgrowth from the food/energy subject of Bellagio. A similar pattern of papers and discussion, prayer and conversation was followed.

The papers will be published in 1978. They include the following:

—"A Comparative Survey of Significant Proposals for a New World Order," by Philip S. Land and other staff of the Center of Concern, Washington, D.C.

—"Man's World: Chaos or a New Order, a Third World Point of View," by Ismail Sabri Abdalla, Director General of the Institute for National Planning, Cairo, Egypt, and Chairman of the Third World Forum.

—"Basic Human Needs and a New International Economic Order: A Northern View," by James P. Grant and John Sewell, President and Vice-President, respectively, of the Overseas Development Council, Washington, D.C.

—"Satisfying Human Needs in a World of Sovereign States: Rhetoric, Reality and Vision," by Richard Falk, Princeton University.

—"The Changing World Order: Challenge to Faith Communities, or, Faith: Challenge to the Changing World Order," by Robert N. Bellah, University of California, Berkeley, California.

Papers giving responses in the light of the Buddhist, Hindu, Jewish, Muslim, and Christian faiths were presented by Lankaputra Hewage, Colombo, Sri Lanka; Devaki Jain, New Delhi; Irwin Blank, Boston; Khurshid Ahmad, London and Karachi; Burgess Carr, Nairobi.

After the publication of these papers in 1978, it is possible that an "interpretative account" of this Lisbon symposium and of other projects of the Interreligious Peace Colloquium will be published in due time.

26

The Food/Energy Situation in 1977

Despite some improved harvests in 1976 and 1977, despite less famine footage in the daily news, the world food crisis continues. While the attention span of the affluent diminishes, under-nourishment goes on as usual among the poor.

In the summer of 1977, Lester Brown of the Worldwatch Institute, Washington, gave me the following data on total grain reserves, in terms of "Days of World Consumption."

Crop Year	Reserve Stocks of Grain*	Grain Equivalent of Idled U.S. Land*	Total Reserves*	Reserves as Days of World Consumption
1971–72	155	78	233	73
1972–73	172	24	196	60
1973–74	127	0	127	37
1974–75	132	0	132	40
1975–76	123	0	123	37
1976–77	126	0	126	36
1977–78	151	0	151	43

*in Millions of Metric Tons

Figures for the last year are, of course, estimates. Total reserves include the modest carry-over stocks in importing countries.

We see that the 1976–77 reserve dropped to only 36 days of supply at current world consumption rates. A move up by seven days, to 43 days of supply, is hoped for in 1977–78. But this is still dangerously below the 60 days of supply that many regard as the safety line.

During the 1960s, annual reserves range from a high of 103 days to a low of 68 days, for a ten-year average of 90 days of supply, at world consumption rates then current. During the 1970s, world food reserves have been reduced by half. During the past five years they are averaging only 39 days of supply at present consumption rates. For over 500 million humans that rate is already much too low. It means undernourishment and protein deficiency, disease and lethargy. Meanwhile, population among the poor continues to increase, at about 2.5 percent each year.

The energy crisis, as expected, has worsened the plight of poorer peoples, and of the hungry in particular. Since 1974, petroleum costs have eaten into funds formerly used to buy food abroad. Reduction of oil imports by food deficit countries has reduced their capacity to produce and store, process and distribute food. External debt of poorer peoples has doubled and trebled. Exports and balance of payments of oil-short nations have fallen drastically.

Western Europe and Japan are also heavily affected, as well as the United States, despite its own domestic oil production. This "trilateral club" has made new attempts at a common strategy on energy and food. Policies of "independence" from foreign petroleum proclaimed for the United States by Presidents Nixon and Ford proved ephemeral. The new president inherited a heavy dependence on imported oil, growing from about 25 percent to over 40 percent of U.S. annual needs since 1973. Mr. Carter has found it necessary to launch an energy program of drastic dimensions, so far-reaching that he has called for sacrifice and effort that are "the moral equivalent of war."

Serious literature on the food and energy situation now abounds, in books, long articles, and monographs. These studies as a whole move away from the crisis mentality of the early seventies to focus rather on food and energy "systems" as they interrelate with wider social, political, and economic structures.

Most admit that crash efforts are still needed from time to time to meet famine here or there. Consequently, assurance is needed that sufficient food aid will be available. Fortunately this is one goal of the World Food Program that has been largely reached, by reserves made available from Canada, Australia, and the United States. (These are the only countries with a regular grain surplus.) Another positive note is attainment of the billion dollars to set up the International Fund for Agricultural Development, with grants of about $500 million each from OPEC countries and from the West.

However, according to most studies, such efforts are infinitesimal in relation to the harsh global reality. Food and energy programs must be placed within the wider matrix of a new world order, which includes a more equitable structure within nations, poor as well as rich. The "New International Economic Order" has become the watchword for this movement toward systems analysis and structural solutions. And proposed solutions are judged by their provision of basic human needs and rights—including "the right to eat."

Actual interdependence among nations is growing, due in part to the food and energy crises. More significantly, in my judgment, consciousness of an acceptance of this interdependence is also growing, among leaders as well as the general public. This seems true in the West, within the OPEC nations, and among Third World peoples as a whole.

The solidarity that has persisted among the oil-exporting group came as a surprise to most western observers. Equally surprising has been the common front that continues between OPEC and the rest of the Third World, despite the economic burden that OPEC prices have placed upon some eighty oil-poor countries. These appear to value the political and economic clout that OPEC now brings to their regions in North-South bargaining as adequate recompense.

This gives the negotiation a sense of realism, of raw power on both sides, which was lacking in debates before the energy crisis loomed in October 1973. In 1977, both energy and food issues are now subsumed within the larger matrix of a more just world order. But they play key roles therein: Energy provides brawn and muscle in the bargaining process; adequate food for all the human family appeals to the heart of humankind, stimulating the political will of nations.

27

Personal Notes

by Joseph Gremillion

I am an ordained minister of the Christian church, a priest of the Roman Catholic church for thirty-four years. For the first fifteen of these, I did pastoral work in my native state of Louisiana.

Most of these years I spent in Shreveport, a city near the Texas and Arkansas borders, in the heart of the Bible Belt. Here the vision of my ministry broke through my inherited parochial limits toward two new dimensions: social justice and human rights, ecumenical and interreligious cooperation.

The plight of the blacks and migrant workers called me to the first awakening. A third of our city and state population was black. In the late 1940s and early 1950s their struggle for justice and civil rights had barely begun in our area. I asked: How could our all-white, upper-middle-class parish pretend to follow Christ on Sunday, then ignore the "Negroes" and their plight on Monday? Mexican cotton pickers came through annually, nameless as locusts. How could we ignore these brothers and sisters in the Lord? How could we help both groups to help themselves?

The dominant churches were Protestant, mostly Baptist and Methodist. We Catholics numbered only about 7 percent in Shreveport, less than 2 percent in the Bible Belt as a whole. I had been born and reared on a cotton farm of eight share-cropping

277

families, in Moreauville, a village 95 percent Catholic, in the French-speaking bayou country around New Orleans. My sheltered boyhood and, alas, my training for the priesthood put me on double guard against Protestants, as heretics and "rednecks."

Before I got to Shreveport, Jews were completely unknown to me. There were none in Moreauville; I met none during my seven years of theological training.

Muslims, Buddhists, Hindus? These "pagans" appeared as footnotes in manuals on the true faith. I awakened to their existence as believing communities only ten years ago, while working in the Vatican and with the World Council of Churches, Geneva.

From my twin Shreveport openings, toward social ministry and interfaith cooperation, I had been called by church authorities to social ministry at national and international levels. From 1960 to 1967 I served as director of social development for Catholic Relief Services, the overseas social agency of the U.S. conference of bishops, with offices in New York and Washington. This plunged me into the Third World.

In 1967, Pope Paul named me executive officer of the Pontifical Commission Justice and Peace, Vatican City. The Vatican Council begun by Pope John had legislated the establishment of this department in the papal "cabinet." Its purpose was to awaken the church to Christ's command of love for all humans, by promoting social justice, concern for the poor and oppressed, development, human rights, and peace.

Until 1974 this was my ministry, with increasing thousands of collaborators. For good reason, members of my own tradition and fellow Christians of the Protestant and Orthodox churches began working together early on. But as we converged toward joint Christian social ministry, we became aware of another parochialism enclosing our new ecumenicity: the parochialism of a "Christian we" formed by only a fourth of the human family. We began to realize that our vision of justice and rights and peace conformed dangerously to the vision of western civilization and its imperial and colonial, technical and cultural domination over most of the globe.

Because we are a graft on Hebraic roots, and because we felt guilt for the recent Holocaust (and so much else before), we western Christians found it natural and necessary to reach out to the Jews. In the nineteen years since Pope John, we Catholics have tried to purge out nineteen centuries of hatred. We have not fully succeeded. The effort continues and brings Jews and Christians together in West and East.

To continue my autobiography of personal ignorance, the reality of Israel and Zionism, of Arab solidarity and Islam and Palestine, began dawning after my arrival in Rome. There I met Muslims for the first time; only in 1975 did I form friendships with Muslims and begin reading the Quran and Islamic history. Simultaneously, together with friends in the Vatican and World Council of Churches, I had growing contacts with Hindu and Buddhist leaders.

Out of this abyss of multiple parochialism, in God's providence, my personal vision for the Interreligious Peace Colloquium came forth, step by step.

One step I wish to note is the visit of Rabbi Henry Siegman to my Vatican office in 1973, to propose concretely the session that became Bellagio. Of the thousands who have opened my personal vision, I wish to cite him by name, and in gratitude.

Appendix

PARTICIPANTS IN THE BELLAGIO COLLOQUIUM

ADEBO, CHIEF S.O., Chairman, National Universities Commission, Nigeria.

AL-NOWAIHI, DR. MOHAMMED, Chairman and Director, Department and Center for Arabic Studies, American University in Cairo, Egypt.

ANANDA THERA, DR. W., Head, Department of Buddhist Studies, International Buddhist Centre, Sri Lanka.

ARNS, PAULO EVARISTO CARDINAL, Archbishop of São Paulo, Brazil.

ASKARI, DR. HASAN, Head, Department of Sociology, Aligarh Muslim University, India.

AVINERI, PROF. SHLOMO, Dean, Faculty of Social Sciences, Hebrew University of Jerusalem, Israel (Director-General, Foreign Ministry of Israel, since July 1975).

BLANK, RABBI IRWIN M., President, Synagogue Council of America, United States.

BORLAUG, DR. NORMAN, Director, West Headquarters Staff, International Maize and Wheat Improvement Center, Mexico.

FAWZI, DR. HUSSEIN, Former Dean, Faculty of Science, University of Alexandria, Egypt.

GREMILLION, REV. JOSEPH, Co-Chairman, SODEPAX, United States.

HANNAH, DR. JOHN A., Executive Director, World Food Council of the United Nations, United States.

HEHIR, REV. J. BRYAN, Associate Secretary, United States Catholic Conference, United States.

HESBURGH, REV. THEODORE M., C.S.C., President, University of Notre Dame, United States.

HORNSTEIN, MR. MOSES, Vice President, Synagogue Council of America, United States.

KLOMPE, DR. MARGA M., Minister of State, The Netherlands.

LAMM, RABBI NORMAN, Professor of Jewish Philosophy, Yeshiva University, United States.

LINOWITZ, THE HON. SOL M., Former U.S. Ambassador to the Organization of American States, United States.

MARTIN, THE HON. EDWIN M., International Bank of Reconstruction and Development, United States.

MBITI, REV. JOHN, Director of the Ecumenical Institute, World Council of Churches, Kenya.

MOELLER, MSGR. CHARLES, Secretary, Secretariat for Promoting Christian Unity, Vatican City.

MOORE, RT. REV. PAUL, Episcopal Bishop of New York, United States.

MURTY, PROF. K. SATCHINDANANDA, Chairman, Faculty of Arts, Andhra University, India.

PALIHAWADANA, DR. M., University of Sri Lanka, Sri Lanka.

PARMAR, PROF. S.L., Department of Economics, Allahabad University, India.

RAUSCH, BISHOP JAMES, General Secretary, National Conference of Catholic Bishops, United States.

ROSSANO, RT. REV. PETER, Secretary, Secretariat for Non-Christian Religions, Vatican City.

SIEGMAN, RABBI HENRY, Executive Vice-President, Synagogue Council of America, United States.

SIVARAMAN, DR. K., Department of Religious Science, McMaster University, Canada.

SMITH, PROF. WILFRED CANTWELL, Chairman, Department of Religion, Dalhousie University, Canada.

SPAE, REV. JOSEPH J., General Secretary, SODEPAX, Committee on Society, Development and Peace, of World Council of Churches, Geneva, and Justice and Peace Commission, Vatican City.

STENDAHL, REV. KRISTER, Dean, Harvard University Divinity School, United States.

TIMIADES, MOST REV. EMILIANOS, Metropolitan of Calabria, Representative of Orthodox Ecumenical Patriarch to World Council of Churches, Switzerland.

VANCE, MR. CYRUS R., Former Deputy Secretary of Defense, United States (Secretary of State since January 1977).

SPONSORS, OFFICERS, AND BOARD MEMBERS

The Colloquium at Bellagio in May 1975 was sponsored by an ad hoc steering committee composed as follows: Rabbi Irwin M. Blank, Rev. Joseph Gremillion, Rev. Theodore M. Hesburgh, His Eminence Iakovos, Mr. Philip M. Klutznick, Mr. Sol M. Linowitz, Mr. Matthew Rosenhaus, Rev. Krister Stendahl, Mr. Cyrus R. Vance, and Rabbi Henry Siegman, who served as Coordinator. The Honorable U Thant was also a member until his death in November 1974.

The Interreligious Peace Colloquium was incorporated in August 1976 according to the laws of the State of New York. The founding directors and officers were Mr. Matthew Rosenhaus, President; Mr. Cyrus R. Vance, Vice-president; Rabbi Henry Siegman, Treasurer; Rev. Joseph Gremillion, Secretary. These served as the Executive Committee of IRPC; Gremillion was named chief executive officer with the title of Coordinator; Vance resigned in January 1977 upon becoming Secretary of State of the United States.

A Board of Directors, named by the Executive Committee, is in formation. As of September 1977, the members included: Chief Simeon Adebo, Rabbi Irwin Blank, Professor Ismail al Faruqi, Rev. Theodore Hesburgh, Mr. Philip Klutznick, Ambassador Sol Linowitz, Dr. Muhammad Abdul Rauf, Mr. Henry Schultz, Mr. Maurice Strong. Rosenhaus, Siegman, and Gremillion are ex officio members of the Board.

OUTLINE AND QUESTIONS FOR WORK GROUPS
(PREPARED TO AID DISCUSSION AT BELLAGIO)

While benefiting from data given by specialists and from interpretations and projections of scholars and public figures, this discussion is not meant to be primarily "academic." It aims rather at our faith communities and at the possibility of influencing them upon our return home. We wish to leave this Colloquium with a core of common accord, if that be possible, concerning:

1. The meaning of a thrust "toward economic interdependence" as a human goal among all the planet's people.

2. The structures, transformations, tensions, obstacles, and other elements involved.

3. A possible joint agenda for faith communities in the future—short-term and long-term (that is, from one to five years,

and from five to twenty-five). It is again stressed that in this discussion and its reports, no one speaks officially on behalf of his or her community; we all participate *ad personam*.

Economic Facts of the Food/Energy Crisis

1. Does my faith community know these facts? To what degree? Through which information network? Can this communication of fast-changing data be improved? Made useful to faith groups? How?

2. Is it possible for several or all faith communities to cooperate in, or at least coordinate, the information process? At local, national, transnational levels?

3. Does my faith community place its study of these facts within the larger context of the global economic system which arose initially from the industrial power of the West and later from that under Soviet leadership? Within the more recent context of inflation, recession, and unrest within the western system? And growing national, cultural, and religio-cultural awareness and identity among other regions?

Interpretation of the Economic Reality

Is my faith community conscious of:

1. The impact of the food/energy crisis upon the economic systems of the respective nations and regions—particularly upon those which lack significant economic resources and power in the global marketplace (often called the Fourth World)?

2. The added degree and growing extension of human suffering caused in these areas by the crisis?

3. The basic transformations in the global economic relations which the crisis has accentuated and accelerated, with grave consequences for world peace and for transnational social justice, which must be built up and undergird peace?

4. The impact of these economic changes upon political relations among nations and regions?

The Role of Religion

1. Does my faith community accept that it has a role in the "secular" field of economic interdependence? How does it conceive this role?

2. Does it view all human beings as "members of one human family"? The planet's space and seas and resources as the gift of the transcendent Power or Person or God or Absolute or One to all people and nations?

3. Can my faith community motivate concern for these problems of economic interdependence, social justice, and peace among its believers, as citizens? Should it do so? Will it? By what measures?

4. Is my faith community open to cooperation with persons and groups of other faiths? If not, is this because of belief or inherited practice or historic events? Related to political or national policies? Cultural or other reasons? Are these obstacles irremovable? Can cooperation be initiated or increased? How?

Economic Structures

1. Does my faith community approach the food/energy crisis as an isolated event or as part of a crisis in the world economic system?

2. Has it any interest in changing the structures in this system? Which in particular?

3. Does it think in terms of a new world economic order? Of a charter of economic rights and duties among nations and regions? If so, which are the principal structures, tensions, obstacles, and other elements to be considered in promoting these goals? (UNCTAD, U.N. Special Session of April 1974, etc.)

On Our Return Home

1. Realistically, what might be done within my faith community at local, national, transnational, and/or global levels?

2. In cooperation with other faiths? With secular lifeviews and bodies?

3. Should we launch a follow-up program to promote a more just economic order, commensurate with other growing awareness as one human family?

4. If so, how should this be done? Will *you* participate? Engage others?

Index

Abraham, ix, 22, 121, 129, 141
Adebo, Simeon, 35, 54–55, 58–59, 64, 65, 166, 253, 280, 282
advertising, 4, 51, 224
affluence: and food consumption, 8; increase of, 4, 180
Africa, 11, 12, 14, 22, 32, 194, 197, 213, 224, 264; see also specific countries
agribusiness, 19
agriculture: development of, 3, 13, 15, 26, 176, 183, 184, 195, 206–7, 214, 245; dignity of, 3, 26, 165, 245, 246; priority of, 23, 31, 172, 176, 184; technology for, 17–24, 162
Algeria, 13, 30
Allah, 14, 141, 227, 241, 256; see also God
Al-Nowaihi, Mohammed, 27, 33, 65, 86, 122, 133–39, 158, 162, 231, 244, 247–48, 257, 280
Ananda Thera, W., 85, 91–108, 153, 233, 249–50, 262, 280
anti-Semitism, 77
Arab nations, 30, 55, 266; see also specific countries
arms race, 39, 51, 197–98, 229–30, 243
Arns, Evaristo, 33, 59, 64, 155, 262, 280
artificial protein: production of, 62
Asia, 11–12, 22, 194, 213, 264; see also specific countries
Askari, Hasan, 25, 28, 29, 31, 55, 86, 122–32, 137, 138, 153, 154, 157, 158, 159, 169, 171, 232, 239, 254, 262–63, 280
Aspen Institute for Humanistic Studies, 60, 222, 223
Australia, 14, 15, 37; grain purchases from, 8
Avineri, Shlomo, 26, 28, 35, 46–49, 55, 59, 60–61, 116, 170, 227–28, 242, 253, 256, 280

Bangladesh, 28, 29, 176; need for petroleum in, 8
Bellagio, vii–ix, 5, 12, 16, 26, 44, 50, 53, 55, 124, 141, 203, 217, 227, 239, 249–50, 256, 259, 264, 266, 271, 279, 282
Bergson, Henri, 143–44, 146
Bhagavada Gita, 79
Black Africa, 265
black theology, 235
Blake, Eugene Carson, 209
Blank, Irwin M., viii, 29, 53, 113, 120–21, 156–57, 220, 280, 282
Boerma, Addeke, 28
Boethius, 147
Borlaug, Norman, 7, 9, 13, 15, 17–33, 40, 46, 49, 162, 165, 167, 170, 221, 228–29, 240, 280
Brazil, 18, 59, 165
"Bread for the World," 209
bread: as a basic right, 3; holiness of, 3, 16, 216, 219–20, 240–41, 249–50
Brown, Lester, 19, 251, 273
Bucharest, 262
Buddha, 91–92, 94–101, 104, 108, 137–38, 233, 251; political and social thought of, 101–8; relationship to society of his day, 99–101; religious concord in the preaching of, 111
Buddhism, 137–39, 153, 232–33, 234, 245, 249–50, 256; and change, 107–8; economic welfare in, 106–7; goals of, 106–8; Hindu response to the proselytizing nature of, 89; ideal of harmony in life of, 93–94, 107–8; ideological aspects of, 110–11; and Marxism, 111–12; notion of common good in, 96–97; and peace and harmony, 74, 79, 93–94, 97–99, 107–8; and relationship to state, 101–3; role of monks in political thought of, 103–5;

Buddhism *(continued)*
  social and political thought in,
    96–108; the Tendai in, 74; Theravada
    School of, 102, 112
Buddhists, vii, ix, 5, 139, 153, 170; at-
    titudes toward food by, 232–33, 245,
    249–50; rivalry among sects within,
    74
Burma, 102, 103, 104

Camara, Helder, 144, 155, 164
Cambodia, 104
Canada, 14, 16; grain purchases from, 8,
    29; protection of fishing rights by, 76
capital investment: for fertilizer pro-
    duction, 8; for food production, 27
capitalism, 40
Center for the Study of World Religions
    at Harvard, 83
Center of Concern, 173, 203, 251
cereal grains: increased production of,
    18–19, 27, 32; relationship to meat
    production, 32
Chad, 32
China, Peoples' Republic of, 12, 162, 165,
    229; Cultural Revolution in 27; food
    production in, 8, 25–28; grain purch-
    ases by, 8; use of fertilizer in, 21,
    27–28
Christian Conference of Asia, 212
Christianity, 144–51, 235, 240, 245, 250,
    277–78; and population control, 83;
    and treatment of Jews, 75; as a force
    for unity, 78, 147–51; divisiveness
    caused by, 75, 78, 81, 142–43; Hindu
    response to the proselytizing nature
    of, 89
Christians, vii, ix, 5, 14, 22, 172
Club of Rome, 142
coal: as source of energy, 67; as source
    of fertilizer production, 21
cocoa: relationship of price and re-
    serves of, 33
Committee on Food Aid Policies and
    Programmes, 15
Committee on World Food Security, 15
Common Market countries, 30
Communist movement, 47, 125
community, viii–ix, 67, 73; and attempt
    to be one, 74; as distinguished from
    society, 77–79, 113–14; one, 74; Hindu
    conception of, 88; of communities,
    116–19, 129, 160–62, 166, 171–72,

249–50; of faith, 79–81; and role of
    transcendence, 76–77, 122–23; of suf-
    fering, 153; and world, 67, 77–79,
    114–19, 160
Conference on Trade and Development
    (UNCTAD), *see* United Nations
conflict between agricultural and in-
    dustrial sectors, 176, 229
Confucius, 251
Congar, Yves, 145
consciousness raising, 221–22
conservation, 38
Consultative Group on Food Production
    and Investment, 13, 20
consumerism, 51, 177, 192, 222
consumption patterns, 4, 8, 32, 177,
    179–80, 212, 230, 234, 246, 251–52
crisis psychology, 253–54
crop failure, 8, 15
Crusades, the, 77, 142
Cullmann, Oscar, 148
cultivation practices: advances needed
    in, 23
cultural colonialism, 31
cultural evolution, 28
cultural values, 9, 31
Cyprus, 266

David, 141
Declaration on Eradication of Hunger
    and Malnutrition, 206, 210
"developed" nations, 13, 41, 58, 60, 191,
    196, 211–12; just distribution in, 3;
    overconsumption in, 32–33, 193–94;
    reliance on energy of, 191; structural
    approaches to food crisis in, 245
"developing" nations, 13–14, 24, 42, 55,
    58, 60, 191, 227, 229; agricultural
    practices in, 23, 28, 184, 189; decline
    of exports in, 183, 188–89; decreased
    dependence of, 43, 63, 188, 190; dis-
    tribution problems in, 3, 176, 182;
    economic gap between "developed"
    nations and, 62–63; growing popu-
    lation of, 18, 177–79, 196–97; solar
    energy in, 67; structured approach
    to food crisis in, 245–46; susceptibil-
    ity to consumerism of, 51
development, 34–35, 58, 59, 63; aid for,
    64; conferences on, 4; as cure for the
    food problem, 175ff; need for struc-
    tural change to insure, 176–78; ob-
    stacles to, 229

Development Assistance Committee (DAC), 14, 37

disarmament, 197–98, 210, 234, 243, 246, 261

disease, 7, 162

Dostoyevsky, Fyodor, 151

Durkheim, Emile: concept of *anomie* in, 76; on religion and community, 75–76, 123

Eastern faiths: Smith on, 69; *see also* specific traditions

East Europe, 12

economic power blocs, 61–62, 190–91

economic structures, 29, 45–48, 58–64, 175, 183

economy and politics: inter-relationship between, ix, 29, 47, 54–67; Martin on, 35–45

education, 23, 210–12, 214, 243

Educational Scientific and Cultural Organization (UNESCO), *see* United Nations

Egypt, 15, 65, 229, 230, 257

elites, 27, 42

Emperor Asoka, 100–02

energy, 3, 152; consumption of, and industrial production, 44; crisis of, 16, 39, 54, 191, 243–44, 252; distribution of, 240, 261; multifaceted nature of crisis of, 72; relationship to food crisis of, 3, 8, 21–22, 30, 43, 158, 243–44, 246, 252; relationship to peace of, 40; relationship to power politics of 243–44; researching sources of, 40; scarcity of, 1, 40; strategies for meeting the crisis of, 173–201

energy-food crisis, 55, 57, 67, 251–52, 265, 283; and nationalism, 44; as a call to faith, 3–4, 64; as a challenge to peace, vii, 3–4; Hannah and Borlaug on facts concerning, 7–24; international conferences on, 1; multifaceted nature of, 66–67, solutions for, 59, 152, 173–225; in 1977, 273–76

environment-consciousness, 20

equality of opportunity, 38, 40, 42

"Establishment of the Rule of Righteousness" (first sermon of the Buddha), 96

ethical systems: and relationship to regional blocs, 12

ethics: assumptions concerning justice, Martin on, 37–38; problems concerning, 31; social, vii

faith: collapse of traditional forms of, 79; community and nature of, 75–79, 113; Hindu conception of, 88, 89–90; ideological aspect of, a Buddhist view, 110–11; nature of, 73; and population control, 83–85; Smith on the divisive and cohesive nature of, 71–85

faith commitments: joint approaches to, ix, 283

faith communities: collaboration among, for human community, 79–81; divisions among, vii–viii; and economic structures, 29, 246–47; and the food crisis, 120–21, 173–236, 246–47; open and closed natures of, 77–79, 153; relationship to global crises of, viii, 4, 64–65, 163–66; *see also* five faith traditions

Farugui, Ismail Al, 282

fascism, 47

fasting, 211

Fawzi, Hussein, 229–30, 234, 239, 250, 257, 280

fertilizer: adulteration of, 182; distribution of, 30, 188, 193, 195; and energy, 21–22, 30, 252; and increased agricultural production, 20, 184; organic, 20–21; prices of, 3, 183, 212; production of, 8, 19–22, 29–30, 47, 246; relationship of petroleum to production of, 8; structure of the international market of, 193; unnecessary use of, 41, 193, 195

five faith traditions: global interdependence among, vii–viii; response to food crisis of, 12, 69–172; response to global issues of, 1

food: adulteration of, 182; as commodity, 3, 31, 181–82, 243, 251–53; distribution of, 15, 29, 176, 181–83, 186, 189, 220–21, 229, 233, 240–42, 261; human right to, vii, 39, 210, 241, 245, *see also* right to eat; price of, 8, 15, 40–41, 176–77, 180, 181; price of, and increased production, 183, 188; price of, and profiteering, 177, 182; price of, and shortage of foreign exchange,

food *(continued)*
41, 183, 189; production of, 8, 11–13,
17–24, 29, 32, 42, 161–62, 179, 181, 183,
185–88, 252–53; production of, and
cash crops, 47, 184, 185; relationship
to politics of, 25–26, 27–28, 35–67, 210,
213, 240, 243; reserves of, 12, 15, 18,
40, 176, 180, 209, 240, 274; scarcity of,
3, 18–19, 39, 162, 177, 189; theological
attitude toward, 31, 120–21, 232–33,
241, 251; and U.S. foreign policy, 29,
50–51, 251; *see also* bread, holiness of
food aid, *see* relief assistance
Food and Agriculture Organization
(FAO), *see* United Nations
food crisis, 15–16, 17, 136, 242; strategies
for meeting, 12–13, 47, 173–236; and
structures of society, 177–88; trends
in, 28, 31, 212–13, 273–76
food program: Hannah and Borlaug on,
7–24; Martin on, 37–45; in 1977, 275
food security, 12–13, 15
food stamps, 15
Ford, Gerald R., 253
Ford Foundation, 83–84
Fourth World, 8, 62, 243, 252, 254; *see
also* specific countries
Francis, John, 125
Francis of Assisi, 256

Gandhi, Indira, 232
Gandhi, Mohandis, 89–90, 156, 165, 199,
202, 216–17, 231, 256
Gaon, Saadia, 114
Germany, 47, 75
Global Information and Early Warning
System on Food and Agriculture, 16
global interdependence, ix, 14, 30; *see
also* interdependence
God, ix, 14, 22, 79, 80, 88, 93, 123, 127–29,
130–32, 137–39, 141, 145–51, 154,
157–59, 162, 171, 227, 235, 284; *see also*
Allah
Graham-Maingot, Linda, 141
grain embargo, 39
grain production, 66; decrease in, 18; increase in, 7–8, 185
grain reserves, 4, 8, 12, 18–20, 40–41, 176,
180; secrecy concerning, 19
"Graymoor Covenant," 212
Green Revolution, 8, 17, 23, 178, 183–86,
207, 228

Gremillion, Joseph, vii–viii, ix, 5, 32, 250,
265, 277–79, 280, 282

Halevi, R. Yehudah, 114
Hammurabi, 251
Hannah, John A., 7, 9, 11–33, 40, 46, 49,
59, 222, 280
Harris, Frank, 173, 202–15
Hegel, 46, 48, 115, 125
Hehir, Brian, 33, 57–58, 160–61, 163, 228,
280
Henriot, Peter, 173, 202–15
Hesburgh, Theodore, 140, 161, 164, 209,
252–54, 261–62, 263, 280, 282
high-yield seeds, 23, 184, 207
Hijaz, 124
Hinduism: and caste system, 89, 256;
and community, 88; divisiveness in,
74, 155–56; and population control,
83; and secularization, 89–90; Smith
on significance of, 80; sociological
rigidities of, 74, 88–89; tolerance
within, 88–89; and universalism, 74,
89–90
Hindus, vii, ix, 5, 80, 136, 155–56, 170,
232, 234, 278
Hitler, 75
Hobbes, 61, 117
Holland, 23, 31
holocaust, the, 75, 266, 278
Honganji Temple: destruction of, 74
Hornstein, Moses, viii, 281
Houtart, François, 110–11
human family, vii, 7, 9, 15, 34, 261, 284
hunger, 42, 80–81, 157, 167, 175, 181, 187,
198, 203, 209, 212, 214, 244; alleviation of, 1, 3, 5, 52; and lifestyle, 32–33,
38, 40, 50–51, 212–13, 216–25, 243,
246–47, 256; as political problem, 28;
as religious problem, 71ff, 80–81; *see
also* food crisis
Huxley, Julian, 128

Iakavos, 282
India, 31, 65, 86, 124, 126, 155, 177, 178,
182–83, 185, 187, 189, 193, 198, 199,
231, 232, 234, 256, 263; food crisis in,
25, 136; invasion of Sri Lanka by,
110; need for petroleum in, 8; and
origins of Buddhism, 93–95, 98; program of population control in, 83; religious divisiveness in, 71

individualism, 60–61, 227–28
Indonesia, 124
Indonesia-Philippines-Malaysia triangle, 266
inflation, 16, 177, 191, 195
interdependence, 30, 67, 188–99, 217–18, 221, 224, 226, 227; among faiths, ix
international aid, 29–31
International Bank for Reconstruction and Development (IBRD), *see* World Bank
International Fund for Agricultural Development, 13–14, 20, 29–30, 246, 276
International Monetary Fund, 13
international monetary system, 16, 44
International Women's Year, 251
Interreligious Peace Colloquium, vii–ix, 1–3, 14, 25, 29–33, 137, 249, 257, 264–73; board of, 282; continuation committee of, viii, 5; officers of, 5; purpose of, 255–56; statement of, 5; steering committee of, vii–viii, 262, 282
Interreligious Task Force on United States Food Policy, 209
Iran, 13, 30
irrigation development, 3, 17
Islam, 14, 122–32, 138–39, 154, 158–59, 228, 230–31, 241, 244, 256, 267–68, 271; and Buddhism, 139; divisiveness in, 74; Hindu response to the proselytizing nature of, 89; monotheistic claim of, 129; Quran of, 130–32, 137–39; Smith on, 70ff, 80
Israel, 14, 74, 114, 120, 123, 141, 165, 266, 267, 268
Italy, 47

Jain, 263
Japan, 14, 37, 44
Jesus, ix, 80, 123, 124, 129, 141, 145–47, 148–51, 155, 232, 251
Jewish-Christian consultation, 116
Jews, vii, ix, 5, 14, 22, 80, 124, 129, 265, 269, 278, 279; attitudes toward food of, 232; treatment of, by Christians, 75; *see also* Judaism
John the Baptist, 219, 232, 235
John the Evangelist, 150
John XXIII, 141, 278
Jordan, 141

Judaism, 113–19, 148, 157, 234–35, 240–41, 264–66, 268; divisiveness in, 74; ethical motivation in, 118; food and hunger within, 120–21; influence on Durkheim, 75–76; notions of community in, 113–15; and observation of seven Noahide commandments, 157; tolerance within, 80; *see also* Jews
justice, vii, viii, ix, 13, 19, 35, 57–58, 108, 122–23, 134, 145, 151, 156, 157, 164, 187–88, 190, 192, 193, 194, 197–99, 210, 212, 215, 230–31, 233, 240, 244, 248, 252–53, 255, 262–63; distributive, 184; Gandhi's passion for, 89; hunger for, 4; Martin on impact of food crisis on, 35–45; population control and, 177–80; relationship to development of, 176; role of religion in struggle for, 69ff

Kabbalah, 115
kenosis, 153
Keynes, Maynard, 59
King, Martin Luther, 52, 156
Kissinger, Henry, 161
Klompe, Margaret, 31, 59, 64, 66, 244, 250–51, 254, 281
Klutznick, Philip M., 282
Kuwait, 13, 30

labor: division of, 59; as a source of wealth, 243
Lamm, Norman, 65, 66, 86, 113–19, 152, 154, 157–59, 161, 164–66, 170–71, 218, 226, 250, 281
land: cultivation practices of, 22–24; limited amount of arable, 17–18; redistribution of, 23, 185, 188, 207, 214
Laos, 102, 103, 104
Latin America, 11–12, 64, 194, 197, 264; *see also* specific countries
Law of the Seas Conference, 76
laws of market, 3; *see also* food: price of, and market system
Lebanon, 266
Leclerc, Joseph, 147
Letter from Birmingham Jail, 156
Libya, 13
Liebnitz, 147
lifestyle, 4, 32–33, 38, 40, 50–51, 213, 215–25, 243–47, 256

Limits to Growth, 142
Lindberg, Charles, 158
Linowitz, Sol, 56–57, 64, 158, 166–67, 172, 282
local food councils, 4

Maize and Wheat Improvement Center, 7
Malachi, 157
malnutrition, 3, 7–8, 16, 40–42, 175, 181, 193, 198, 218; alleviation of, 1, 4
"man-made famine," 182
Maritain, Jacques, 151
market system, 28, 41, 47, 181–82, 209
Marshall Plan, 37
Martin, Edwin M., 37–45, 50, 57, 58, 62–63, 66, 161, 281
Marx, Karl, 46–48
Mauriac, François, 150
Mbiti, John, 170, 232, 242, 281
McNamara, Robert, 42
meat: and grain consumption, 8, 32, 180–81, 192–93
Mexico, 26
Middle East, 22, 124, 136, 141, 266, 269; religious divisiveness in, 71; *see also* specific countries
military expenditures, 51; *see also* arms race, disarmament
missionary movement: revising the aims of, 81
Moeller, Charles, 86, 129, 140–51, 154–55, 168, 171, 281
Moltmann, Jürgen, 148
Moore, Paul, 35, 50–53, 64, 166–68, 251, 281
Moses, ix, 121, 123, 124, 141, 155, 251
Muhammad, ix, 123, 124, 137–39, 141, 157–59, 251
Muller, Max, 93
multinational business, 60
Murty, Satchidananda, 86, 155, 165, 172, 231, 256, 263, 281
Muslim countries: rising influence of, 14, 30; support of Special Drawing Rights, 13
Muslims, vii, ix, 5, 14, 22, 54, 86, 138, 172, 265; attitudes toward food of, 232, 244; *see also* Islam
Myrdal, Gunnar, 231

Nasser, Gamal Abdal, 229
National Council of Catholic Bishops, 212

National Council of Churches, 212
national food councils, 4
nationalism, 43, 61, 75–76, 122, 124, 152, 160–63, 168
national security argument, 51
natural gas: conservation of, 38; and fertilizer production, 8; flaring off of, 21–22
neocolonialism, 31, 65
New International Economic Order (NIEO), 43–44, 59, 62–63, 208–10, 261–62, 267
New Zealand, 14, 37
Niebuhr, Reinhold, 130
Nietzsche, Friedrich, 150
Nigeria, 13–14, 35, 165
nitrogen, 8, 20, 21
Nixon, Richard M., 253
Nongovernmental national food councils, 240
Northern Ireland: religious divisiveness in, 71
nuclear energy, 40, 65, 66
nuclear power: control of, 62, 66–67; development of, 66–67; threat to peace of, 39, 54, 66–67
nutrition, 11, 41

oil-producing nations: embargo by, 49; increased economic power of, 14, 44; responsibilities of, 30; *see also* Organization of Petroleum Exporting Countries
OPEC, *see* Organization of Petroleum Exporting Countries
Organization for African Unity, 55
Organization for Economic Cooperation and Development (OECD), 14, 37
Organization of Petroleum Exporting Countries (OPEC), 12–14, 28–30, 43–44, 55, 61, 183, 254; *see also* oil-producing nations
Orthodox Churches, 55
overconsumption, *see* consumption patterns
Overseas Development Council (ODC), 60, 209, 222, 251–52

Pakistan, 136, 198; religious divisiveness in, 71
Palestinians, 266
Palihawadana, M., 86, 91, 109–12, 133, 137, 250, 262, 281
Pannenberg, Wolfhart, 148

Paraguay, 18
Parmar, Sam L., 29, 56–60, 64, 155–56, 163–64, 172, 173–99, 202, 216–17, 222, 224, 227–34, 251–53, 281
Pastoral Constitution on the Church in the Modern World, 140, 144–46, 148–49
"Pastoral Plan of Action," 212
Paul the Apostle, 153, 278
Paul VI, 140, 209–10
peace, vii, ix, 13, 22, 79, 108, 122–23, 132, 145, 147–53, 229, 234, 240, 243, 254, 261; and energy crisis, 66–67; and food crisis, 46–67, 197–98; Martin on food crisis and, 37–45; role of religion in search for, 69ff
Peace of Westphalia, 160
Perry, Edmund F., 103
Peter, 140
petroleum, 30, 40, 47, 49, 66; conservation of, 38; and fertilizer production, 8; price increase in, and food supply, 8; price of, 14, 54–55
Philippines, 124
phosphorous, 8, 20
Pius XI, 146
pluralism: role of, in community formation, 79
plutonium, 67
political action by religious bodies, 207–10
political will, 1, 9, 194
politics: interrelationship with economy, 29, 37–45, 47, 54–67, 178, 188
Pontifical Commission Justice and Peace, 211
population, 3, 32–33, 83–84, 135–36, 160, 162, 175, 177–81, 196–98, 212, 224, 230, 234; in Fourth World countries, 8; growth rate of, 7; and food production, 13, 18–19, 42; zero growth in, 62
potash, 8, 20
Potter, Philip, 209
poverty, 7, 108, 179, 185, 187–88, 192, 198, 209
power, 39, 48, 58–63, 182, 188, 198, 208, 218, 226–32, 243–44
pragmatism, 169
prayer, 5, 224–25
Protestant churches, 212, 256, 270, 278
purchasing power, 212

Quaddafi, Muammar Al, 228
Qatar, 13

Quran, *see* Islam, Quran of

Rauf, Muhammad Abdul, 282
Rausch, James, 32, 61, 164, 166, 244, 281
raw materials: conferences on, 1
relief assistance, 13, 15, 26, 41–42, 60, 64–66, 182, 195, 204–5, 228, 240
religion: distortion in, 73; evaluation of programs of, 212–15; factors motivating response of, 203–4; influence in politics and society of, 71–151; influence on public policy of, 59, 64, 69–172, 244–48; power structures of, 226–36; programs supported by, 205–12; promotion of community by, 75–76; promotion of divisiveness by, 71ff, 156, 164; role in food crisis of, 72–73, 255–56; subject/object polarity within, 82–83
religious values, 9; primacy of, in Buddhist countries, 103
repentance: for divisiveness by religious communities, 74
resources: redistribution of, 4, 31, 34, 56, 219, 244
rice: 16; basic right to, 3
right to eat, vii, 3–4, 56, 210, 216
Rockefeller Foundation, viii
Rosenhaus, Matthew, viii, 5, 264, 265, 282
Rossano, Peter, 154–55, 281
Roszak, Theodore, 125
Rousseau, 221
Russell, Bertrand, 166–67
Ryan, William, 5

Sahel, 8, 17, 30, 31, 175–76, 182, 190
St. Bartholomew Massacre, 142
Sarah, 121
Saudi Arabia, 13, 22, 30
Schultz, Henry, 282
Schweitzer, Albert, 144, 155, 219
Second Vatican Council, 129, 140, 144–46, 148
secularity: as basis for world order, 73; failure of, 115–16; Hindu response to, 89; religious fallacies promoted by, 75
Shinto: communitarianism of, 74
Siegman, Henry, ix, 5, 60, 163, 166, 232, 261, 264, 265, 281, 282
Sivaraman, K., 86–90, 114, 154, 281
Smith, Adam, 181, 251
Smith, Wilfred Cantwell, 25, 69–85, 87,

Smith, Wilfred Cantwell *(continued)*
109–10, 112–15, 118, 128, 134–37,
141–42, 153–56, 160, 167, 169–72, 203,
250, 254–57, 271, 281
social change: religious motivation for,
52–53, 64
social democrat movements, 47
socialism, 61
social justice, *see* justice
social responsibility, 61
SODEPAX, 142, 211
solar energy, 42, 67
Soviet Union, 12, 49, 75, 229, 266; crop
failure in, 18; grain purchases by, 8,
30, 49; opposition to grain reserves
by, 40
Spae, Joseph, 27, 29, 62, 153, 281
Special Drawing Rights (SDR), 13
Sri Lanka, 91, 102–3, 109–10
starvation, 3, 7–8, 29, 49, 72, 108, 126,
128, 136, 157, 181, 218, 252, 254
Stendahl, Krister, 5, 32, 62, 66, 167–68,
170, 173, 216–25, 229, 231–32, 234–35,
239, 249, 281, 282
Strong, Maurice, 282
structural change, 46–48, 57, 58–63, 228,
230, 232–33, 244–48; and the alleviation of hunger, 1, 25, 39, 163, 173–99,
210; Avineri on, 46–49; and development aid, 66
Sudan, 31
Suez Canal, 229
Synagogue Council of America, viii, 120,
211, 270

Taizé community, 223
Talmud, 118, 120, 157
Tamils, 110
Tantur Ecumenical Institute, 140–41,
150
Tanzania, 65
Taoist: vision of peace among, 74
technical assistance, 13, 31, 41
technology, 9, 123, 125, 266; and food
production, 17–24, 27, 44
Teilhard de Chardin, Pierre, 148
Tendai, *see* Buddhism, the Tendai in
"Ten Days for World Development," 212
Thailand, 102, 103, 104
Third World, 8, 44, 62, 208, 252, 254; *see
also* specific countries
Third World Forum, 44, 63
Tillich, Paul, 150

Timiades, Emilianos, 281
Toynbee, Arnold, 155
trade, 29–31, 191–92, 208
transcendence: and community, 75, 79,
122–27; ideology and, 169–71; and
immanence, 144–47
"trickle down theory," 66, 184
trusteeship principle, 235–36

U Thant, 282
United Arab Emirates, 13, 30
United Nations: Conference on Trade
and Development (UNCTAD), 261;
Educational Scientific and Cultural
Organization (UNESCO), 62; Food
and Agriculture Organization
(FAO), 11, 28, 195, 208; Group of 77,
12; Sixth Special Session of the General Assembly, 1; World Food Conference, 1, 8–13, 15–16, 20, 41, 161,
195–96, 206, 208–10, 228, 253; World
Food Council, 4, 7, 11–16, 31–32, 50,
174, 232, 239–40, 242, 246, 254
United States, 14, 15, 29, 49, 56, 196, 223;
civil rights movements in, 52; credibility gap within, 51; grain purchases from, 8, 30, 39; livestock production in, 32; nationalism and, 75;
nonessential use of fertilizer in, 193;
opposition to grain reserves of, 40,
176; responsibilities of, 30, 209; support of repressive regimes of, 51, 56;
and world hunger, 50–51
Upanishads, 245

Valery, Paul, 143
Vance, Cyrus R., ix, 5, 255, 264–65, 281,
282
Venezuela, 13, 30
Vietnam, 234
violence, ix
Voltaire, 154

Waldheim, Kurt, 1, 189
war, 162, 168, 261
Ward, Barbara, 261
waste, 4, 21–22, 32–33, 38, 179, 183, 213,
222–23, 233, 243, 247
Watergate, 51
wealth: accumulation of, 61; redistribution of, 253
Weber, Max, 96
Weil, Simone, 165

Welles, Orson, 119
Whitehead, Alfred North, 166–67
World Bank, 12, 20, 37, 42, 193; Consultative Group on Food Production and Investment in Developing Countries, 37
World Conference on Religion and Peace (WCRP), 209–10
World Council of Churches (WCC), 202, 209, 211, 270; Program on Dialogue with People of Living Faiths and Ideologies, 217

World Economic Survey, 1973, 182
World Food Conference, *see* United Nations
World Food Council, *see* United Nations
world monetary system, 240
World War II, 47–48

YMCA, 38

Zetland, Marquess, 98
Zionism, 268
Zoroaster, 137–38

ACKNOWLEDGEMENTS

In their Foreword, Cyrus Vance and Henry Siegman expressed gratitude to benefactors who provided the funds for the Bellagio meeting. Two years later, appreciation is voiced to persons and institutions who have helped since that first event. On behalf of the officers and directors, thanks are extended to the DeRance, Ford, Rockefeller, and Rosenhaus Foundations for their substantive grants. Four couples from my hometown, Shreveport, Louisiana, and one priest friend have made financial contributions; to these I add my personal gratitude to the formal expression conveyed for IRPC officers.

I also wish to thank Sister Bonnie Raine for preparing the Index, and the several typists who deciphered my scribble. Among the latter, I must single out my secretaries, Ms. Anne Schmitz and Mrs. Gwendolyn Twiggs.